POLITICAL UNTOUCHABLES
The Tories and the '45

Political Untouchables

The Tories and the '45

Eveline Cruickshanks

Duckworth

First published in 1979 by
Gerald Duckworth & Co. Ltd.
The Old Piano Factory
43 Gloucester Crescent, London NW1

© 1979 by Eveline Cruickshanks

ISBN 0 7156 1334 0

Printed in Great Britain by
Ebenezer Baylis and Son Ltd.
The Trinity Press, Worcester, and London

Preface

The story of the '45 in Scotland has been told so often that the late Sir James Fergusson suggested there ought to be a law to prevent any more books on the subject. Yet these works have largely ignored the European context out of which the '45 arose and in which alone it could succeed. Historians on this side of the Channel have assumed that for the French the rebellion was a useful 'diversion' from the war in Flanders, without taking any systematic look at French sources. French historians, who knew that Louis XV was in earnest in seeking to restore the Stuarts, did not appreciate that conditions in eighteenth-century England made open expression of Jacobitism impossible. Being part English, part Scottish, and part French, I may have an excuse for an undertaking which will most probably arouse the ire of historians of all three nations. At any rate, alternate education in England and in France has convinced me that European history seen in purely national terms will not do.

I am grateful for permission to use the manuscripts of Her Majesty the Queen, of the Duke of Beaufort, the Duke of Bedford, the Duke of Devonshire and the trustees of the Chatsworth Settlement, the Duke of Northumberland, the Earl of Harrowby, the Treasurer and Masters of the Bench of Lincoln's Inn, and in France those of M. Martial de la Fournière of the Quai d'Orsay, M. le Général Guinard of the service historique du Ministère de la Défense Nationale, and M. le Contre-Amiral Fliche of the service historique de la Marine.

I am indebted to Professor Ian Christie for making a number of suggestions on the contents of this book, to John Brooke and Howard Erskine-Hill for useful discussions on some points made, to John Kerslake of the National Portrait Gallery for advice on illustrations, and to Peter Hasler of the History of Parliament Trust for reading the final draft. Dr Linda Colley has kindly allowed me to read her thesis on the Tory party from 1727 to 1760, and I have benefited from several exchanges with her. My greatest debt is to the late Romney Sedgwick, a staunch Whig, whose wit and erudition I greatly admired, for a series of discussions, heated at times, but, as I well know, much enjoyed on both sides.

E.C.

Contents

Illustrations

'On the Abjuration'

Our fathers took oaths as we take our wives
For better for worse, and kept them their lives,
But we take the oaths like whores, for our ease,
We whore and rogue, and part when we please

(anonymous poem in the manuscripts of the
Duke of Beaufort at Badminton)

Abbreviations

Add.	Additional manuscripts in the British Library.
AECP Ang.	Archives étrangères, correspondance politique, Angleterre at the Quai d'Orsay.
AEM & D. Ang.	Archives étrangères, mémoires et documents, Angleterre.
CJ	*Journals of the House of Commons.*
Guerre	Manuscrits du departement des forces terrestres at the château de Vincennes.
H. Walpole Corresp.	*The Correspondence of Horace Walpole,* Yale ed.
HC	*History of Parliament, The House of Commons 1715–1754;* ed. Romney Sedgwick.
HMC	*Historical Manuscripts Commission reports.*
Marine	Manuscrits du departement de la marine, in the Archives Nationales, Paris.
Parl. Hist.	Cobbett's *Parliamentary History.*
SP	State Papers in the Public Record Office, London.
VCH	*Victoria County History.*

All the dates in England are given in the Old Style with the year beginning on 1 January. Documents written on the Continent are given in both Old and New Style.

Quotes in foreign languages have been translated.

1

The Tories and the Party System

Politics in the reigns of the first two Georges (1715–1760) have usually been looked at from the point of view of the reign of George III (1760–1820), which is viewing them through a distorting mirror. Political thinking was still dominated by the great events of the Revolution of 1688 and the Restoration of 1660, much as ours still is by those of the Second and First World Wars. In dealing with the eighteenth century, and with the Tory party in particular, historians have often been guilty of hindsight and of knowing consistently better than contemporaries.

Traditionally the Tories stood for the support of the Crown and the Anglican Church, and for hatred of a standing army which they equated with the rule of Oliver Cromwell. Basking in the sun of royal favour under Charles II and in the early years of James II's reign, they had enjoyed a monopoly of office to the exclusion of the dissenters and Roman Catholics. They showed little concern at the private religion of James until he threatened their entrenched position by the rashness with which he attempted to force through the repeal of the Test Act and Penal Laws and the admission of dissenters and Roman Catholics to office. This alienated those who would have been his strongest adherents, so that when, in answer to an 'Invitation' sent by a small group of influential people, some Whigs, some Tories, known to history as the Immortal Seven, William of Orange landed at Torbay in November 1688 with an army of 15,000 veterans from the wars against Louis XIV, he met with virtually no opposition. James's army had been increased from 20,000 to about 30,000 since his accession, despite protests from prominent Tories in the 1685 Parliament, but part of it was in Ireland, and with Protestant officers in England refusing to act with

Roman Catholics it soon 'melted away'.[1] Many Tories, especially
in the west, welcomed William in the belief that he had come over
to bring his father-in-law to his senses, rather than to take the
crown. After the Revolution, most of them accepted him as king
de facto if not *de jure*, though driven into a false position by the
imposition of the oaths of abjuration by which the Whig Junto
endeavoured to drive them out of office. Although some leading
Tories engaged in plots with James and Louis XIV, and although
their belief in a foreign policy based on seapower rather than inter-
vention on the Continent conflicted with William's aims, he
resolutely refused to place himself in the power of one side only,
so that their party also enjoyed its share of Crown and Government
patronage at national and local level. Leading Tories in opposition
joined Whigs in opposition in the 1690s in an influential country
party, which secured the passing of the Triennial Act, of legislation
to reduce the number of placemen in Parliament, and secured the
disbandment of the army after the peace of Ryswick on the grounds
that the militia was the only constitutional force in peace time. The
whole Tory party rejoiced at the accession of Queen Anne, a devout
Anglican, whose heart, as she proclaimed was 'wholly English', but
she resolutely refused to make herself dependent on only one party,
and until just before her death resisted demands by Convocation
and by High Tories for an end to the practice of occasional con-
formity by which dissenters qualified for office by taking the
sacrament once in a while. They opposed bills to naturalise foreign
Protestants from 1709 to 1748 because, be they Dutch, German or
French, they were dissenters and invariably became Whigs once
they were in England.[2]

The system of mixed ministries had worked well enough to carry
the country through its immense war effort during Marlborough's
wars, even though the court party tended on occasions to fragment
on party lines. For this latter reason, the ablest party managers
would have liked single-party governments. Thomas, Marquis of

[1] J. R. Jones, *The Revolution of 1688* 289; C. Dalton, *English Army Lists and
Commission Registers* ii, pp. v, xxvii. For the general implications of the
Revolution, see J. P. Kenyon, *Revolution Principles*; Mark Goldie, 'Edmund
Bohun and *Jus Gentium* in the Revolution Debate 1689–93', *Historical Journal*
xx (1977) 569–86.
[2] See H. Horwitz, *Parliament, Policy and Politics in the Reign of William III*;
G. Holmes, *British Politics in the Age of Anne*; W. A. Speck, *Tory and Whig*.

Wharton, the greatest electoral magnate of his time, wanted Tories excluded from the Administration after the Whig victory at the 1708 election. Similarly, Henry St John, later Viscount Bolingbroke, could see little sense after 1710 in retaining in office Whigs who would not support the Government, while there were not enough places to go round for loyal supporters. This would have produced a two-party system, by which the Crown could call on one or the other to govern, and the organisation of the court party was certainly more efficient after 1715 under single-party ministries.

In the months which followed the death of Queen Anne in August 1714, the unforeseen happened. There was a ruthless purge of Tories from places apart from the very few who had life patents, and this was followed by a complete proscription which lasted forty-five years.[1]

During the last years of Queen Anne, overshadowed by the struggle for power between Robert Harley, Earl of Oxford, and Bolingbroke, the attitude of most of the Tories to the succession had been very Micawberlike, and they never really faced what would happen if the Queen died. Though the idea of the Hanoverian succession was distasteful to them and at best a necessary evil, the party was not mainly Jacobite and the figure of 80 Jacobites in the 1713–14 Parliament which has been given may be too high as it included some who had gone into opposition with Argyll.[2] Bolingbroke, who was more aware of possible danger in the event of the sudden death of the Queen, attempted in January 1714 to get James II's son, James the Old Pretender, to change or dissemble his religion, well knowing his party's traditional attachment to the Stuarts and their dislike of excluding the person nearest in line. James's refusal to do either put an end to further progress in this direction, while Oxford's flirtation with the court of Saint Germain seems to have been designed merely to get the Jacobite vote in Parliament. However, the Hanoverian envoys, reporting to the Electoral Prince (as the future George I was styled), represented the whole Tory party, apart from the small but influential group of Hanoverian Tories, as committed Jacobites and enemies to the Hanoverian succession. Another reason for George I's hatred of the Tories—the word is not too strong—is that they had long been

[1] *HC* i 62.
[2] Holmes 279.

represented as the friends of France, particularly at the time of the Exclusion Crisis and the renewal of hostilities with France in 1701, and he would not forgive them for what he regarded as their betrayal of the Allies at the peace of Utrecht and their refusal to pay arrears due to the Hanoverian troops in 1714. George I knew no English and depended on Baron Bothmer, a former Hanoverian envoy to London, as an intermediary, and it was Bothmer who advised him to employ only Whigs, who welcomed him with open joy, whereas the Tories, as the baron wrote in his diary, 'stood sullenly aside or even took the Stuart's part'.[1]

What took place in 1715 was not a change to an all-Whig ministry, it was a whole social revolution. Tory gentlemen could no longer provide for their younger sons in the traditional manner since places in the Army (the Navy was a partial exception), the Civil Service, or ecclesiastical livings in the gift of the Crown were denied to them. Tory army officers lost their commissions, sometimes without compensation, which was against all precedents. Tory lawyers could no longer become judges or K.C.s. The lower clergy, who were overwhelmingly Tory, could not become bishops, and resented the Whig bishops, who formed the most servile part of the House of Lords, and who acted, more often than not, as electoral agents for the Whigs in the constituencies, the most notorious being the Bishop of Lichfield who threatened his Tory chapter with ecclesiastical censure for incontinency if they would not vote for the Whig candidates at the 1727 election.[2] Tory merchants could no longer get government contracts, or directorships in the Bank of England or other great public companies. Moreover, many Tories, from old parliamentary families, could no longer afford to stand for Parliament, once deprived of office, that great restorer of men's estates. They were made to serve the expensive and troublesome office of sheriff in all but election years when Whigs were appointed to handle the writs, and likewise the Tories were excluded from the county lieutenancy. Though Tory Members were included in the commissions of the peace, they were swamped by Whig justices,

---

[1] See my article 'The Tories and the succession to the Crown in the 1714 Parliament', *Bulletin of the Institute of Historical Research* xlvi (1973) 176–85; R. Pauli, *Zeitschrift des Historischer Verein für Niedersachen* (1883) 83. I am grateful to Alex Hughes for translating a difficult passage in the diary.

[2] *HC* i 319.

often men of inferior rank in Tory counties.[1] Yet some historians have argued that the Tories did not want office under the first two Georges, mainly because some Tory knights of the shire did not want places after the fall of Walpole for fear of not being re-elected.[2] Of course they did not. Knights of the shire did not want to become placemen themselves under Queen Anne or George III either, but they wanted places for their relations and their dependants, and if Tories did not want office *per se*, why did they take it before 1715 and after 1760? The meaning of the proscription was put most eloquently by George Lyttelton in his *Letter to the Tories* (1747) in which he urged them to abandon Jacobitism:

> We are kept out of all public employments of power and profit, and live like aliens and pilgrims in the land of our nativity;... no quality, no fortune, no eloquence, no learning, no wisdom, no probity is of any use to any man of our unfortunate denomination, ecclesiastic or layman, lawyer or soldier, peer or commoner, for obtaining the most deserved advancement in his profession, or any favour of the Crown; whilst, to our additional and insupportable vexation, the bare merit of hating us, and everything we love and hold sacred, daily advances dunces in the law and church, cowards in our fleets and armies, republicans in the King's house, and idiots everywhere!

Thus half the nation was driven into the wilderness—and the greater half, since Tories tended to represent counties and larger constituencies and would have won every general election between 1715 and 1747 had the number of seats obtained been commensurate with the number of votes cast. The Tory vote was remarkably steady as well as numerous, with little shift or splitting.[3] The point was put by Archibald Hutcheson, a Tory, who wrote to Sunderland:

> The foundation is to make it a demonstration to the whole nation, that his Majesty relies on the affections of his people, as the only solid guarantee for the protestant succession; that he is equally the king of all his people, and that no part, much less the far greater part, may not lie under the impression that they are considered only in the

---

[1] Stuart mss. Box 1/299.

[2] John Owen, *The Rise of the Pelhams* 214; B. W. Hill, *The Growth of Parliamentary Parties 1689–1742*, 192–3.

[3] See polls in *HC* vol. i. I am indebted to Edward Johnson for giving me the results of his detailed work on poll books for the period.

nature of proscribed persons, and thereby irresistibly determined to lay hold of the first opportunity which shall offer, of freeing themselves from what they esteem an intolerable oppression.[1]

And by Bolingbroke, who wrote that a Prince who 'renders his sceptre the rod of one set of men, and the tool of another, will be esteemed by his subjects and by foreigners the King of half his people, that is half a King'.[2]

It was the proscription which turned the Tory party into a Jacobite one. Bolingbroke wrote to Sir William Wyndham: 'If milder measures had been pursued, certain it is that the Tories had never universally embraced Jacobitism. The violence of the Whigs forced them into the arms of the Pretender.'[3] This is confirmed by Iberville, the French ambassador, who knew Tory leaders and records many conversations with them, and who reported on 31 October 1714: 'I see that the number of the Jacobites, who before the death of the Queen was not by far as great as some believed, increase daily by the accession of all the Tories, moderate Jacobites or Hanoverians, moved by a violent rage against the King at their exclusion from office.'[4] A few Hanoverian Tories who had been offered places had refused them, as they would not break with their party. Early in 1715 he noted that the Prince of Wales (the future George II) seemed to hate the Tories as much as his father and that they seemed to be 'heading for civil war which they regard as their only resort'.[5] This was a counsel of despair at the purge, followed by the impeachment of Oxford and the driving into exile of Bolingbroke and Ormonde who joined the Pretender in France. The passing of the Riot Act after Jacobite riots all over England in the spring of 1715 was followed by the suspension of the Habeas Corpus Act, and by an increase in the army (from which Tories had been weeded out) to 15,200 in England and 12,000 in Ireland, as well as 6,000 Dutch troops which could be called upon under the Barrier Treaties. By August 1715, the French envoy described the Tories

[1] To Sunderland, 3 April 1722, Marlborough mss. from Blenheim, now in British Library.
[2] *Lyttelton Memoirs* i 196–7.
[3] *HC* i 62.
[4] AECP Ang. 265ff. 51. An example of an Hanoverian Tory who became a Jacobite is Sir Henry Bunbury (*HC* i 506–7).
[5] AECP Ang. 265ff. 70, 84.

as in a state of 'stupefaction and fear'.[1] They had been promised arms but no troops by Louis XIV, in the exhausted state of France, despite Bolingbroke's plea that a tenth of what the Prince of Orange had in 1688 would do, and when even that prospect had disappeared with Louis's death they would have abandoned any idea of rising had not the Scots started the rebellion without consulting the English.[2] To make matters worse, the plans in the west where the English rising was to be centred were betrayed by one of Ormonde's agents, thus enabling the Government to seize the ringleaders. The arrest of Members of Parliament, including Sir William Wyndham and Sir William Carew, and of peers like Lord Lansdowne, was notified to Parliament, but there were other preventive detentions in the west, most of them Tory Members of Anne's Parliaments. In the circumstances the Tories rather strove 'to smother their own contrivance than to bring it to bear'.[3] Lord Gower, who was said to have set out to join Thomas Forster, the leader of the rising in Northumberland, the day of Forster's defeat at Preston, went home when he learnt the news. Thereafter, Gower was always lampooned on this score.[4] Overconfidence and lack of secrecy had proved so disastrous that henceforth the Tories deliberately ridiculed in public any threat of a rising.[5] The other lesson they had learnt was that they needed regular troops.

In the diplomatic field too, the Whig government turned the tables on the Tories. France was then the greatest power in Europe as England became in the next century, and knowing that the greatest threat to the Hanoverian succession would come from there the Whig government negotiated an alliance with the Duke of Orleans, who had set aside the will of Louis XIV and assumed power as Regent on behalf of the young Louis XV. This was an amazingly bold step in view of the vilification of France as the arch-enemy by the Whigs ever since 1678. The negotiations, conducted between Stanhope and the Regent's favourite, Dubois, provided for the recognition of the Hanoverian succession and for the expulsion

---

[1] AECP Ang. 265ff. 158, 161.

[2] *HC* i 62; H. T. Dickinson, *Bolingbroke* 138–41.

[3] *HC* i 62; Morice mss. at the Bank of England, Walter Moyle to Humphry Morice, 26 Sept. 1715, and Sir N. Morice to Humphry Morice, 7 Oct. 1715.

[4] Stuart mss. 216/111; *Westminster Elections 1741–51*.

[5] G. G. Mounsey, *Carlisle in 1745* 25.

2

of the Pretender from France. Iberville, who was left out of them, was still in London and was then an unhappy man. He reported in 1717 that his friends in the Tory party 'who have become almost all Jacobites' reproached him with the ingratitude of France, and that his windows were being broken in turn by Tory mobs, and by Whig mobs who disapproved of the French alliance. Most of the Tories, he added, blamed Oxford for everything that had happened.[1] Bonet, the Prussian envoy, still thought that the Tories would never accept the Pretender because he was a Roman Catholic, but Bonet was a strong partisan of the Whigs and had no contacts among the other side.[2] Even Oxford was so indignant at the harsh treatment he had received from the House of Hanover (and he had been chiefly instrumental in securing the passing of the Act of Settlement in 1701) that he wrote to the Pretender from the Tower in September 1716 offering his services.[3] Acting through Charles Caesar, treasurer of the Navy under Queen Anne, and William Bromley, secretary of state under the late Queen, who like Caesar corresponded with the Pretender, Oxford directed the Swedish Plot of 1716–17. This was a plan for a new rising if Charles XII of Sweden, who was determined to revenge himself on George I for having as Elector of Hanover taken advantage of his difficulties to dispossess him of Bremen and Verden, would assist by sending troops. Money was collected in England to pay for their use in bringing about a restoration. In January 1717, the English Government, against all diplomatic practice, seized the papers of Gyllenborg, the Swedish envoy.[4] In one of these, Gyllenborg said that the Pretender derived the strength of his party from his being English whereas George I was a foreigner, and without that the Pretender would have had few supporters however strong his hereditary claims.[5] Charles XII's death, followed by the failure of a Spanish expedition under Ormonde at the beginning of 1719, put an end for the time being to any prospect of help from abroad.[6]

[1] AECP Ang. 293ff. 25, 34; 294ff. 13–14.

[2] Hill 138.

[3] Lord Mahon, *History of England from the Peace of Utrecht 1713–1783* (1858 ed.) i 279.

[4] *HC* i 63.

[5] *Letters which passed between Count Gyllenborg, the Barons Görtz, Sparre and others*, London 1717, 23.

[6] *HC* i 63.

The widespread discontent in England caused by the burst of the South Sea Bubble seemed to present an opportunity to the Tories. Sunderland, George I's prime minister, seeking Tory votes to save himself from impeachment, and to safeguard his future since he had no hopes from the Prince of Wales in the event of the death of George I, made large promises to the Tories. Bromley was against dealing with Sunderland, and Oxford, who was out of the Tower but in retirement, was not consulted. Atterbury, Bishop of Rochester and Dean of Westminster since Queen Anne's days, as the Pretender's chief representative in England dealt with Sunderland mainly through Archibald Hutcheson, an able Tory lawyer who administered Ormonde's affairs in England. What Sunderland was asked for at first was a free Parliament, that is one elected without any Crown or Government pressure on elections. This had been the universal request at the Restoration and at the Revolution of 1688, and what the *English Advice to the Freeholders of England*, distributed by the Tories at the 1715 election, had called for. It would seem that Sunderland tried to oblige, for according to a report from the Jacobite agent in London, at a meeting of the Cabinet in February 1722, with George I presiding, Sunderland—

> opposed the buying the ensuing elections, that it was a method very expensive, which the present situation of affairs could not dispense with, so that it was impossible for the Treasury to hold out by procuring pliable persons to be elected, who after they were chosen must be maintained with places and pensions etc. . . . Mr Walpole asked with some heat if his Lordship was bringing in the Tories and having a Tory Parliament? To this the Earl [Sunderland] replied that the Tories and the Whigs were equally entitled to a share in the Administration, and that he was not for governing by brigades. King George stared the Earl of Sunderland in the face at the name of a Tory Parliament, for it seems nothing is so hideous and frightful to him as a Tory.

With the apparent connivance of Sunderland, the Tories then entered into a scheme for a rising in each county, assisted by the Irish regiments in the French service and those under Ormonde in Spain. The plan was revealed by Dubois to Walpole and Townshend the day of Sunderland's death, 19 April 1722.[1] Walpole's way of

[1] *HC* i 63-5, 494; Archibald Hutcheson, 28 and 30 July 1721, 23 April 1722,

handling the Atterbury plot was to terrify the Tories by bills of pains and penalties against the underlings while taking no proceedings against the Members of Parliament or peers named in it apart from Atterbury himself. This was so successful that afterwards, the Tories, who still formed the bulk of the Opposition, hardly dared attend Parliament 'thinking it better to lie still and to give no provocation'.[1]

It was in this situation that Bolingbroke, who never forgave the Pretender for dismissing him for negligence in failing to send over any arms during the '15 rebellion, and who had succeeded in detaching his friend Sir William Wyndham from the Stuart court, returned to England having obtained a pardon by bribing the Duchess of Kendall, George I's mistress. Although he was never able to live down his past, although he, one of the greatest orators of his time, was deprived of a voice in the Lords, his sheer intelligence and restless energy enabled him to play a crucial part behind the scenes. His first step was to make overtures to Walpole on behalf of three Tory leaders who were his friends, Lord Bathurst, Lord Gower and Sir William Wyndham, explaining that they were 'ready to enter into any measures' with Walpole and Townshend, being 'desirous to rid themselves of the disagreeable situation they were in by renouncing Jacobitism'. Next year, having got nowhere with Walpole and carrying with him his friend Wyndham, Bolingbroke allied himself with Pulteney, the head of the new Whig opposition, with a view to forming a coalition of the two opposition parties to bring down Walpole.[2] On the accession of George II in 1727, the Tories, who had been in the wilderness for twelve years, hoped for a change of heart from the new king. Charles Caesar reported to the Pretender on 27 June:

> Some of the Tories, particularly such as Lord Bolingbroke would influence, had shown an inclination to quit their principles in hopes of preferment, and upon the Duke of Hanover's death and his son's succeeding him, your steady friends found that many more would do the same, they could not tell where it would stop, they thought that

---

Marlborough mss. For Atterbury's part in the plot, see also G. V. Bennett, *The Tory Crisis in Church and State*.

[1] *HC* i 65–6.
[2] Dickinson, 140–2; *HC* i 66–7.

the only way to prevent a considerable breach amongst the Tories upon this occasion was to go one and all to court.

George II, however, was no more inclined to employ them than his father had been. They were divided among themselves, Wyndham as 'the head of those who called themselves Hanoverian Tories' supporting a coalition with the opposition Whigs, which was opposed by William Shippen and the 'veteran staunch Jacobites'.[1] To some Whig contemporaries at this time the number of true Jacobites did seem small.[2] Repeated disappointments had brought despair. The identity of the party seemed lost in the coalition, and the Tories now read the *Craftsman*, which preached that the only real distinction was between Patriots and a corrupt Administration, and that party distinctions had ceased to matter.[3] Political realities were very different. The belief of some historians that Wyndham led the bulk of the Tories who were loyal to the House of Hanover, while Shippen led a group of about fifty Jacobites, does not stand up to a close examination of the politics of the time.[4] There is very little evidence that Shippen led a party within a party, and the expression which is most frequently applied to him in reports of parliamentary proceedings is 'Shippen alone'. Wyndham owed his position in Parliament to being the best speaker on the Tory side and to the advice of his friend Bolingbroke, who was surpassed as a parliamentary strategist only by Walpole, but he had few personal followers. Speaker Onslow wrote that Wyndham—

formed such a new set of principles with regard to the public, and from them grew to think that the religion and liberties of the nation so much depended on the support of the present family to the throne, that he lost all confidence with the Jacobites and the most rigid of the Tories, and it is thought would have left them entirely if he could have stood the reproach of that in his county or could have maintained a prevailing interest there without them; and upon that footing would willingly have come into a new Whig Administration upon the exclusion of Sir Robert Walpole, with whom he would never have acted, and with the admission of some few of his Tory friends who in

[1] *HC* i 67.
[2] *Lord Hervey's Memoirs*, ed. Romney Sedgwick, i 3–5.
[3] Stuart mss. Box 1/299.
[4] Coxe, *Sir Robert Walpole* i 294; Hill 192–3; Owen 214.

company with him would willingly also have left their party for such a change.[1]

Wyndham's strategy of uniting with the discontented Whigs was deeply distasteful to the Tories, who again and again refused to act with the Whigs in opposition, and had not succeeded in ending the proscription. Nor was his zeal for the House of Hanover sincere, as we shall see. In 1730 the Tories suddenly appeared 'in perfect coalition' with the Whig opposition. This was brought about by a circular letter from the Pretender sent through Ormonde urging his friends in Parliament to 'unite in the measures against the Government and even with those who oppose it for different views than theirs', especially those 'which tend to promote a misunderstanding between the English Government and any foreign power, but most especially France'. In the short term it was linked with the attack on the Government for allowing the French to restore the port of Dunkirk contrary to the terms of the Peace of Utrecht. In the long term, it was connected with the arrival in Rome in January 1731 of Lord Cornbury, the great-grandson of Lord Chancellor Clarendon, to whom Bolingbroke was to dedicate his *Letters on History*. In secret meetings with the Pretender, he elaborated a plan for a restoration by offering places to leading Whigs and Tories in opposition. The project was directed on the English side by Lord Arran (Ormonde's brother), Lord Strafford, Lord Bathurst and Lord Gower, while Cornbury went on to Paris to negotiate with Chauvelin, the French foreign minister, who favoured a more aggressive foreign policy than the chief minister Cardinal Fleury, whom it was thought he would succeed.[2] In London, the French envoy Chavigny, a protégé of Chauvelin, had several meetings with Bolingbroke and Wyndham with whom he was on the closest terms. Chavigny reported in 1732-3 that they had told him that the Tories could not reconcile themselves to the Hanoverian succession and wanted a free Parliament. They thought that the Hanoverian family was as unpopular as ever. Looking on the character of the Pretender as a major obstacle to a restoration, Bolingbroke set his sights on Charles Edward, the Young Pretender, then twelve years old, who

[1] *HC* ii 563.
[2] *HC* ii 164; for Chauvelin and French policy under Fleury see P. Vaucher, *Walpole et la politique de Fleury*.

was regarded as forward as well as handsome, and whose portrait was everywhere in London. He then elaborated a plan for the education of Charles Edward and his younger brother Henry, saying that if he and Wyndham 'could but get hold of the children' there was nothing they could not do with the Tories.[1] Bolingbroke intervened directly by sending his secretary Brinsden to Paris with a proposal that James should resign his claims to his eldest son Charles Edward, who was to be educated as a Protestant under Ormonde in Switzerland or France. The Pretender refused to comply point blank.[2] Cardinal Fleury, however, was a peace-loving old man, who used Chauvelin as a bogey but kept him on a tight rein, and he was still on close terms with Horatio Walpole,[3] Sir Robert's brother, who had been British ambassador at Paris and still expressed feelings of the warmest friendship for the old Cardinal. Lord Orrery observed that while 'the duty of every Englishman to hate the King of France' was preached as the 'eleventh commandment', 'we are at present like wooden puppets, squeaking, strutting and acting solely for the machination and dexterity of the nimble fingered Cardinal'.[4] Walpole did not rely on Fleury's goodwill alone. Sniffing something in the wind, he had made overtures to Col. William Cecil, the Jacobite agent in England and a kinsman of Orrery and the Earl of Exeter. Under the guise of seeking his advice, Walpole flattered Cecil into meeting him alone. Cecil always denied having revealed anything of importance, but Walpole certainly learnt of Bolingbroke's plan, and Cecil was hopelessly compromised.[5] Disheartened with what he regarded as French breach of faith and accusations from the Tories of having disclosed the secret of his negotiations to his friend Bolingbroke, Cornbury broke his connexion with the Pretender in 1735.[6] The same year Bolingbroke withdrew to France, living at Chanteloup in Touraine.[7]

[1] Dickinson, 232; AECP Ang. 376ff. 247–73; 377ff. 126–31; 379f. 164; 330ff. 205–7, 228.

[2] Stuart mss. 157/29; 158/156.

[3] To avoid repeating 'old' and 'young' Horace Walpole, Walpole's brother has been called Horatio Walpole and his son Horace Walpole throughout.

[4] *Orrery Papers* i 105–6.

[5] Stuart mss. 144/6; Horace Walpole, *Memoirs of the Reign of George II* i 73. For Cecil see *HC* i App. pp. 113–14; for Orrery, see next chapter.

[6] *HC* ii 164.

[7] *Lyttelton Memoirs* i 63.

2

War with Spain and the Fall of Walpole

Bolingbroke, Horace Walpole wrote,

> who had sowed a division in the Pretender's court, by the scheme for
> the father's resigning his claim to the eldest boy, repeated the same
> plan of discord here, on the first notion of the Prince's disgusts; and
> the whole Opposition was instructed to offer their services to the
> Heir Apparent against the Crown and the Minister.[1]

Though Bolingbroke and Wyndham could not afford to separate
themselves from the Tories, without whom they would have been
generals without troops, the party could and did differ from them.
When in 1737 the Prince of Wales decided to apply to Parliament for
an increased allowance, Wyndham said 'that he would answer for his
whole party, as well as for himself; that he was very happy that an
occasion presented itself to convince his Royal Highness, by their
zealous and hearty appearance in support of his interest, how far
they were from being Jacobites and how much they were misrepresented under that name'; but in the event, though he spoke he
did not vote for the application, on which 45 Tories abstained, with
the result that it was defeated by a majority of 30, an example of what
Bolingbroke called 'the absurd behaviour of the Tories, which no
experience can cure'.[2] Next year an attempt by the Prince to come to
terms with the Tories broke down on Wyndham's stipulation that
'the Prince's people should join in reducing the army'. In the ensuing
debate on the army estimates political realities came through the
constitutional proprieties. Lord Noel Somerset, brother of the 3rd
Duke of Beaufort, who was regarded as 'the rising head of the Tory

[1] *Memoirs of the Reign of George II* i 73.
[2] *HC* i 68-9.

interest',[1] pointed out that the people of England were 'totally unaccustomed to military discipline and unprovided with arms'. Supposing they could be overawed by 'a large mercenary army' and that an administration could get control of both Houses of Parliament by corrupt means, then 'by the Revolution principles, it would be very lawful to resist such a government; but if it had a standing army to support it, they could not be able.' Replying, Walpole declared:

> No man of common prudence will profess himself openly a Jacobite; by so doing he not only may injure his private fortune, but he must render himself less able to do any effectual service to the cause he has embraced; therefore, there are but few such men in the kingdom. Your right Jacobite, Sir, disguises his true sentiments, he roars out for revolution principles; he pretends to be a great friend to liberty . . . These are the men we have most reason to be afraid of: they are, I am afraid, more numerous than most gentlemen imagine, and I wish I could not say they have been lately joined, and very much assisted by some gentlemen, who, I am convinced, have always been, and still are, very sincere and true friends to our present happy establishment. By the accession of these new allies, as I may justly call them, the real but concealed Jacobites have succeeded even beyond their own expectation; and therefore I am not ashamed to say I am in fear of the Pretender.

Pointing out that if the Pretender landed at the head of five or six thousand men 'there is no question but that they would meet with many, especially of the meaner sort, to join them', he went on to say that the army was also needed to suppress the smugglers as the local militia, in most cases, co-operated with rather than acted against them, an interesting fact in view of the close connexion between the smugglers and the Jacobites.[2] It obviously served Walpole's turn to brand all Tories as Jacobites, and to tar their Whig allies with the same brush for acting with them. Walpole was certainly obsessed with the danger of Jacobitism at home and abroad, and this concern has been thought akin to paranoia. But it was the sort of madness which kept him one jump ahead! Obviously, since any expression of Jacobitism, indeed any opposition to the Hanoverian succession,

[1] Dr Linda Colley, 'The Loyal Brotherhood and the Cocoa Tree', *Historical Journal* xx (1977) 81.
[2] *HC* i 68–9; *Parl. Hist.* x 375–467.

was treason, punishable by death and loss of estates, he had no means of knowing exactly how strong it was. But by a widespread and costly intelligence system at home and abroad, he was able to defeat most Jacobite schemes.[1] Conversations recorded in the diary of Sir Dudley Ryder, the attorney general, one of the most important new sources for the period, show that Walpole really believed the Tories were Jacobites, and this is confirmed by his brother Horatio and his son Horace.

While correspondence between leading Tories and the Pretender, always a risky business even if conducted in cypher, had fallen off since there was no positive plan afoot, the flow of funds from England sent anonymously through the Pretender's bankers in Paris continued. Nor had the Tories ceased to turn their sights towards the Stuart princes. A Frenchman who was in Rome in 1739 reported that it was well known there that the Pretender was getting large sums of money from England. The English who flocked to Rome, he wrote, were eager to see the Prince of Wales and the Duke of York, as the Stuart princes were styled, and since going to the Stuart palace was a capital offence in English law they asked him and other foreigners where the princes would appear in public in order to meet them.[2] That Jacobitism was not extinct was shown on the outbreak of the war with Spain in 1739. In the City of London, the common council on which the Tories had a majority led by Humphrey Parsons, a Tory alderman who was twice lord mayor of London and a zealous Jacobite, joined the friends of Frederick Prince of Wales there and on the court of aldermen, in fanning the agitation for war by petitions and addresses. Commenting on these proceedings, Walpole told Dudley Ryder that 'the disaffected are endeavouring to get the city into declarations and addresses that may distress us', which, he added 'did its mischief at once, in that such a thing as this came to the court of Rome and other foreign courts as the sense of the people for the Pretender, and that they want nothing but a standard and 5,000 men to begin with'. Though Whigs and

---

[1] See P. Fritz, *Jacobitism and the English Ministers*; and below, chapters 3 and 4.

[2] Receipts from England through Waters in Paris for sums usually between £100–£300 occur in most volumes of the Stuart mss.; Charles de Brosses, *L'Italie il y a cent ans, ou Lettres écrites d'Italie à quelques amis en 1739 et 1740*, ed. Columb., ii 93–100.

Tories in opposition were united in pressing for war, they did so for different reasons. Walpole told Ryder in October 1739 that there was—

> a great difference between the Jacobites and the patriot Whigs, particularly those of the Prince's court; and they had a meeting in the vacation when one of the Prince's friends proposed a revolution in favour of the Prince, saying that the King's interest was entirely lost, and he could not support it, but the Jacobites said if there was to be an alteration, it should be a restoration. This broke off the treaty. He assured me this was told him by one present at the meeting.[1]

Pulteney at this time thought Bolingbroke's counsels obnoxious, and was particularly critical of the fiasco of the secession on the Spanish Convention moved by Wyndham, whereby most of the Opposition left Parliament.[2]

The Scots took the initiative to secure a restoration. On the outbreak of the war with Spain, seven Scottish lords formed an association and issued an Invitation to James Stuart on the model of that sent to William of Orange in 1688. They were the Duke of Perth, his uncle Lord John Drummond, Lord Lovat, Lord Linton (who in 1741 became Earl of Traquair), his brother Hon. John Stewart, Donald Cameron the younger of Lochiel, and Sir James Campbell of Auchenbreck. Their secretary was William Macgregor of Balhaldy, the chief of the outlawed clan Macgregor, who was a cousin of Lochiel and an intimate of Lovat's. The disastrous consequences of having started the rebellion in Scotland in 1715 without consulting the English was always present in James's mind, and he replied that nothing could be done in Scotland without co-operation from his friends in England, and that France must be approached with a request for arms and regular troops. The English had in fact made strong objections to a purely Scottish project, as an enclosure in the correspondence of Murray of Broughton, the Jacobite agent in Scotland, states:

> The King [the Pretender] is informed, that his friends in England being apprehensive that some project might be forming in Scotland,

---

[1] *HC* i 69–70; ii 282, 326–7.
[2] *Marchmont Papers*, ed. Rose, ii 179–80.

for his restoration, without an attempt being made in England and by consequence without a sufficient prospect of success, his said English friends had advised those in Scotland not to proceed in any such project without hearing from the King. That no project should be examined in which both nations have not their share and will himself never authorise or agree to any that hath not a reasonable prospect of success.[1]

In order to ascertain the intentions of his leading supporters in England, James sent Col. Arthur Brett, an experienced army officer who, on the accession of George I, had been dismissed as lieutenant-colonel of the regiment which became the Royal Welch Fusiliers.[2] Those Brett dealt with were Lord Orrery, Sir John Cotton, Sir Watkin Williams Wynn, Lord Barrymore, and William Shippen. John Boyle, 5th Earl of Orrery [I], also sat in the English House of Lords as Baron Boyle. He had large estates in co. Cork, including Rathgoggan and the borough of Charleville, but lived mainly in England at Marston near Frome in Somerset. He had inherited his father's literary tastes, and moved in the circles of Pope and Swift. The friend and correspondent of Lord Barrymore and Dr King, the Jacobite principal of St. Mary's Hall, Oxford, he much admired Thomas Carte's Life of the first Duke of Ormonde, which he regarded as 'the first and best history of those times that has yet appeared'. He had made his maiden speech in the Lords in 1732 against the standing army, which he called 'an emblem of distrust between his Majesty and his subjects', and answered a whip from Col. William Cecil for the Lords early in 1739 when he spoke strongly against the Spanish Convention. Politically, he was a strong opponent of Walpole and had dealings with Chesterfield and Boling-broke as well as with the Stuart court.[3] Sir John Hynde Cotton, 3rd Bt., Member for Cambridge and a Lord of Trade under Queen Anne, was descended from an old Cambridgeshire family who had acquired the manor of Madingley near Cambridge by marriage, and was the head of the Tory party in that county. His predominant interest at Cambridge, however, was weakened by a series of expensive contests. He lost the allegiance of the corporation as soon as they

[1] Stuart mss. 209/7; *Memorials of Murray of Broughton* 364.

[2] Dalton, *Army Lists* vi 101, 197, 341.

[3] *Orrery Papers* i xii–xix, 111, 133, 176, 183, 193, 231–2, 252–3, 256, 264–6, 287, 301–2, 320.

realised he was not spending quite as much in the borough as he used to, and he transferred in 1741 to Marlborough the pocket borough of a Tory peer. Described by William Cole, the Cambridge antiquary, as 'one of the tallest, biggest, fattest men I have ever seen', he had to have a special set of chairs made at Madingley to take his weight. 'He was supposed,' Cole wrote, 'to be able to drink as much wine as any man in England without being disgusted by it', saying, on being told that it would be better for his gouty leg if he drank less, that 'if it would not bear his usual allowance of six bottles it was no leg to him'. Dr King, as well as Cole, was a frequent visitor to Madingley, where Cotton gave a home to Thomas Carte, who catalogued his library, including the greatest collection of pamphlets on the civil war then in existence. Cotton was related to the Wogans, Jacobite exiles, several of whom were in James's service. In Parliament, Cotton was the best speaker on the Tory side next to Wyndham. 'He had wit,' Horace Walpole wrote, 'and the faithful attendant on wit, ill nature, and was the greatest master of the arts of the House, where he seldom made but short speeches, having a stammering in his elocution, which, however, he knew how to manage with humour.'[1]

Sir Watkin Williams Wynn, 3rd Bt., Member of Parliament for Denbighshire, was the grandson of Sir William Williams, Speaker of the House of Commons under Charles II and solicitor-general to James II, who purchased a large estate at Llanvorda across the border into Shropshire and married the heiress to Glascoed in Denbighshire. Acquiring Plasyward in the same county through his mother, he inherited, on the death of his first wife's father, Llwydiarth and Glanllyn in Montgomeryshire and Llangedwin in Denbighshire, and the next year succeeded to Wynnstay, which he made his seat, as well as Rhiwgoch in Merioneth under the will of his mother's cousin Sir John Wynn, whose name he assumed. His vast estates, great electioneering activity, and personal popularity soon made him the head of the North Wales Tories, and such a dominating figure in Welsh politics that he was called 'Prince of Wales'. In preparation for an expected county election in 1720 he came at the head of 500 horsemen and wrote: 'To-morrow I roast a very large ox and hind, and intend to drink the town of Wrexham

[1] *HC* i 201, 584; Lady A. Houblon, *Houblon Family*, ii 36–40, 112–13; J. Nichols, *Literary Anecdotes of the 18th Century* ii 480–1.

dry.' At the time of the 1722 election and the Atterbury plot he and his friend Lord Bulkeley 'audaciously burnt the King's picture and the several pictures of all the royal family'. Wynn was the leading member of the Cycle of the White Rose, a secret Welsh Jacobite society whose membership extended into Cheshire and Lancashire, and he helped his fellow members Sir Robert Grosvenor and Lord Barrymore (who was his life-long friend) in their elections. At the 1732 election, when Grosvenor was under violent attack from Government supporters, Wynn came to the rescue accompanied by his liveried servants and 900 colliers from Wrexham. When he was elected mayor of Chester in 1736, the *Gentleman's Magazine* reported that 'the feasting continued several days, in so much that little business was done but by cooks and confectioners. Such appearance of gentlemen were never seen since Lord Delamere was mayor at the Revolution.' Nor was Wynn's popularity confined to his own part of the country, for when he came up to London to attend Parliament, Welshmen came out as far as Finchley and escorted him to town in a great procession. George Kelly, Ormonde's secretary, whom Wynn had financially supported during his imprisonment in the Tower as one of the chief agents in the Atterbury plot, wrote to the Pretender in 1737 that Wynn ought to be consulted before Charles Edward was sent on any foreign travels.[1] James Barry, 4th Earl of Barrymore [I], Member for Wigan, had been a colonel of foot under Queen Anne serving with distinction in Spain, where he first became connected with the Duke of Argyll. He had a seat at Castlelyons in co. Cork and large estates in the same county, and got a fortune of £10,000 by his first wife, a sister of Charles Boyle, 2nd Earl of Burlington. His second wife, with whom he eloped in 1706 when her father, Earl Rivers, opposed the match, was a great heiress, and by 1721 Barrymore had managed to get possession of all the Rivers estates in Lancashire, Cheshire, Yorkshire and Essex, and control of one seat at Wigan. Like his kinsman and friend Lord Orrery, he did not live in Ireland but in England, at the Rivers' houses of Rock Savage and Marbury in Cheshire and Wardley in Lancashire. He had lost his regiment on the accession of

---

[1] *HC* ii 543–4; P. D. G. Thomas, 'Jacobitism in Wales', *Welsh History Review* i (No. 3) (1962) 288–95 and 'Wynnstay versus Chirk Castle', *National Library of Wales Journal* xi (No. 2) (1959) 105–23; A. Roberts, *Wynnstay and the Wynns* 9–11; Stuart mss. 194/10.

George I and never forgave the House of Hanover, though he decided against joining the '15 rebellion after the arrest of the West Country Jacobites. In Parliament he was a fairly frequent speaker and attended regularly, writing at the time of the split in the Whig party in 1717:

> Nobody has more thorough contempt for ministers and what is called men in great offices than I have. I cannot remember they ever did true service to their country, they minded indeed strengthening themselves to carry on private piques and getting as much money as they could, but I have observed that when such people fall out, now and then some good come on it, so it may prove now; for which reason I would not be absent at this juncture. It may be in a man's vote at this time to do some good which, perhaps, may never again be in his power.[1]

Shippen, a wealthy lawyer not a great landowner, had mellowed with age and took no considerable part in Jacobite affairs after this time. Such were the principal Pretender's friends in England. They were committed Jacobites, but had a great deal to lose—some, a very great deal to lose.

A report to the Pretender on these negotiations dated 28 March 1740 stated:

> Col. Brett found the King's [the Pretender's] friends more timorous and backward than heretofore, and as full of good inclinations as ever. It was absolutely impossible to form any plan of business with them; they shudder at the thought of an attempt when it can be compassed, and yet wish it, and even seem to long for it . . . Lord Orrery has been all the winter in Ireland but left word that he would return if the King should think fit. Mr. Shippen trembles . . . Sir John Hynde Cotton doubts, or seems to doubt of others, but answers clearly for himself; Watkin Williams is hearty and may certainly be depended on. The gentry, yeomanry, commonalty are well disposed, better than ever for a restoration. The City of London is full of spirit and gives effectual proofs of it; but with all this it is impossible to bring them into any measures that can give sufficient encouragement to any foreign minister.[2]

[1] SP 44/104/46; *HC* i 440. M. Cox, 'Sir Roger Bradshaigh and the electoral management of Wigan', *Bulletin of John Rylands Library* xxxvii. 120–64; Lodge, *Irish Peerage* i 309–12.

[2] Stuart mss. 221/109 and 131.

The chief reasons for their backwardness, was said to be 'the Duke of Hanover's [George II's] violence, Walpole's vigilance, the present appearance of an army and a fleet, a long series of disappointments, and a confirmed habit of despondence and indolence'. Shippen, in fact, proved 'so weak upon the prospect of real business' that he was left out of the consultations altogether. The others, Brett reported, declared they would 'not fail to join such troops as the King of France shall send to their assistance'. Cotton agreed to remain in London in order to settle 'a correspondence with proper persons in different parts of England by messengers without trusting anything to writing'. Everything depended upon whether France would provide regular troops.[1] A memorandum in the French Foreign Office says that at this time persons of the greatest distinction, gentlemen and noblemen, came over from England to see Cardinal Fleury asking for assistance, but as nothing was put in writing by Fleury, we do not know who they were except for Lord Barrymore, who wrote to the Pretender from Paris 12/23 May 1740:

> Your faithful servants think by many incidents lately happened that the present juncture is much the most favourable that has been for many years, and if anything can be had from this side, I should not fear of success, but to make any attempt, unless a sufficient force was at hand to resort to, would only add strength to your enemies and certain ruin to your Majesty's friends; what can be expected from hence I fear are only fair words, I wish I may be deceived, but am sure I succeeded in demonstrating the feasibleness of the undertaking.[2]

Barrymore asked the Pretender to destroy the original of his letter; this was done, but a copy was kept. These developments were not to the liking of Bolingbroke, who wrote to Wyndham:

> Of all the causes of our present public misfortunes, which are easy to be traced, a principal one is this: the Whigs have always looked on the protestant succession, and the Tories on the restoration of the Stuarts, as sure means to throw the whole power of the government into the hands of one or the other of them, and to keep it there: the former were encouraged and confirmed by the weak conduct of my Lord Oxford; by the characters of the late and present King, different

[1] Stuart mss. 222/33 and 107; 223/129.
[2] J. Colin, *Louis XV et les Jacobites* 12–13; *HC* i 440; Stuart mss. 222/128.

indeed, but suited to their purpose; and by the absurd behaviour of the Tories, which no experience can cure.[1]

Wyndham suddenly arrived in Paris in the spring of 1740, first to confer with his friend Bolingbroke, and then on to see Cardinal Fleury. Col. Daniel O'Brian, the Pretender's representative at the French court and one of the army officers who had lost his commission in 1715, wrote: 'Though Lord Bolingbroke's behaviour has been all along such as you know, and though Sir William Wyndham's has been for some time very unaccountable, yet they both seem to dread any business of the King's should be thought of without them.'[2] On Wyndham's death in June, George Lyttelton, a leading member of the Whig opposition and a protégé of his kinsman Lord Cobham, wrote:

His influence with the Tories was the only means of keeping that party in any system of rational measures. Now he is gone . . . it is much to be feared that resentment, despair, and inability of conducting themselves may drive the Tories back into their old prejudices, heat and extravagance.[3]

In other words, they might not so easily be persuaded to play the game of the Whig opposition, and in a different international situation, might play their own under the new leadership of Cotton and Wynn. On his side, Walpole had not been inactive. He made overtures to Thomas Carte, the historian, in 1739–40 through Avery, a London merchant and a supposed Jacobite, telling Carte he was averse to the shedding of blood and asking him to procure assurances in James's own hand for the maintenance of the constitution in Church and State and the safe retreat of the Hanoverian family. A clergyman who had become a nonjuror on the accession of George I, Carte had been secretary to Bishop Atterbury at the time of the plot and was said to have stirred up Jacobite riots at the Coventry election of 1722. Pursued by the King's messengers, he had made his escape to France in 1723, but had returned to England about 1730 when Queen Caroline obtained leave for him to do so, a favour of which

---

[1] Coxe, *Sir Robert Walpole* iii 524.
[2] Stuart mss. 221/178. For O'Brian's career under Anne, see C. G. T. Dean, *The Royal Hospital, Chelsea*, 183, 190.
[3] *HC* i 70.

he availed himself but which he had not solicited. He was at the centre of Tory politics, living with Sir John Cotton at Madingley, and received grants from the common council of London, the Goldsmiths' and the Vintners' Companies towards his history of England (of which the first volume only was completed before his death). His letters in the Stuart papers give some of the best reports of parliamentary debates, the details of which he obtained directly from Cotton or from his friend Sir John St. Aubyn, knight of the shire for Cornwall, and of the proceedings of the corporation of London, told him by his friends Sir John Barber and Humphrey Parsons, both of them aldermen and lords mayor. The Pretender gave him such a letter as Walpole had requested, adding: 'as for the Princes of the House of Hanover, I thank God I have no resentment against them, nor against any one living.' Carte then handed over to Walpole James's letter, which the minister asked to keep. Suddenly Carte found himself being threatened: 'He put me in mind that the warrant against me was not called in but still lay in the messenger's hands', whereupon he protested that he had come at Walpole's invitation. The minister then tried another tack. Saying he knew Carte was poor, he offered him a handsome annuity or the deanery of Windsor in exchange for information. When Carte refused indignantly, Walpole laughed, saying how could he 'learn the Jacobites' designs but from the Jacobites themselves?' He then saw Carte to the door with every courtesy and advised him to have nothing to do in future with such men as Avery.[1] When Walpole attempted to continue his 'negotiations' with James, the latter replied that if Walpole was in earnest let him send his son (Horace), who was due to go on the grand tour, and he would talk to him! Carte was regarded as 'honest and zealous, but indiscreet', but it was thought better to let Carte and Cecil 'go on, because both Sir Robert Walpole and Lord Ilay [brother of Argyll and Walpole's manager for Scottish elections] were apprised of all their motions, and seemed to believe that the King [James] had no other correspondents'.[2] In

---

[1] Nichols, *Literary Anecdotes* ii 471–518; Robert Digby to William, Lord Digby, 18 Nov. 1722, Digby papers formerly in the possession of Miss Fiona Digby. AEM & D Ang. 76ff. 73–92; Vaucher, App. ii pp. 455–8; Lord Mahon lii–liii.

[2] Stuart mss. 219/111 and 148; 253/154; James Browne, *History of the Highlands* (1852–3 ed.) ii 458, 468–9.

any case, while Cardinal Fleury lived there was no real prospect of a restoration with French assistance. Walpole knew this, telling Ryder 'France would certainly not go into a war with us during the life of the Cardinal, but after his death, he believed she would, for the majority of the council were for it'.[1] He was absolutely right.

Co-operation between the two wings of the Opposition had virtually ceased with the death of Wyndham. The motion for the dismissal of Walpole in February 1741, Carte reported,

> was set on foot by the Duke of Argyll and the party of the Old Whigs without either concerting measures with the Tories or acquainting them with the matter, so that when it was moved in the Commons, Sir John Hynde Cotton and Sir Watkin Williams were forced to go about the House to solicit their friends to stay the debate, which they were vexed should be brought on without their concurrence

whereupon 'Parsons, Lord Mayor, and most of the Tory party left the House', including Shippen who 'retired into Solomon's porch, and would not vote either way'. Oxford's son Edward Lord Harley and his nephew Edward Harley left the House. Carte went on:

> Had all Sir Robert Walpole's actual opposers stayed he would not have carried the question by above 50 votes but the retiring of so many encouraged others to stay and even vote for him who durst not else have done it. Among those who voted were Lord Cornbury, Lord Quarendon the Earl of Lichfield's son, Mr. Bathurst, son of the Lord of that name, and Lord Andover, son of the Earl of Berkshire, though the fathers of the last three voted against Sir Robert Walpole in the Lords.[2]

It is a fact that at this time most Tories preferred Walpole to their Whig allies in Opposition. After his ruthlessness at the time of the Atterbury plot, he had gone out of his way to conciliate them by being more Anglican than the Church party, defeating the efforts of the Whig dissenters to secure the repeal of the Test and Corporation Acts, though this was of course to prevent them raising the cry of 'the Church in danger', their most effective call to battle in Anne's

---

[1] *HC* i 70.
[2] Stuart mss. 232/13; *HMC Egmont diary* iii 192.

days.[1] Shippen did not conceal his dislike of the opposition Whigs, saying: 'Robin and I are two honest men; he is for King George and I for King James; but those men with the long cravats [meaning Sandys and his associates] only desire places, either under King George or King James', and gave as his reason for walking out that 'he would not pull down Robin upon republican principles'. The motion was also disliked by the Tories because their 'principles abhor even the shadow of bills of pains and penalties', and this applied particularly to the Harleys because of Oxford's sufferings under such a bill.[2] There were also political reasons, since the Tories

> were not to be employed, they had rather Sir Robert was at the head of affairs than that the malcontent Whigs should take his place, of whose warmth they had less opinion than of Sir Robert's coolness, whose personal behaviour towards the Tories has always been obliging although an enemy to them as a party, and . . . they had too much pride to be the tools of the discontented Whigs, and put their hand under the stirrup to mount them into the saddle.[3]

The Tories formed over half the Opposition, and without their vote Walpole could not be brought down. Leading Whigs in Opposition at this time despaired of ever being able to encompass it.[4] Blaming the conduct of some of these Whigs for the defection of the Tories, Dodington, a follower of Argyll, criticised—

> that foolish manner of discourse . . . which is, that we are such immaculate Whigs, that if any change should happen, we should be as sorry as the minister that a Tory should be employed, and would use all endeavours to keep any share of the administration out of their hands. How impudent is this! What man, or body of men, will act with another, to be made professedly the scaffolding of his fortune, and then swept away with the rest of the rubbish?[5]

At constituency level, Whigs and Tories co-operated together at the general election of 1741 which left Walpole with a majority of only

---

[1] N. C. Hunt, *Two Early Political Associations*. For the Church in danger debate under Anne, see G. Holmes, *The Trial of Dr. Sacheverell*.

[2] *HC* ii 111, 423; Stuart mss. 232/13.

[3] *HMC Egmont diary* iii 192.

[4] *Lyttelton Memoirs* i 178–93.

[5] Coxe, *Sir Robert Walpole* iii 573–4.

16. This made concerted tactics in Parliament all the more essential. In retrospect, it would appear that the section of the Whig opposition led by Argyll, Chesterfield and Cobham were either ready to pay, or willing to appear ready to pay, the Tory price for bringing down Walpole: a restoration. In August 1741 Chesterfield set out for France, writing of Pulteney to Dodington 'the silly, half-witted, zealous Whigs consider him as the only support of Whiggism, and look upon us as running headlong into Bolingbroke and the Tories . . . if the Duke of Argyll sounds to battle, I will follow my leader.' In Paris he saw Bolingbroke, and then went on to Avignon to meet his kinsman, the Duke of Ormonde.[1] Walpole was alerted at once. It is difficult for us to realise the immense prestige Ormonde had retained with the Tories. Vilified by the Whigs for obeying as commander-in-chief the 'restraining orders' putting an end to hostilities with France before the Peace of Utrecht, he was regarded by fellow Tories as 'the best bred man of his age'.[2] In exile, he behaved with unfailing dignity before every reverse and kept aloof from the quarrels and recriminations to which the Jacobites were all too prone. The sequel of Chesterfield's visit to Ormonde, was a letter from James to his friends in England dated 16/27 September 1741 and sent through Col. Cecil:

I must earnestly recommend to all those with you who wish me well that they should pursue vigorous and unanimous measures in the next sessions of Parliament. They will probably have many occasions of greatly distressing the present Government and ministry, and will perhaps find some who will concur with them in that, though not out of good will to my cause, and even if the first proposers of measures which may tend to that end. In such cases I hope my friends will make no scruples in joining heartily with them for whatever their particular motives may be, anything that tends to the disadvantage of the present Government and to the bringing it into confusion cannot but be of advantage to my cause. Opportunities may offer during the next sessions, which if lost, may return no more, and besides the consequences that my friends showing a proper spirit may have at home, nothing certainly can more effectually encourage Cardinal Fleury to declare for us. Enfin, I take my friends' behaviour next session to be a matter of the greatest importance, and I doubt not but

---

[1] *Letters of Lord Chesterfield*, ed. B. Dobrée, ii 468–70; *HC* i 71.
[2] Dr William King, *Political and Literary Anecdotes* (1819 ed.) 9.

when they consider seriously what they owe both to themselves and to
me, they will not be wanting in anything that may contribute to our
common welfare, and indeed that of our country. I desire you will
communicate this letter or the contents of it to as many as you can
with safety and prudence.[1]

Walpole said he had proof that over one hundred copies of this letter
had been distributed, that it was procured by Chesterfield through
Ormonde, and that the loss of the crucial divisions leading to his fall
'was the effect of these summer negotiations'.[2] When the new Parliament met in December 1741, the Tories came up early, contrary to
their normal practice, and in their fullest numbers. A well-informed
ministerial supporter immediately noticed the change: 'Notwithstanding the personal candour that was shown upon the motion last
year, there is some cement that holds the Opposition together now,
stronger than I believe any consideration will be able to break
through.'[3] The Tories voted with the opposition Whigs in division
upon division until Walpole had to resign.

Early in 1742, just before Walpole's resignation, copies of a letter
from the Pretender dated 14/25 May 1741 was sent round to Tories
and opposition Whigs by the penny post. In this he referred to a
Declaration he had just signed:

It contains a general indemnity, without exception, for all that hath
passed against me and my family. A solemn engagement to maintain
the Church of England as by law established in all her rights,
privileges, possessions and immunities whatsoever. And as I am
utterly averse to all animosities and persecution on account of
religion, it also contains a promise to grant and allow a toleration to
all Protestant dissenters.

I also express in it an utter aversion to the suspending of the
Habeas Corpus Act, as well as to the loading of my subjects with
unnecessary taxes, or the raising of them in a manner burthensome
to them, and especially to the introducing of foreign excises, and all
such methods as may have hitherto been advised and pursued to
acquire arbitrary power at the expense of the liberty and property of
the subject. And besides there is a general article of my readiness to

---

[1] *HC* i 71; Stuart mss. 236/73; Add. 9224ff. 2–4.
[2] *HC* i 71; Ryder diary 4 Dec. 1741, Coxe, *Sir Robert Walpole* i. 687n.
[3] *HC* i 71.

settle all that may relate to the welfare and happiness of the nation both in civil and ecclesiastical matters by the sincere advice and concurrence of a free Parliament.

George Heathcote, Member for London and a leading opposition Whig, sent his copy to the Duke of Newcastle, the Secretary of State.[1] James Erskine, Member for Stirling Burghs, was the brother of the late Lord Mar who had led the '15. Erskine had been prominent in concerting the tactics of the Opposition since 1734 and was connected with Pulteney and Cobham as well as Gower while corresponding with the Pretender.[2] He discussed the contents of this letter with John Proby, Tory Member for Stamford and Gower's brother-in-law. Proby approved of it, but he criticised James's advisers, especially Col. Cecil, whom he called 'a foolish man', and James Murray, Lord Dunbar, Secretary of State in Rome. Erskine replied that if Proby would care to suggest 'the most proper persons among the Tories to take the direction of H.M.'s affairs in England' he would transmit his proposals. The Pretender had written to Erskine to desire he should assure his friends among the opposition Whigs that if 'they enter seriously and heartily into measures for bringing about my restoration . . . there is no reasonable demand they can make, either on behalf of themselves in particular, or of the country in general, that I shall not readily and cheerfully comply with'. Just before Walpole's fall, Erskine gave Pulteney a copy of the Pretender's letter of May 1741. At their next meeting, Pulteney returned it, saying: 'Take your papers, I do not love to have such papers!' Erskine then pointed out the dissatisfaction of the Tories, and how difficult it had been to hold the Opposition together, upon which 'Mr. Pulteney answered that he had done exceedingly well, but now he thanked God that they were out of the power of the Tories, for Sir Robert Walpole . . . had sent to them and agreed to resign his offices and leave them to form a ministry such as they found proper'.[3]

For over twenty-five years the Tory party had been kept together, with only a handful of defections, a remarkable enough feat since its leaders had no rewards to offer. Their main concern was to negotiate

---

[1] SP 36/60/131–6. I am obliged to Dame Lucy Sutherland for this reference.
[2] *HC* ii 14–17; *Marchmont Papers* ii 2–4, 18, 58, 128–9, 167.
[3] Stuart mss. 240/140; 242/112; *HC* ii 16.

from strength and make terms as a party and not allow their political opponents to split them. This was, of course, normal political behaviour, but it was denounced by those whose ends were checked by it as obstinacy and short-sightedness. The public demands of the Tory party were: a reduction of the army, the organisation of an effective militia (in which they would be allowed to serve), a foreign policy based on the national interest, a repeal of the Septennial Act, the Riot Act, the Waltham Black Act and the Smuggling Act.[1] In other words they wanted all the repressive legislation passed since 1715 swept away. These demands were expressed in many instructions sent to Tory Members from all parts of England and Wales, and one was sent from Scotland to James Erskine. Those sent to Sir Watkin Williams Wynn from Denbighshire denounced 'standing armies in time of peace' who 'like the locusts of Egypt cover the face of the land, living in sloth and idleness, and devouring the labours of the industrious'. These instructions also demanded bills to prevent corruption at elections and the 'villainous practices of returning officers', and vigorous inquiries into the corruption and mismanagements of the late administration.[2]

A non-Jacobite Tory noticed at this time that 'the body of the Tories are suddenly listed under a new general, the Duke of Argyll'.[3] At a meeting of the whole Opposition at the Fountain Tavern in the Strand on 12 February 1742, Argyll called for the formation of a Government based on the principle of 'the Broad Bottom, a cant word which corresponding equally with the personal figure of some of their leaders [Cotton] and the nature of their pretensions, was understood to imply a party united to force the Tories into the Administration'. Wynn was doing his utmost to secure for Argyll the post of commander-in-chief of the army—to act as the General Monck of a second Stuart restoration. On Argyll's refusal to accept this office unless his Tory friends were given places,

> Sir Watkin Williams Wynn, with a considerable number of other Parliament men, repaired to his Grace, and exposed to him that

[1] *The Conduct of the late and present ministry compared*, 1742, quoted in A. Foord, *His Majesty's Opposition*, 234. For the Black Act, see E. P. Thompson, *Whigs and Hunters*. For the effects of the Smuggling Act, see below Chapter 4.
[2] *Gentleman's Magazine* 1742, 216–17.
[3] *HC* i 612.

unless matters were in a further way of settlement, they should all break to pieces next Thursday, when the Parliament was to meet; that when the question about the army should come on, he and the rest were determined to oppose continuing the same number unless his Grace were at the head of it, and therefore they pressed him hard to accept his Majesty's offer to restore him to his posts.

The next day, Argyll and 'the chiefs of the Tory party . . . waited on the King whose rooms had not been seen from the beginning of the reign so crowded', when 'the King was surprised to see such a number of new faces, gentlemen and lords of great property and interest in their countries [i.e. counties], but expressed himself troubled that (as he had heard) some of them said they would come but that once'.[1] Ryder wrote that Argyll 'stands out, and insists he will come into no accommodation till some of his friends are brought in, and particularly that Lord Gower, Lord Bathurst, Sir Watkin Williams Wynn, and Sir John Hynde Cotton are provided for'. On 17 February, the day before Parliament met, it was agreed that Argyll should be restored to his former offices, that Cobham should have a regiment with the rank of field marshal, and that Bathurst, Chesterfield and Gower should be provided for as soon as suitable vacancies occurred. On 10 March, Argyll resigned because the King would not accept his nomination of Sir John Cotton and Barrymore's brother-in-law Lord Granard as lords of the Admiralty.[2] At another meeting of the Opposition at the Fountain Tavern the next day, Argyll declared that a few were engrossing to themselves 'the exclusive right of nomination', adding:

The choice of those already preferred having fallen upon the Whigs, is an ill omen to the Tories. If these are not to be provided for, the happy effects of the coalition will be destroyed, and the odious distinction of party be revived. It is therefore highly necessary to continue closely united, and to persevere with the same vehemence as ever, till the Tories obtain justice, and the administration is founded upon the broad bottom of both parties.

Pulteney replied it must be the work of time 'to remove suspicions incalculated long and long credited, with regard to a denomination

[1] *HC* i 71–2; *HMC Egmont diary* iii 257–8.
[2] *HMC Egmont diary* iii 254–6, 257–8; *HC* i 52–3; Ryder diary 17 Feb. 1742.

of men, who have formerly been thought not heartily attached to the reigning family'.[1] Privately, Pulteney told Bishop Newton that the Tories would have had justice had it not been for their 'mad ideas'.[2] Bussy, the French envoy in London, who for reasons of his own was on the closest terms with the English ministers,[3] reported that Argyll and Chesterfield bitterly attacked Pulteney and Carteret for taking office to the exclusion of the Tories. Walpole feared above all that Carteret would agree to 'a Tory Parliament [i.e. a free Parliament] which must naturally end in the Pretender'. Pulteney was said to have waited on Frederick Prince of Wales, advising him he should insist on office for Bathurst, Gower, Lord Carlisle, Lord Westmorland, Cobham and Sir John Cotton. The real obstacle was George II's 'unconquerable aversion' for the Tories.[4] To try to satisfy the clamours of Tories and some of the opposition Whigs, particularly those in the City of London, Pulteney presented a bill in March to prevent false returns at elections and secured the passing of a watered-down place bill introduced by Sandys, but a bill sponsored by Thomas Carew, a Jacobite Tory, to prevent court pensioners from sitting in Parliament was thrown out in the Lords by a large majority.[5]

In the spring of 1742, most of the Tories, especially Carew and John Philipps, warmly supported a motion to send the army to Flanders, but opposed proposals to bring a corresponding number of troops over from Ireland, deriding the possibility of an invasion or a Jacobite insurrection.[6] A memorandum in the French Foreign Office commented that Carteret's policy of sending all available troops to the Continent was precisely what the Tory party had always wanted.[7]

In June 1742 the news broke out that the Duke of Argyll had given his brother, Lord Ilay, to hand over to the King, two letters he had received from the Pretender. At first, Argyll said he had them from Col. Cecil, which Horace Walpole thought unlikely since

---

[1] Lord Perceval, *Faction Detected*.
[2] Foord, 224.
[3] See below Chapter 4.
[4] Add. 33004f. 86; Ryder diary Feb. 1742.
[5] *HMC Egmont diary* iii 262.
[6] Owen 132-3.
[7] AEM & D Ang. 78ff. 5-9.

Argyll had not seen Cecil for two years. Then Argyll admitted that 'upon recollection he thought it right to say he had received those letters from Lord Barrymore'. The first, in the Pretender's own hand, was 'to thank Mr. Burnus [the Duke of Argyll] for his services and that he hopes he would answer *the assurances* given of him'. The second, a copy of a circular letter from the Pretender to his friends in England dated 25 April 1742 was as follows:

Though I am very impatient to hear from you, I cannot delay any longer expressing to you my satisfaction at the late behaviour of my friends in Parliament, and I take it as a great mark of their singular regard for what I wrote to you some months ago, because I am sensible that some of them were not entirely of opinion that Mr. Tench's [Sir R. Walpole's] removal would be for my interest: as affairs have fallen out that even proves more to my advantage than could have been well expected, which will I hope encourage my friends the more to pursue the most vigorous measures during the remainder of this session. Whatever step they take, or measures they may pursue which can any ways tend to the ease of the people and good of our country will always be encouraged and applauded by me, though I were to draw no personal advantage by it myself, but that is not like to be the case in the present circumstances, and it must surely appear now very visible to all impartial men, who will allow themselves to reflect, that my and my family's restoration is the only effectual remedy for the evils the nation groans under, but it cannot be expected that it should be brought about of a sudden. My friends late conduct does them honour, it shows the whole nation the greatness of their influence and what they are able to do. I should much encourage them to continue what they have begun till they have perfected the work they have at heart. It is not a single member being removed that will alone effect it, but a steady, vigorous and constant pursuit of all such measures as may effectually tend to the distressing the present government and whoever shall be the chief ministers and directors of it, to the overthrowing all entirely at last, as the only effectual means to provide for the welfare of the nation. Let therefore all other views and considerations give place to this great and single object, let no private jealousies and party animosities obstruct a perfect union amongst themselves or hinder them from going heartily with whoever has their country's interest at heart, and shall even add with cheerfulness and sincerity, let them think neither of me, nor my family, but in as much as we may be the instrument of relieving our country from its present oppression and restoring it to its former glory and happiness for I shall always be happy enough when I see my country so. It is the only thing in general I can express to you, it is you on the place that can only determine on particular measures according to the different circumstances of things and I desire you would communicate this to as many of our friends as you can with prudence and safety.[1]

James Erskine was indignant, writing of Argyll:

His conduct to Lord Barrymore is condemned by all the earth. He has long lived in great friendship with that Lord, and professed great honour and respect for him as a man of sense and worth, and one of the best officers in Britain, and though his Lordship was several days within a few miles of his Grace's house after delivering the Chevalier's [the Pretender's] letter to him, and so he exposed his friend to be caught napping for a treasonable fact, though it could not have imputed anything against his Grace to have given his friend previous notice of the danger he was to bring him into.[2]

Carteret, not wishing it to be known that the Whig opposition, in part at least, had acted in concert with the Pretender, suppressed the Pretender's letter, so that 'nothing was done upon it'. Walpole's verdict on this was that Argyll 'was got into the Pretender's scheme but when Colonel Cecil sent him a letter from the Pretender he had not the courage to stand by his promise'. Barrymore left immediately for Ireland where he remained till the end of the year. As to Argyll, after this he lived 'retired, hardly seeing anybody, or speaking to the few admitted to him, but as one moped, indolent, dejected and broken-hearted' until his death in October 1743.[3]

During the summer recess, Cotton met Dodington to agree measures for a new opposition, which opened next session. In the debate on taking 16,000 Hanoverian troops into British pay on 10 December 1742, Carte reported:

Sir Watkin Williams Wynn declared that England was made a mere province of Hanover, and when there were some for taking the words down, Sir J. H. Cotton got up, averred it to be so in fact, repeated and justified the words so that the House acquiesced . . . Sir John St.

[1] *HC* i 72; Add. 9129ff. 123–4; Stuart mss. 241/52.
[2] Stuart mss. 249/83.
[3] *HC* i 72, 114, 441; Stuart mss. 241/52; Ryder diary June 1742.

Aubyn . . . declared it to be his sentiment, that we lived under a Prince who being used to arbitrary power in his dominions abroad, was minded to establish it here, that all his measures were calculated for that end, and that of the Hanoverian troops in particular . . . This speech made him in a moment the darling toast of London.

Sir John Philipps (now a baronet) declared 'it is Hanover and Hanover only that seems now to be our care', giving detailed figures purporting to show that £392,697 were charged for the Hanoverian troops by the King as Elector, though they cost him only £100,000. Lord Gower and his friends also weighed in against the Hanoverians. The Tories made all the political capital they could out of the open preference George II showed to his Hanoverian officers and his tactlessness in wearing the yellow sash of Hanover at the battle of Dettingen in June 1743. Although George II had shown personal bravery in leading in person the army that defeated the French at that battle, the Opposition, led by Chesterfield and Cobham, turned the battle into a propaganda defeat. Even the Duke of Newcastle, riled because he and Pelham were having to support in Parliament 'Hanoverian' policies in Europe without being consulted, denounced 'German politics, German measures, and (what is near as bad as either) German manners' and thought that the Hanoverian troops would have to be sacrificed to popular clamour.[1]

[1] *HC* i 72; Owen 157, 183–7.

3

The Plans for a Restoration

The death in January 1743 at the age of 90 of Cardinal Fleury who had retained complete power until the end, changed the European situation. No first minister was appointed to succeed him and in theory Louis XV was to govern personally as Louis XIV had done. In fact his successors were the secretaries of state, 'the four kings of France' as Frederick the Great called them, who conducted business without consulting the great nobles on the council of state.[1] Their aims and policies were quite different from Fleury's, and since they play a central part in this story some account of them must be given. They were led by the one longest in office, Jean-Frédéric Phély-peaux, Comte de Maurepas, Secretary of State for the navy since 1723 and a member of one of the oldest ministerial families in France. In spite of Fleury's policy of strict retrenchment, by con-centrating on quality rather than quantity, Maurepas had rebuilt an effective French navy from the ruins of that of Louis XIV. He was also the minister in charge of French trade and the colonies. Beneath the appearance of a court wit, with a formidable reputation as a writer of epigrams and lampoons, he was a hard-working and able minister.[2] The Comptroller General of the Finances, the next most influential member of the ministerial group, was Philibert Orry, Comte de Vignory, who had held this post since 1730. He had the reputation of a competent, honest minister, rather than a brilliant one, and was regarded as common sense personified. By economy and more efficient administration of existing taxes, helped by the long period of peace under Fleury, he had refilled the treasury left

[1] Frederick II, *Oeuvres Complètes*, Berlin 1790, ii 187; *Mémoires du Duc de Luynes* v 86; *Journal et Mémoires du Marquis d'Argenson*, ed. Rathéry, i 340-1.
[2] Lacour-Gayet, *La Marine militaire de la France sous Louis XV* 88; Luynes v 89; Add. 32747f. 292.

empty by the wars of Louis XIV.[1] The Secretary of State for War, Pierre de Voyer de Paulmy, Comte d'Argenson, came like Maurepas from a ministerial family. He was regarded as one of the most accomplished and handsome men of the age, not only a good minister, but a leader of the Enlightenment, a friend of Montesquieu and a patron of the Encyclopedists.[2] Last and least was Amelot de Chaillou, Secretary of State for Foreign Affairs since 1737. He had been treated as a clerk rather than a minister by Fleury, and now looked to Maurepas for guidance on all matters of importance.[3] These ministers had very much disapproved of but been powerless to prevent France's entry into the War of the Austrian Succession under pressure from the great court nobles, whose only career was the army and only means to fame and promotion the battlefield. Even Fleury could not withstand the torrent. A great league of German princes to vote for the Elector of Bavaria, the French candidate for Emperor, was negotiated by the Comte de Belle-Isle, nephew of Fouquet, Louis XIV's minister. He was assisted by Chavigny, who was against a restoration of the Stuarts ever since the failure of his friend Bolingbroke's plan in the thirties. The agreement of most German princes was won by the simple device of buying most of them, at enormous prices. George II as Elector of Hanover was cowed into signing a convention for the neutrality of Hanover in 1741, and even to promise to vote for the Elector of Bavaria and to try to stop English attacks on French shipping by the threat of a French invasion of his electorate. This was backed up by military operations against Austria, successful at first but ending in the disastrous retreat from Prague in which Belle-Isle lost most of his army.[4] These policies had cost France millions, brought her no real benefit and were now discredited. In the light of this situation, the ministers began to review favourably the plans for a restoration of the Stuarts submitted to Cardinal Fleury since 1740, to which the cardinal had given nothing but fair words. The reasons why this policy was adopted were spelled out only in 1745, but logically they should be

[1] Marion, *Histoire financière de la France depuis 1715* i 30, 162; Argenson iv 198-9.

[2] Balteau, *Dictionnaire de Biographie Française*; Luynes v 90.

[3] Balteau; Argenson iv 239-40; Luynes v 89-90.

[4] See M. Sautai, *Les Préliminaires de la Guerre de Succession d'Autriche*, and *Les Débuts de la Guerre de Succession d'Autriche*.

given at this stage. They were as follows. An alliance with England
had been regarded as beneficial for French trade since the days of
Charles II, and had been so since 1716. The partnership with the
House of Hanover had begun to break down in the late thirties,
and since the outbreak of the war against Spain France had
been engaged in hostilities with England as an auxiliary of Spain,
though not officially at war with her. A Stuart king would not inter-
vene in Continental affairs in the way the Electors of Hanover had
done. Austria, still regarded as the greatest enemy of France, would
be deprived of a valuable ally, Sardinia would have to make terms,
and Holland would be neutralised. The Anglo-Spanish war would
end. France had no territorial claims against England, and if she had
any views on English colonies they were not stated.[1]

It was in this situation that Francis, Lord Sempill, who had superseded Col. O'Brian as the Pretender's representative at the French
court, went to see Amelot in the spring of 1743 with a message from
the Duke of Beaufort, Lord Barrymore, Lord Orrery, Sir Watkin
Williams Wynn, Sir John Hynde Cotton and Sir Robert Abdy,
asking for French assistance for a restoration.[2] A member of one of
the oldest families in England, the 3rd Duke of Beaufort was one of
the four wealthiest men in England. His father, the second duke, had
been lord lieutenant of Hampshire and Gloucestershire under Queen
Anne, and had obtained places and favours of all kinds for his friends
and protégés.[3] The third duke had *nothing*. Sir Robert Abdy, 3rd Bt.,
member for Essex, was a large landowner and a friend of Cotton's.[4]
As Lord Sempill plays an important part in the origins of the '45,
something should be said of him. Murray of Broughton's portrait
of Sempill is an attempt, an all too successful attempt, at character
assassination. Sempill befriended Murray, praised him to James,
introduced him to the French ministers, in return for which Murray
(whose testimony when checked against the French sources shows
him to have been a liar) did all he could to discredit Sempill. The
son of a Scottish peer who was out in the '15 and whose forfeited
estates were granted to a Whig relation, Francis Sempill had been
employed in missions in England ever since the days of the Atterbury

[1] AEM & D. Ang. 78f. 212; Luynes v 343 and n.l.
[2] AEM & D. Ang. 82ff. 67–8.
[3] See 2nd Duke of Beaufort's letterbook at Badminton.
[4] *The Houblon Family* 40.

plot. The dowager Lady Sandwich, a Jacobite living in Paris, welcomed his appointment, writing to the Pretender 'his sagacity, penetration, and integrity are employed in Your Majesty's service with so much vigilance and prudence, that I cannot make a better wish than that all who have the honour to be employed in Your Majesty's affairs may be endowed with such qualities as he possesses'. His papers at the Quai d'Orsay and the French foreign archives show him to have had ready access to French ministers and to have been on good terms with influential people at the court of Versailles, as well as devoted to the Stuarts. James later wrote to Charles Edward that no one had as much influence over his friends in England as Sempill. Sempill's message fell on sympathetic ears, but he was told by Amelot that he and his colleagues would require more substantial proof of support in England.[1] Balhaldy, the secretary of the associated Scottish lords, who was a close friend of James Erskine and had probably come to know the Tory leaders through Erskine, went over to England in June 1743 to see what could be arranged. There, Cotton had made it an absolute precondition that Col. Cecil must be kept out, observing that—

> the Government was not and could not be ignorant of Col. Cecil's correspondence with Your Majesty [the Pretender] and yet suffered it to go on, notwithstanding of which he did not judge Col. Cecil to be a traitor but a fool, concluding as Lord Barrymore and Lord Orrery had done that it was proper to keep him in temper in order to avoid the effects of his resentment.

This being agreed, they and those 'in the concert the City of London' undertook 'to procure all reasonable satisfaction to the King of France'.[2] They all refused to give pledges under their own hands—as the Immortal Seven had refused in 1688, signing their Invitation in cypher only—as being 'dangerous and useless'. Louis XV arranged to send James Butler, a kinsman of Ormonde, and his master of the horse (*premier écuyer de la grande écurie*) to England under the pretext of purchasing horses for the royal stables. Louis XV was passionately fond of horses, and Butler's knowledge

---

[1] Boyer, *Political State* xxv 394; AEM & D. Ang. 78f. 19; Browne ii 449. For Lady Sandwich, see Duke of Manchester, *Court and Society from Elizabeth to Anne*; Stuart mss. 283/1.

[2] AEM & D Ang. 75f. 196; 82ff. 62–9; *HC* i 585 and App. p. 114.

4

of horseflesh had made him something of a favourite at court. He had been several times to England before on similar errands, so that his presence would not arouse the suspicions of the English Government. He spoke English fluently, which would avoid the danger of misunderstandings. Louis XV briefed him personally before he left Versailles, telling him to assure the Tory leaders that all their demands would be met 'provided he (Butler) was enabled to vouch for what was affirmed'.[1]

Butler arrived in London in the first fortnight in August. He was entertained by twenty to thirty members of the corporation, and had private talks with Robert Willimot, the lord mayor and Member for London until 1741; Robert Westley, the alderman next in the chair, who would be lord mayor when the attempt was made; and with four aldermen: Heathcote, Gibbon, Benn and Lambert.[2] George Heathcote, a radical Whig, had been sent the Pretender's letter of 25 May 1741 after the fall of Walpole and had then sent it to Newcastle. He 'opened himself' to Sir John Cotton at this time and thereafter became one of the most zealous Jacobites in England. He was an important gain, not only as an effective speaker in Parliament, but as one of the most influential men in the City. Edward Gibbon, Member for Southampton, the historian's father, was the son of a successful merchant, army contractor under William, who, the historian wrote 'would have contracted with more pleasure, though not, perhaps at a cheaper rate, for the service of King James', and had had considerable losses in the South Sea Bubble. Alderman Gibbon had been brought up in a household where 'in the daily devotions to the family the name of the King, for whom they prayed, was prudently omitted', and by a nonjuring tutor. Going on to Westminster and Cambridge, he was a scholar and a gentlemen, not a merchant, and soon found the duties of an alderman irksome. William Benn, who was known to have been an active Jacobite, was a member of the powerful city lands committee of the corporation, which controlled a good deal of its patronage. Daniel Lambert, Member for London, a Portugal merchant, had been very active in the agitation for war against Spain.[3] They were reported to have

[1] AEM & D. Ang. 77ff. 44–5; 76f. 209; 82ff. 62–92; Stuart mss. 250/169; 251/127; 252/40; 253/154. For Butler, see Luynes v 421.
[2] AEM & D. Ang. 85f. 82.
[3] AEM & D. Ang. 82ff. 71–2; 77f. 46; *HC* ii 121, 546; Beaven, *Aldermen of*

shown 'great zeal for a revolution'. A list of the corporation of London (in a hand not identified) was given to Butler, dividing it into Jacobite Patriots, Patriots, Hanoverian Whigs and Whigs, which gave 176 Jacobite Patriots out of 236 members of the common council (see Appendix II). According to the unknown author of this list, the City was said to have chosen—

the most zealous and distinguished Patriots, governors of their public hospitals, and its advisers in affairs of moment, to wit Sir John Hynde Cotton, Sir Watkin Williams Wynn, the Earl of Lichfield, Sir William Carew, Sir John St. Aubyn, Sir Robert Abdy, Mr. Bramston, and others of the same kidney.

Butler was also told that the bitter opposition to the Court shown by the Independent Electors of the City of Westminster, an organisation which had wrested control of Westminster from the Court in 1741, stemmed from 'their attachment to their rightful King'. Later, John Sample, one of Walpole's spies, told Newcastle that most of the plans for the French invasion had been concerted with Sir Watkin Williams Wynn and Sir William Carew under cover of the meetings of the Independent Electors.[1] Butler left London on 6 September for the Lichfield races, where he was met by Sir Watkin Williams Wynn and 'most of our friends', who expressed 'great joy' at being informed that Charles Edward would lead the proposed expedition.[2] Though nothing was put in writing, it was implicit in all the arrangements made that James would resign the Crown to Charles Edward, and according to a well-informed source in France, it had been made a precondition for French assistance.[3] The Lichfield races were a gathering of Tory gentlemen, usually presided over by Lord Gower and Sir Watkin Williams Wynn.[4] We do not know whom Butler met privately there, for he never wrote a report, and what we know of his

London i 195; ii 127, 129, 197; SP 36/60/131–6; Gibbon, *Memoirs of My Life*, ed. Bonnard, 12–8; Ryder diary 28 Jan. 1746.
   [1] AEM & D. Ang. 76f. 202; Stuart mss. 254/154; *HC* i 286; SP 36/63/102. For John Sample, see Fritz 116, 121–2, 141–2.
   [2] AEM & D. Ang. 86f. 214.
   [3] *Journal et Mémoires de Barbier*, ed. Villegille, ii 385–6.
   [4] Anne J. Kettle, 'The Lichfield Races', *Lichfield and S. Staffs. Arch and Historic Society* vi 39–44 (*ex. inf.* Dr Linda Colley).

mission comes from Sempill's papers, Balhaldy's letters to the Pretender and a memorandum drawn up for the French ministers by a clerk of the French Foreign Office. According to these Butler met a good many 'honest' (i.e. Jacobite) gentlemen, who drank King James's health, presumably over the water. Butler left Lichfield on 16 September, went to 'meet some friends in the neighbourhood of London' towards the end of the month, and did not see Sir John Cotton and Sir Robert Abdy, who had been in the country all the while until the beginning of October, and it is presumably because of this that Murray of Broughton (who knew of Butler's mission at second-hand through Lord Traquair, as representative of the lords of the Scottish association) wrote that Cotton was 'shy' at first more from 'timorousness than want of inclination'.[1]

The actual military plans agreed upon were not communicated in full to the Pretender or to the Duke of Ormonde, because they were thought to have been surrounded by spies of the British Government. For this reason, there is more information about them in the French archives than in the Stuart manuscripts. These precautions were necessary. In the Pretender's case, besides the agents already known to historians, there was another and much more dangerous one: an ecclesiastic called Rota, who was in charge of cyphers at the Papal Court, and professed the greatest attachment to James while he was in the pay of the English Government.[2] Beaufort, Orrery, Wynn, Barrymore, Cotton and Abdy asked for 10,000 French troops and arms for 10,000. This was not to be like the '15, a rising of amateurs against professional troops. It was to be, as in 1688, an invasion by a foreign army at the invitation of influential people in England, who pledged themselves to join as soon as the troops had successfully landed. The people for whom the ten thousand arms were asked were not tenants of the country gentlemen, but the officers on half pay and the soldiers who had been broke, who, it was thought, would join. The most essential part, the French were told, was to secure London as soon as possible as the centre of the government and most of the financial resources of the country. Maldon near Colchester in Essex was chosen for the landing because London could be reached from there without crossing the Thames, because there were said to be many Jacobites

---

[1] AEM & D. Ang. 86ff. 214–15; Stuart mss. 353/154; *HC* i 585.
[2] For Rota, see Add. 32751f. 179; 32776ff. 73, 410–12.

in Essex, and because the English fleet did not patrol that coast. The Tory leaders asked for Maurice of Saxony, the natural son of Augustus II, Elector of Saxony and King of Poland, to command the French army, not only because he was regarded as the best general in the French service, but because he was a Protestant and was known personally to most of them. In order to conciliate the Scots, a separate French expedition to Scotland was requested under the command of Lord Marischal (the Earl Marshal of Scotland, who had been in exile since the '15). Absolute secrecy being vital to the success of the enterprise, the plans were made known to only a handful of people.[1] Apart from the six already mentioned, the secret was communicated to Sir John St. Aubyn, 3rd Bt., Member for Cornwall, owner of St. Michael's Mount and of large tin mines, who had been one of the leaders of the Atterbury plot in 1722 and had told Carte in 1739 that he could raise the tinners for the Pretender's service; Sir William Carew, 5th Bt., Wynn's friend, Member for Cornwall and a large landowner there; Sir Henry Slingsby, 5th Bt., Member for Knaresborough in Yorkshire; and John Baptist Caryll, Baron Caryll in the Jacobite peerage, the grandson of Pope's friend John Caryll, and the owner of Ladyholt and other substantial estates, but ones much encumbered with debts. He was the only Roman Catholic involved. Because of the landing place chosen, another five were let into the secret: Charles Gray, Member for Colchester, a successful lawyer who had acquired substantial estates by marriage, a scholar and a reformer who had brought proceedings for corruption against the corporation of Colchester of which his Whig father was a member, which had led to its dissolution and to his father disinheriting him; Samuel Savill, also Tory Member for Colchester; Thomas Bramston, Member for Essex, one of the ablest of the parliamentary lawyers, who had secured the passing of an Act of Parliament in 1732 to impose a £100 p.a. property qualification on justices of the peace in an attempt to prevent the inclusion of landless justices in Tory counties in order to secure a Whig majority; Mr. Read, who was described as a gentleman of great property in the country of Essex, probably Henry Read of Earl's Fee in Barstable, Essex; and Sir Edward Smith, 3rd Bt., of Hill Hall in Theydon Mount,

[1] AEM & D. Ang. 82ff. 65–95; 76ff. 186–7.

Essex.[1] The Duke of Bedford, through his father-in-law Lord Gower, was said to have given assurances of support for a restoration at this time, though Bedford was not to be 'trusted with anything before execution'. Gower had just been elected president of the Loyal Brotherhood, the Tory club (or board as it was called), in succession to the 2nd Earl of Lichfield, an office which by this time was considered tantamount to being the head of the Tory party. Like Lord Bathurst, Gower had not been active in the Pretender's affairs since the days of Lord Cornbury's negotiations, but he had presumably met Butler at Lichfield, and was regarded as committed at this time, which helps to explain subsequent Tory resentment against Gower and Bedford.[2]

Butler was given a list of the nobility and gentry in English counties and in Wales 'who could be relied upon' (Appendix I). Published in extracts (in a not invariably accurate translation) from a copy sent to the Pretender by Balhaldy and wrongly attributed to Butler, the list has been treated heretofore as showing men pledged to *rise* in 1745.[3] Drawn up in England, the list (in a hand that has not been identified) is now printed exactly as it was given to Butler. It was meant to convey 'the general inclination of the nation' and included people who were expected to 'rally to their legitimate sovereign' by 'declaring' for a restoration by way of a free Parliament, as had been done in 1660.[4] It was in fact the equivalent of the lists drawn up by Danby before the Revolution of 1688 of 'the names of the men of real position and influence throughout the country who might be expected to countenance a movement against James' in the event of a successful invasion by William.[5] Only those in the concert were expected to ride out to meet Charles Edward when the landing took place, and it was recognised on both sides that the advantage would be not only secrecy, but the fact that if the attempt failed, it would look like an unsuccessful French invasion, and no one in England would be implicated. Obviously the amount of support expected was probably much magnified in order to

[1] *HC* i 81–2, 529; ii 401–2, 425; *Quarterly Review* cxxxix 367–95; Howard Erskine-Hill, *The Social Milieu of Alexander Pope* 81, 83, 101–2; Morant, *Essex* i 259.

[2] Stuart mss. 242/40; Add. 32804ff. 286–7; *HC* ii 431; see below Chapter 7.

[3] Eardley-Simpson, *Derby and the Forty Five*, App. pp. 235–61.

[4] AEM & D. Ang. 85f. 92.

[5] A. Browning, *Thomas Osborne, Earl of Danby* iii 152–3, 157–63.

persuade the French. In sending a copy of the lists to the Pretender, Balhaldy wrote, 'as to the list of nobility there cannot well be many more depended on than those who are named there; and that in the state of the counties, it was not possible to make them fuller or distincter in the time or the season of the year, when every creature was in the country'.[1] It was a list of people expected to declare for a restoration provided a successful landing had been effected by French troops with Charles Edward at their head, conditions which were never fulfilled. Nevertheless, an attempt has been made not only to identify all the persons on this list, but also to define, wherever possible, the line they took in the different circumstances of the '45. It is interesting to see that most of the Whigs on this list were connected with Cobham, Bedford or Chesterfield.

How widespread was the wish for a restoration at this time is not a question that, on the face of it, can ever be answered. For the Tories it did seem indeed the only means left of ending a proscription which had now lasted twenty-eight years. Balhaldy at this time defines the problem of counting heads as far as Jacobites were concerned:

The many sanguinary penal laws since the Revolution, whereby the crime of Jacobitism is rendered more horribly dreadful in its consequences than murder, witchcraft or even open deism or atheism . . . has brought such a habit and spirit of dissimulation on them, that a Jacobite can never be discovered by his words. It must be his actions that decypher him.[2]

Sir Lewis Namier noticed long ago that Tory family papers are non-existent for the reigns of the first two Georges.[3] Many would have been destroyed through the accidents of time, but in collections where they have survived before 1715 and after 1760, it seems a reasonable assumption to think there was something to hide. A nineteenth-century antiquary who had seen many such collections concluded that it was 'the custom in Jacobite days to destroy all letters with any hint of political or religious feeling in them'.[4] It ought to be easier to identify the non-Jacobite Tories, since declaring

[1] Stuart mss. 253/154.
[2] Stuart mss. 253/154.
[3] *Crossroads of Power*, 35.
[4] J. Robinson, *The Delaval Papers*, 56.

one's loyalty to the Crown was not fraught with danger and was indeed much encouraged by the Government; yet in the parliamentary Tory party, after every effort was made to find them, they turned out to be a small proportion of the whole. Some historians have regarded the bulk of the Tories as overwhelmingly well-affected to the House of Hanover.[1] If they were, why did they not say so? After all, the Tories were forward enough in expressing their loyalty to Queen Anne or George III. Popular Jacobitism is almost virgin territory,[2] but again almost impossible to explore after the passing of the Riot Act. Jacobite demonstrations did take place at elections when the troops had to be drawn away from constituencies, in Westminster, Coventry, Chester and elsewhere, but it is difficult to say how representative they were.[3] Again the Jacobite riots among the Cornish tinners, the West Country clothiers, or the Newcastle keelmen, were most probably economic rather than political in origin.[4]

The other papers prepared by the Tory leaders in the concert in the late summer of 1743 was a proposed council of regency for Charles Edward to consist of 'the Duke of Beaufort, the Earl of Barrymore, the Earl of Orrery, Sir Watkin Williams Wynn, Sir John Hynde Cotton, Sir Robert Abdy, the Earl of Westmorland, and Lord Cobham'. Westmorland and Cobham were included 'because of their reputations and abilities, if they can be brought at first to his Majesty's standard which is not much questioned'. John Fane, 7th Earl of Westmorland, had been returned by his friend Lord Cobham as Whig Member of Parliament for Buckingham. In 1734, he had been deprived of his regiment, the Life Guards, for voting against the Government without being allowed to sell out, thus losing £6,500. His resentment had 'led him to imbibe' what Horace Walpole was pleased to call 'all the nonsensical tenets of the Jacobites', and with the zeal of a convert he became one of the most active of them all. Cobham, a dark horse in politics, was a man to be reckoned with as the patron of the Cobham cubs, some of the ablest young men in the Commons, men such as William

---

[1] Hill 192–3; Owen 214.
[2] See N. Rogers, 'Popular Protest in early Hanoverian London', *Past and Present* lxxxix (1978) 70–100.
[3] *HC* i 203–4, 285–7, 339–40.
[4] See Carte's memo of 1739, Stuart mss. 216/111.

Pitt, the Grenvilles and George Lyttelton, though it is not, of course, suggested they knew anything of his game. The Pretender complied, adding to the council the names of Chesterfield, Sir John St. Aubyn, Sir Henry Slingsby and the lord mayor of London (Westley).[1] A safe means of correspondence between the Tory leaders, the French Court, and Sempill, was assured through John Lefebure, foreign secretary to the Post Office, and a secret Jacobite. Lefebure, whose 'zeal, fidelity and services' were said to be well known to James and Charles Edward, was in charge of the secrets department of the Post Office where intercepted mail was opened. His letters to Sempill show that he not only revealed whose letters were being opened but that he suppressed information most damaging to individual Jacobites from 1740 onwards. He was assured that no changes would be made in the Post Office on a restoration without consulting him.[2] Butler was given, besides the lists of the corporation of London, the nobility and the well-affected in the counties, a list of the exact size and disposition of the forces then in England, obtained from a John Mill, clerk to the Paymaster of the Army, and a secret Jacobite like Lefebure, through whom he continued to send military intelligence. Mill's lists gave 10,683 troops in England, 3,500 of them near London, and 4,530 in Scotland.[3]

The Declaration of King James, signed by him on 23 December 1743, deserves some attention as it was drawn by the six in England, to be printed and distributed there when the landing took place. As it represents the points most likely to appeal to their supporters, it may be worth quoting at some length:

We have seen our people, for many years, groaning under the weight of most heavy taxes, and bearing many of the calamities of war, while the rest of Europe enjoyed all the blessings of peace. We have seen the treasures of the nation applied to satiate private avarice, and lavished for the support of German dominions, or for carrying on of ambitious views, always foreign and often contrary to the true interest of the nation. We have since seen the nation involved in wars, which have been, and are carried on without any advantage to Britain, and even to the manifest detriment and discouragement of its trade, and a great

[1] AEM & D. Ang. 76f. 206; Stuart mss. 254/104; 254/152; *HC* i 286.
[2] AEM & D. Ang. 86ff. 70–109; Stuart mss. 254/152. For Lefebure, see K. Ellis, *The Post Office in the Eighteenth Century* 65–7, 80.
[3] AEM & D. Ang. 75f. 201.

body of Hanoverians taken into the English pay and service, in a most extraordinary manner, and at a most expensive rate; nor could we behold without indignation, the preference and partiality shewn on all occasions to these foreigners, and the notorious affronts put on the British troops. We have beheld, with astonishment, an universal corruption and dissolution of manners, encouraged and countenanced by those, whose example and authority should have been employed to repress it, and a more than tacit connivance given to all irreligion and immorality. Bribery and corruption have been openly and universally practised, and no means neglected to seduce the great council of the nation, that it might be more effectually enslaved by those who ought to be the guardians of its liberty. The manufactures of England are visibly going to decay, trade has been neglected, and even discouraged, and the very honour of the nation made a sacrifice to the passions of those who govern it . . .

We see, with a sensible satisfaction, the eyes of the greatest part of our people opened, and their present deplorable situation, and that they are convinced they can find no relief but by restoring their natural born Prince, whose undoubted title will of course put an end to the many calamities they have suffered during the Usurpation; and our satisfaction would be complete, could we owe our mutual happiness to ourselves and subjects alone, without the assistance of any foreign power; but should we find it necessary to employ any such, let our good subjects be assured, it is only to protect ourselves and them against those shoals of foreign mercenaries, with which the Elector fills the kingdom whenever he thinks himself in danger; and therefore, to disperse all fears and jealousies from the hearts and minds of our subjects, and to convince them, as such as in us lies of the happiness they may enjoy under our Government, we have thought fit to unfold to them, in this solemn and public manner, the sincere sentiments of our royal and truly English heart.

The declaration went on to promise a general pardon; 'to call and assemble a free Parliament, wherein no corruption, nor undue influence of any kind whatsoever, shall be used to bias the votes of the electors, or the elected' and to govern only by its advice; to support and maintain the Church of England; and to allow a toleration to all Protestant dissenters, 'being utterly averse to all persecution and animosity on account of conscience and religion'. The manifesto of the Duke of Ormonde as commander-in-chief, also drawn up at this time and to be distributed on the landing with the declaration, stated that the existence of a large standing army, many of them foreigners maintained 'contrary to the constitution of the Kingdom' made it necessary to call on a contingent of regular troops rather than to rely on the people of England alone. It stressed that friendship between England and France 'for 200 years with few interruptions before the Revolution of 1688' had led to commercial prosperity, whereas continental land wars since had proved ruinous to the nation; that the King of France had no territorial ambitions in England, and that the disciplined troops under Count de Saxe, a Protestant, would be under his (Ormonde's) command, and would be withdrawn as soon as a restoration was achieved. Convocation, which had never been allowed to meet since the accession of the House of Hanover, would once again sit regularly, and 'unworthy' bishops would be removed which would restore the rest 'to the public esteem they formerly enjoyed'. Judges would no longer be chosen from among those 'who have prostituted their vote in the Commons for years at the dictates of the ministry'. The commissions of the peace would only be composed of men of substance, and gentlemen from the oldest families in the land would no longer have to sit on the bench with 'mean, inferior people'. Younger sons of Tory gentlemen would have preferment open to them once again. Country gentlemen would not be made to pay virtually all the taxes (the land tax) to support foreign interests they detest. The House of Stuart having no interests separate from those of England, a restoration would end all the ills of disputed succession, and lead to the repeal of the 'incredible number of penal laws imposed to preserve a foreign monarch' and which 'made free speech impossible in the land'. Ormonde was to pledge himself personally to secure the repeal of the Septennial Act, the passing of a rigorous place act and the maintenance of a free Parliament with no government interference in elections. English officers placed on half pay and others deprived of their commissions because of their convictions would be fully compensated.[1]

There was an alarm before Butler's return to France in mid-October that Carte, who knew Butler, might have learnt the real purpose of his visit and talked too much, but it proved groundless.[2]

---

[1] AEM & D. Ang. 76ff. 235–7; 82ff. 32–38; 85ff. 97–8; Stuart mss. 254/92.
[2] Stuart mss. 254/152; G. H. Jones, *The Main Stream of Jacobitism* 222, thinks that Carte learnt of the invasion plans, but there is no evidence for this in the Stuart papers and they were not betrayed by him.

At Versailles Butler had a long interview with Louis XV, who professed himself satisfied. Butler wrote to the Pretender: 'I discovered, during my stay in that kingdom, a very fair prospect of success.'[1] In November Amelot summoned Sempill to inform him officially that the King of France had decided to restore the Stuarts. In December Saxe went over to England to reconnoitre, as Walpole later discovered, and attempted to establish a correspondence of his own with the six, but Lefebure warned that Saxe's letters were being opened, and Lord Barrymore insisted that all communications must go through his cousin Dr Peter Barry, a London physician, living in Craven Street near the Strand by the method already settled.[2] James wrote to Ormonde on 23 December:

> I really cannot tell myself when this may be delivered to you, because you will receive it only at the time when all is ready for the execution of the enterprise. The King of France is resolved to undertake in my favour. His Majesty required so great and strict a secret in the affair, that I was not at liberty to mention any thing of it to you before. He will take care you should have all proper lights and instructions, and I have only time to tell you that the affair has concerted with people in England, and that your old friends have a great share in it; and I hope you yourself will be in a condition to perform that great part which I have all along designed for you.[3]

While all this had been going on, the difficulties of the English Government increased. Carteret, who pursued a pro-Hanoverian foreign policy, had the ear of the King but little following in the House of Commons, while Newcastle and Pelham who commanded a majority in the House, were not consulted by the King. Carteret, in search of followers, was making overtures to the Tories, but they would have nothing to do with him. Pelham wanted to retain Gower as Privy Seal despite his continued Toryism and his opposition to the Hanoverian troops and to gain Cobham, who had closely associated with Gower. Newcastle wrote to Walpole, now Lord Orford, who was still being consulted behind the scenes:

The taking in the Cobham party and the Whigs in Opposition, with-

[1] AEM & D. Ang. 82ff. 91–5; 77ff. 42–3; Stuart mss. 250/189.
[2] AEM & D. Ang. 82f. 93; 76f. 42; 77f. 143; Ryder diary 26 Feb. 1744.
[3] Browne ii 450.

out a mixture of Tories, is absolutely impracticable, and therefore, the only question is, whether, in order to get the Cobham party, etc., you will bring in three or four Tories, at least, with them; for without that, they will not come.[1]

Orford was becoming concerned about Cobham's politics, writing to Pelham 'sure the Cobhams are not the authors or printers of the *Constitutional Journal*! That is such express and confessed Jacobitism that he must be gone as far as the late Duke of Argyll was if they are in that scheme.' Cobham's associate in promoting the *Constitutional Journal* was Chesterfield.[2] Gower insisted on 'the absolutely laying aside the thoughts of the Hanover troops' and the dismissal of Bath's (Pulteney's) friends, whereupon the negotiation collapsed and Gower and Cobham resigned. Horace Walpole's comment was:

All is distraction! no union in the Court: no certainty about the House of Commons: Lord Carteret making no friends, the King making enemies: Mr. Pelham in vain courting Pitt, etc. Pulteney unresolved. How will it end? No joy but in the Jacobites.[3]

[1] Owen, 167, 190, 193–4, 197; Coxe, *Pelham* i 94.
[2] Coxe, *Pelham* i 105; *Lyttelton Memoirs* i 217–18.
[3] Owen, 197.

4

The French Invasion

At the end of November 1743 preparations for the French expedition began, and in early December Louis XV informed his kinsman and ally Philip V of Spain that he was resolved to restore the Stuarts. France was prepared to meet all the requests of those in the concert in England with the exception of setting out a separate expedition to Scotland. Although amphibious operations are notoriously difficult, and were especially so in the eighteenth century when success depended on favourable winds and tides, the ministers concerned, Maurepas, Amelot and Orry set to work with enthusiasm and reported to the King without consulting the other members of the council of state. Despite his normally indolent temperament, Louis XV showed unaccustomed energy in issuing repeated orders and writing letter upon letter to say that everything must be done to make the expedition a success and that nothing must be allowed to delay its departure fixed for January 1744. Lord Barrymore, who pledged that all those in the concert would join the French as soon as they landed, suggested that they should come over in fishing boats—a kind of Dunkirk in reverse—to avoid attracting the attention of the English Government. The French thought that his plan would have been feasible in the summer but that they could not risk the pick of their army on fishing boats in the Channel in January without any protection from attack, and appear to have considered that their fleet, though smaller, was in better shape than Sir John Norris's at Spithead which, they believed, consisted of old ships manned by newly-pressed seamen.[1]

[1] AEM & D. Ang. 82ff. 80–8; 76ff. 209, 219; 85ff. 97–8; 86ff. 108–9; Marine B3/421/71–2; Colin 35, 36. As some documents are misdated by Colin and he does not give his sources, references have in every case been given to the originals as well as to Colin.

The Tory leaders were surprised at the scale of the French preparations, but expressed themselves delighted and agreed to send pilots who knew the Essex coast, a code of signals, and some persons of consideration to accompany the expedition one of whom should have naval experience. Suddenly, at the end of December Dr. Barry wrote to say that the six requested a postponement until after the debates on taking the Hanoverians into English pay. This was done at the insistence of Sir John Cotton, who said that if they left Parliament at that time the Government would become suspicious and 'upon the least alarm' would suspend the Habeas Corpus Act and arrest all their friends, whereas once the main business was over they could leave under the pretext of disgust at the Court getting their own way, adding that it would have the further advantage of the debates stirring public feeling against the House of Hanover. Lord Barrymore had been very much against this because the weather in February might be bad, telling Dr. Barry that some who might ride on horseback in fine weather would not turn out in the worst of the winter, that 'fat Sir John' might be one of them but that they would do without 'the effeminate and the lazy'.[1] The change did not suit the French who replied that though the concentration of troops along the coast might not attract attention since the Flanders campaign was over and they were in winter quarters, the Brest squadron was ready to sail and a large number of merchant vessels from the ports of Picardy, Normandy and Brittany had been taken to Dunkirk to transport the troops and ammunition under the pretext of setting out an expedition to America, but delay might enable the English Government to learn its true destination. Moreover, success depended on easterly winds, which are prevalent in the Channel in January, whereas in February westerlies blow more frequently which might prejudice the whole attempt. They had, however, no choice but to comply.[2] Whipped in by Wynn, Cotton and Philipps, the Tories voted in force in the division on the Hanoverians of 18 January 1744. In the Commons, they remained in the background in the debates, but in the Lords Westmorland and Lichfield supported Cobham, Bedford and Chesterfield in demanding that they be disbanded.[3] Meanwhile,

---

[1] AEM & D. Ang. 76ff. 219–20; 90f. 369.
[2] AEM & D. Ang. 82ff. 89–90; 91ff. 357–60.
[3] Owen 199; *Parl. Hist.* xiii 232–74.

Balhaldy had taken to Rome the drafts of the declarations drawn up
in England and asked Charles Edward to leave immediately for
France with as much secrecy as possible, travelling back separately.
Leaving Rome under the pretext of a hunting party in the country,
Charles Edward arrived in Antibes on 12/23 January 1744, but
was held in quarantine for a week because there was plague in Rome.
The delay enabled the English Government to learn of his presence
in France, but it was thought he meant to serve on a French campaign in Flanders or that he was looking for a wife.[1] Against his
arrival, the French struck 15,000 silver medals with the portrait of
Charles Edward on the one side and the arms of the three kingdoms
on the other to be distributed after the landing. A declaration was
drawn up for Maurice of Saxony stating that the King of France
had no territorial ambitions in England and had imposed no conditions on King James; that England and France had only differed
because of the separate interests of the Elector of Hanover in
Germany which were not those of England; that the French troops
would be withdrawn just as soon as a restoration was effected; and
that the ensuing friendship between England and France would
bring commercial prosperity to both.[2] Military intelligence from
England obtained from Mill and sent in a letter from Lefebure to
Sempill stated there were now 11,550 officers and men in England
and 2,800 in Scotland, giving their location and also details of the
troops in Flanders and Ireland. Lefebure added that the greater
part of London would welcome the Prince.[3] The French expedition
consisted of 10,029: 334 officers and 9,695 soldiers, all French as
the six in England had requested that no Irish regiment in the
French service nor the newly-raised *Royal Ecossais* under Lord
John Drummond should take part, since their mere presence on
the coast would alert the English government at once. Balhaldy
had gone over to England in early January to proceed with the
final arrangements, and had meetings with Beaufort, Barrymore,
Orrery, Cotton, Abdy, St. Aubyn,[4] Slingsby, Bramston and Sir

---

[1] AEM & D. Ang. 82ff. 80–92; Colin 28–9, 154–5; *H. Walpole Corresp.*
xviii 378, 385.
[2] Barbier ii 385; AEM & D. Ang. 86f. 340.
[3] AEM & D. Ang. 86ff. 119–27; 90f. 323.
[4] Dr Linda Colley has suggested that Sir John St. Aubyn co-operated with the
Admiralty at this time to repel the French invasion, citing letters (whose present

William Carew who expressed their zeal for success, but all refused a new request from the French to give pledges under their own hand. Balhaldy returned accompanied by Richard Barry, second son of Lord Barrymore, sent by his father as 'a pledge of fidelity worth more than the signatures the King of France had demanded and which they did not dare to give in case they fell into the hands of the English Government', and Lord Caryll, both of whom were to sail with the expedition. Obviously Caryll and Richard Barry had less to lose than the others in the concert, but, after all, those who came over with William of Orange in 1688 had nothing to lose but their debts. Barry was a lieutenant in the Royal Navy and his experience was relevant. He told the French that several naval officers would come over to Charles Edward, giving as their signal a white flame on their top mast. He named two as his and his father's friends, and commanders of two of the larger ships in the Downs.[1] The first was Christopher O'Brien, a relation of Lord Clare who commanded one of the Irish regiments in the French service. O'Brien had served in the English navy, then went into Russian service becoming an admiral in the Russian fleet, and returned to England in 1742 when he became captain of the *Princess Royal*, and commander of the *Royal Sovereign* the following year. The second was Hon. Fitzroy Lee, who had succeeded O'Brien as captain of the *Princess Royal* and was the uncle of the 3rd Earl of Lichfield. They asked that, in case of miscarriage, they should be given equivalent rank in the French navy. O'Brien, in fact, died at sea soon after giving these assurances.[2] Much less welcome to the French was the request for yet another change of plans. Instead of landing at Maldon as agreed, the French were asked to do what the Dutch

---

location she has discovered) from St. Aubyn to Borlase the Cornish antiquary. But this series of letters ranging from 19 April to 17 July 1744 (after any threat of a French invasion had disappeared) really concerns unsuccessful requests from the gentlemen of Cornwall to the lords of the Admiralty to obtain convoys for the tin ships and to protect the pilchard fisheries from foreign privateers.

[1] AEM & D. Ang. 76f. 44; 77ff. 140-1; 83ff. 163-4; Colin attributes to Sempill in 1743 a memorandum written by Carte in 1739, with no relevance to the French invasion.

[2] AEM & D. Ang. 82ff. 95-8; 76f. 44; 77ff. 140-1. For O'Brien and Lee see *Gentleman's Magazine* 1744, 53, 108; Charnock, *Biographia Navalis* iv 195.

had done in the Medway in 1667, that is sail up the Thames where Tilbury was defended only by a company of invalids, and to go as far as the Hope where they would be met by pilots familiar with those reaches of the Thames to guide them as far as Blackwall where those in the concert would join them. Blackwall was only two miles from London which would thus be taken by surprise. Those in the concert in London would foment a general insurrection in the capital. Pilots to guide the French as far as the Hope would be sent to France.[1]

Maurepas's plan was to send the Brest squadron out to sea with secret orders to be opened off Ushant. There, its commander, Roquefeuil, a veteran of La Hogue, was ordered to go and cruise off the Isle of Wight to prevent Sir John Norris from coming out of Spithead, but, if he could not, to draw him off towards the West and engage him in combat. While the Downs were left unprotected, five ships of the Brest squadron under Barrailh were to detach themselves from Roquefeuil and sail to Dunkirk to escort the troops to be embarked on merchant ships for the mouth of the Thames.[2] The instructions to Maurice of Saxony and to the French admirals said that Louis XV had decided no longer to recognise the Elector of Hanover as King of England and, at the request of persons of the highest distinction in England, had resolved to restore the legitimate King, James III. They were to act as auxiliaries to Prince Charles Edward as Regent of England. In the event of a civil war, enemies of King James were to be treated as enemies in war, but if King James's supporters were unable to maintain themselves, Maurice of Saxony was to return to France. The Comte d'Argenson, in a separate letter, thought it highly unlikely that persons who ran such risks would not do their utmost in the very sight of their Prince, and when given an opportunity which might occur but once.[3] On the *Dauphin Royal*, Barrailh's flagship, were to embark: Charles Edward, Maurice of Saxony, Richard Barry, Lord Caryll, Charles Radcliffe (brother of Lord Derwentwater executed after the '15), and Ormonde, who was not to be summoned until the very last

---

[1] AEM & D. Ang. 82ff. 96–8; 83ff. 179–80; 77ff. 85–6; 90f. 324; Colin 55–7, 65, 70–2 (Sempill's letter dated by Colin 29 February is 29 January).

[2] Colin 47, 55–74, 87–9; AEM & D. Ang. 77ff. 84–5, 113–14, 140–1; Guerre A1/3034/19.

[3] Guerre A1/3034/19, 55 and 82; AEM & D. Ang. 91ff. 264–5.

minute as all his movements were being watched in England. There were other Englishmen to embark. One was John Cotton of Steeple Gidding in Huntingdonshire, a nonjuror who had formerly lived in France after his escape from England as a Jacobite at the battle of Preston in 1715, and who had inherited in 1731 most of the Huntingdonshire estates of his uncle Sir John Cotton, 4th Bt. of Conington, Hunts. Member of Parliament for Huntingdonshire 1710–13. Another was a Mr Ashby, brother of Thomas Ashby, Member of Parliament for St. Albans 1734–43. The third was Read of Essex, one of the people at the talk with Butler in 1743, who was expected to bring over the pilots familiar with the reaches of the Thames.[1] An embargo was imposed on all English ships in the Channel ports under pretext of searching for contraband.[2]

In the first fortnight of February, the English Government had no inkling that England was about to be invaded. The Brest squadron was sighted at sea, but Henry Pelham, writing on 4 February, concluded 'they intend to intercept our ships coming in and going out . . . possibly to make us recall a part of Matthews's squadron [in the Mediterranean], or at least to prevent our sending any succour, or provisions', and thought it unlikely they were making for Ireland, as some people believed. However, he ordered Sir John Norris to go to Spithead to 'get his fleet ready as soon as he can', adding: 'I am much afraid we are not so forward in our marine here as we should be, however, I hope we shall be able to cope with this squadron.' As it was, Norris came out of Spithead two days before Roquefeuil was off the Isle of Wight.[3] At this stage, Newcastle was approached by '101' a secret agent with an offer that, in exchange for £2,000 in cash, he would give information of the highest importance to the English Government. 101 was the biggest catch in Walpole's intelligence service. François de Bussy, the illegitimate son of an impoverished noblewoman, had through her become secretary to the French ambassador at Vienna and then a senior clerk in the French Foreign Office. Greed and arrogance

---

[1] AEM & D. Ang. 75f. 201. *Gentleman's Magazine* 1731, 82; Stuart mss. 256/61–66; H. Broxap, *The Later Nonjurors* 310–11, 230.
[2] Guerre A1/3034/43.
[3] Chatsworth mss., Henry Pelham to the Duke of Devonshire, 4 Feb. 1744; Colin 154; *H. Walpole Corresp.* xviii 392–3; Add. 33,004ff. 59–61.

were his chief characteristics. He was recruited by Lord Waldegrave, the British ambassador in Paris, from whom he had borrowed money. One of the questions he was asked in 1735 was 'had France any intention of assisting the Pretender?' to which the reply was 'no'. In 1737 he was sent on a special mission to Sir Robert Walpole, as he spoke fluent English and Walpole bad French, receiving a special gratification of £1,000 from the minister's hands. Sent as envoy to London in 1740 he communicated the terms of the Franco-Spanish alliance to England and secret French orders to attack the English fleet in the West Indies. Ironically enough, it was Bussy who was sent to Hanover in 1741, where he reduced George II to tears for fear of an invasion of Hanover by a French army massed on its frontiers and bullied him into signing the convention for the neutrality of Hanover, a treaty he later disavowed under pressure from his English ministers when the threatening army was withdrawn. All the while 101 made increasingly heavy demands on his English paymasters. Newcastle paid the £2,000, and in return received a long coded message in which Bussy gave away the whole plan for the invasion of England, naming the Duke of Beaufort, Lord Barrymore, Sir Watkin Williams Wynn and 'Monsieur de Cotton' as the instigators. Newcastle asked if Sir John Hynde Cotton was meant or another of that name, to which Bussy replied that it was the Cotton who had escaped 'after the affair at Preston' in 1715, which Cotton was of course involved, but on the French side of the Channel. 101's message was decyphered on 14 February.[1] The very next day, the King sent a message to Parliament that he had received reliable information that a French invasion was preparing 'assisted by disaffected persons from this country'. After a debate lasting until seven at night 'not one (professed) Jacobite speaking', a loyal address was carried 287 to 123. The Opposition moved for an enquiry into the state of the navy, insisting upon a division in order, as some Government supporters thought, 'to show the French what numbers in the House they may depend upon'. Chesterfield moved the same amendment in the Lords, seconded by Westmorland, but the peers did not divide. Bedford's

---

[1] Add. 33,004ff. 22–3, 30–1. For Bussy, see my article in *History Today* April 1969, 273–6; Vaucher 311–12; C. Piccioni, *Les Premiers Commis des Affaires étrangères au xviie et xviiie siècles* 236–8; Sautai, *Les Débuts de la Guerre de la Succession d'Autriche* 300, 303, 497–8.

speech on this occasion, as Philip Yorke (Lord Chancellor Hardwicke's son) noted in his diary, 'had the most Jacobite tendency of any speech that was ever pronounced in Parliament'. There were then about 10,000 troops in England Ryder wrote, of which only 7,000 could be assembled around London. Orders were sent for 6,000 Dutch to come over as well as 7,000 from Flanders and another 4,000 from Ireland. Sir John Norris was ordered to attack the French fleet, and if the French came near the mouth of the Thames or the Medway all lights were to be extinguished and buoys cut adrift. On 24 February an address for increasing the armed forces was opposed only by Admiral Vernon, an opposition Whig and a national hero since his taking Porto Bello 'with six ships' only in 1740, and he was seconded by his friend Sir John Philipps, three Tories including Daniel Lambert voting against. Philip Yorke commented:

It is observable that none of the leaders amongst the Tories, either on this occasion or on that of the King's first message, showed the least sign of zeal and affection to the government; on the contrary, they treated the whole affair from beginning to end with the utmost indifference and ridicule.

Yorke added:

The troops which were ordered up to London from different parts of the country, met with the kindest reception imaginable on their march . . . The Jacobites, to soften the unpopular sound of a French invasion and a Popish Pretender, began to spread it about, that the general who commanded was a Lutheran, and the young man himself is a firm convert to Protestantism, and that when his father reproached him with having changed his religion, his reply was, he would not lose three kingdoms for a mass.[1]

The 1st Lord Egmont, another Whig, reported rumours that the Young Pretender 'is come only to relieve the English dominions from the oppression they lie under', adding: 'believe this who will: so said the Prince of Orange when he came in 1688, but nevertheless he accepted the Crown.' The Whigs, who had very good reasons

[1] *HC* i 73; SP 36/63/91; *H. Walpole Corresp.* xvii 399–400; *Parl. Hist.* xiii 643–5; *HMC Egmont diary* iii 285–6; Add. 35,337f. 47.

to be satisfied with the Hanoverian Succession, could not believe there was support for its overthrow among those who did not share in its blessings. Loyal addresses began to pour in. The London address, which George Heathcote had opposed, was presented by the lord mayor, Westley, and the two sheriffs, Lambert and Willimot, acting *ex officio*, as it was their function to present petitions and addresses from the corporation, and were knighted as was customary. Horatio Walpole was not impressed, writing 'notwithstanding the many zealous addresses, and particularly of this city, I don't wish to see a French army in England. Richard Cromwell was wont to point at an old trunk he had in his chamber of the lives and fortunes of the good people of England.' He thought there might well be 'a disposition in a great many to receive a new King, and an indifference in many more with respect to this family' and that 'the people may perhaps, look on, and cry "fight dog, fight bear", if they do no worse'. He was 'persuaded that the old leaven of the High Tories still exists' and that 'their principles in favour of the Pretender will appear as strong as ever upon the first occasion'. To Walpole, who watched every move, it was his life's nightmare come true. Bolingbroke, who was against any restoration of the Stuarts except on his own terms, wrote: 'The crisis is terrible—much to be feared—little to be hoped. God help us!'[1]

Arrests began very soon. Col. Cecil was taken on 24 February at his house in Masham Street and sent to the Tower on suspicion of high treason, and Thomas Carte was also seized; neither of them had had anything to do with the invasion. Lord Barrymore, 'the Pretender's general' as Horace Walpole called him, was woken up at 5 a.m. at his house in Henrietta Street, Cavendish Square, and was placed under house arrest with an officer always in his room and soldiers posted at his door. His house was ransacked to find evidence in his papers; messengers were sent to search Marbury, and Castlelyons was also examined on the orders of the lord lieutenant of Ireland for proof, but nothing was found. Examined by the Privy Council Barrymore said:

I have, my Lords, a very good estate in Ireland, and, on that, I believe

[1] *HMC Egmont diary* iii 284; *HC* ii 121–2; 196; 546–7; *HMC 14th Rep.* ix 92–3; Ryder diary 15 and 28 Feb. 1744; Chatsworth mss., Lord Hartington to Duke of Devonshire, 16 Feb. 1744; *Marchmont Papers* ii 327.

fifteen hundred acres of very bad land; now by G–d, I would not risk the loss of the poorest acre of them to defend the title of any king in Europe, provided—it was not my interest.

Egmont, one of the Whigs who thought there were few Jacobites left, had known Barrymore for years as a member of the Irish 'lobby' in Parliament and often visited him, but he was of opinion Barrymore was not a Jacobite! Dr John Beaufort, a London physician, was also arrested, apparently because he had been with Lord Barrymore, who was his patient, the day before. When questioned, he was reported to have stated that his only connection with the French was drinking a bottle of their best claret a day, and that he saw none but sick people. A list sent to Sempill of those arrested or questioned during the emergency gives the name of the Duke of Beaufort as well as that of Dr Beaufort. There is no indication in Government sources of the duke being arrested, but he may have been questioned. At any rate, though he was in the process of divorcing his duchess, he ceased to attend the House of Lords between 22 February and 15 March. Released in April on a £60,000 bail, Barrymore left London, and the Duke of Beaufort was later said to have done the same 'neither inclining to put their persons a second time in the hands of the Government'. John Mill, the clerk in the paymaster's office, was questioned after a servant of the Duke of Perth (who had been taken in Scotland) was followed to his house, but nothing against him was found, and he kept his place. Orders were sent to arrest Caryll, who naturally was not found in Sussex, but escaped further inquiries because he was thought to be hiding from his creditors. No one was charged or brought to trial. When on 28 February, the House of Commons was informed that Lord Barrymore, a Member, had been arrested on suspicion of treason, Wynn, Cotton and Philipps and 'some of the Tories' objected that he had been arrested before the suspension of the Habeas Corpus Act and before the House was notified, whereas in 1715 the House was asked for leave before any of its Members were taken, to which Pelham replied that it had then enabled some to escape.[1]

---

[1] *Gentleman's Magazine* 1744, 107, 165, 277; *H. Walpole Corresp.* xviii 408; *HMC 15th Rep. VII*, 328–9; *HC* i 73, 441; SP 36/63/102, 148–52, 154–5, 189, 197, 280, 282, 289, 373, 374; *HMC Egmont diary* iii 286, 289, 291, 293; AEM &

Not knowing what was happening in England, since Lefebure had forbidden Dr Barry to write as soon as the emergency began, Maurice of Saxony was awaiting the arrival of Read with the pilots and of Barrailh's ships in Dunkirk to escort him to England. On 15/26 February, he wrote to Argenson that he would already have landed in England if Barrailh had arrived instead of amusing himself by capturing English ships, and complained he had not seen anything of the English pilots promised, but that he was still pressing on 'since the wine is drawn, we must drink it'. The next day Barrailh turned up, but 'Monsieur Red', as the French invariably called Read, could not be found though searched for in all the Channel ports. It turned out that Read, who had volunteered for the task, had got to London from Essex on 16 February, the day after the King's message to Parliament on the threatened invasion and, in the circumstances, neither Barrymore nor Orrery thought that the secret of the expedition could be trusted to pilots, and that suitable people familiar with the mouth of the Thames could be found in the Channel ports, so that they sent Read alone. He arrived in France on 20 February/3 March, and, with little command of French could find neither Charles Edward nor Balhaldy, took fright, as Balhaldy later wrote, at the thought of the loss of 'his beef and pudding' and returned to England, leaving a letter for Saxe (not now extant) to say those in the concert in England asked the French to come over immediately.[1] As it was, there were available two captains of smuggling ships familiar with the Thames estuary: Thomas Harvey and Robert Fuller. There had long been a thriving illicit trade between England and France, smuggling wool out from the Kent, Sussex and Hampshire coasts to Dunkirk, Calais and Boulogne, and returning loaded with French brandy which was smuggled back in. The Smuggling Act of 1719 had only temporarily checked that trade, but it made the smugglers outlaws with 'nothing to look for from King George but a rope'. Traditionally, they carried the Jacobite agents to and from the Continent into England, and many were said to have taken the oaths to the King

D. Ang. 77ff. 206–7; 83ff. 189, 198; Northumberland mss. from Alnwick, Lady Hertford to Lord Beauchamp, 2 April 1744; Stuart mss. 260/108; *Parl. Hist.* xiii 669–70.

[1] AEM & D. Ang. 77ff. 129–31, 140–1, 194; AEM & D. Ang. 86f. 115; 83ff. 176–7, 179–80; Colin 105–8.

of France. At this time some of them near Rye were said to have publicly drunk the health of King James, success to Charles Edward's arms, and 'confusion to King George', without anyone daring to apprehend them. Harvey and Fuller, who were said to be zealous Jacobites like most of the smugglers, were held *incommunicado* but with orders to navy officials to treat them in the handsomest manner possible as they were married to Frenchwomen in Boulogne, and were very popular in that town, and any complaint from them might cause a riot there. At this point, secret orders were sent to Maurice of Saxony that if he was not met at the Hope not to proceed but to return to France. In fact, English pilots were already waiting at the Hope, and were later pressed into the English navy.[1] On 22 February/5 March, the embarkation began, and continued all next day, in the hope of coming over before any of the additional troops called for had arrived, and relying on Roquefeuil to hold Norris in check. On 24 February the Brest fleet lay at anchor off Dungeness with 15 ships of the line. Norris with 19 was anchored off Hythe within sight of them. Crowds of people began to gather on the hilltops to watch the expected naval battle. Then 'about three in the afternoon it began to rain', and this was followed by—

> a dreadful storm of wind which put every ship in great disorder, and everybody in great consternation, some ships driving one way, and some another, and all in great danger of driving foul of each other. This storm lasted that night and all next day.

Eighteen of Norris's ships were damaged, five were put out of action and one, the *Prince Frederick*, was rammed and went down with all hands. Most of the ships out in the Downs sank. During the storm, Roquefeuil slipped anchor, and placing himself before the wind was able to return to Brest with several ships dismasted but no losses. The storms which blew straight into the harbour of Dunkirk and continued for several days more drove aground eleven of the

[1] 9 Geo. II Cap. 11; Stuart mss. 288/172; Edward Carson, *The Ancient and Rightful Customs* 96–7 (I am indebted to John Styles for this reference); Cal Winslow, 'Sussex Smugglers' in *Albion's Fatal Tree* 119–66; Add. 32,702f. 149; Marine B2/322/31; B3/421/51; Colin 102–5; AEM & D. Ang. 83ff. 189–90; 91f. 306; Colin 109–11.

smaller ships carrying the troops to the larger ships in the Road, and wrecked six of the latter. There was a loss of only a dozen lives, but the material damage was extensive. Six months' supplies of stores, provisions, tents and ammunition were destroyed, and the transports had lost their anchors, tackle and sloops.[1] Maurice of Saxony, who had been naturally irritated by two changes of plans dictated from England, was now in a flaming temper, writing to Argenson on 25 February/8 March that the men on board Barrailh's ships were more suitable to drive carts than to navigate; that Lord Caryll hesitated about everything; that Charles Edward looked for guidance to Richard Barry who was 'the innocent victim of his father's ideas'. He didn't know where Roquefeuil was and blamed James's friends in England for not letting him know that Norris was out in the Downs with the ships salvaged from the storms. He was impressed with the loyal address from the City of London, and showed so little understanding of conditions in England that, after expecting those in the concert to plan an invasion through letters sent by the English Post Office, he was surprised to find that none of them had 'taken off the mask' when arrests had begun and before the landing! He need not have worried, for there was no hope of getting across without running straight into Norris now, nor in repairing the transports or getting new supplies before the Dutch and other troops reached England. On 28 February/11 March he wrote to Charles Edward to say that the French government had decided to abandon the expedition for the time being.[2]

England made representations to France on the projected invasion, and on the Young Pretender being on French soil contrary to existing treaties. The French replied that since His Britannic Majesty did not honour the treaties he had signed, alluding to the convention for the neutrality of Hanover, His Most Christian Majesty saw no reason to keep faith with him, and declared war on England. From The Hague, the British envoy Robert Trevor wrote to his friend Horatio Walpole on 9/20 March:

[1] Chatsworth mss., Lord Hartington to Duke of Devonshire, 25 Feb. 1744; SP 36/63/142–52; *H. Walpole Corresp.* xviii 107; Colin 147–51; H. W. Richmond, *The Navy in the war of 1739–48* ii 82–84; HMC *Egmont diary* iii 288; Luynes v 370.

[2] Guerre A1/3034/91 and 113; AEM & D. Ang. 83f. 175; Colin 146–77.

The enterprise is certainly postponed for the present; but, as the French court has now discovered how sore and tender we are in this place, I do expect she will give us a *quietus* all this campaign; but keep holding the young man upon her fist.[1]

[1] AEM & D. Ang. 82ff. 106–10; Coxe, *Horatio, Lord Walpole.* ii 73–4.

5

A Time of Waiting

In the spring of 1744, despite the personal risks involved, Charles
Edward sent Balhaldy to England to find out what was happening.
Balhaldy reported on 11/22 May (given as decoded):

> The King's friends and Lord Barrymore's great apprehension is for
> the Channel, they cannot conceive by what means you propose to
> effect a landing while the Duke of Hanover is master of the Channel,
> otherwise they are as certain, as zealous and warm as ever . . . The
> King's friends [opinion] was then and is at present not to lose time
> but to come away as fast as you can with any considerable body of
> men. You will be in peaceable possession of England in a few days,
> for in a short time we shall be in a situation much wished by the
> King's friends. The Duke of Hanover goes abroad in about a week's
> time. The Dutch are to go back, five regiments more to be sent
> immediately to Flanders, so that you would have nobody remaining to
> oppose you, provided you are master of the Channel, or landed at the
> place you proposed, for Lord Barrymore thinks that the best place,
> because the Duke of Hanover's credit will be immediately blown up
> . . . There is nothing wanting but a standard, for God's sake let them
> have it, and it will be well attended. The suspension of the Habeas
> Corpus Act and the last penal law has exasperated the people, and to
> use Lord Barrymore's expression, it will be over shoes, over boots,
> once landed. When a landing was long expected the King's friends
> spoke to some of the leading aldermen particularly Heathcote, their
> answer was that you had nothing to do but to come. They are still in
> the same disposition and sentiment, so are the people of England
> (placemen and stockjobbers excepted) . . . The King's friends recom-
> mend in the strongest manner to have an embarkation for Scotland
> at the same time you intend an embarkation for England.[1]

[1] Stuart mss. 257/55.

The 'last penal law' was a bill introduced in April 1744 by Nicholas Fazakerley, a non-Jacobite Tory, to prohibit correspondence with the Pretender's sons, but he strongly opposed the clauses added by the Lords attainting the Pretender's sons if they attempted to land in England and instituting forfeiture of estates for such correspondence, describing them as 'one of the most pernicious and unconstitutional provisions ever devised'.[1] The Tory leaders attributed Barrymore's arrest to the old business of his having sent letters from the Pretender to Argyll, and blamed Col. Cecil for not having destroyed all his (Cecil's) papers, though nothing material had been found in them by the Government. The correspondence through Lefebure, which went through Holland, was restored with a change of cypher, and an additional means of contact with London was established through the smugglers.[2] In order to encourage the French to make a new attempt, from April to August batch upon batch of English pilots began to arrive in the French channel ports, though one group mutinied after finding out where they were sent! On 24 July Charles Edward wrote to Louis XV that he had just received an express from his friends in England saying that the kingdom was denuded of troops, and that another attempt could be made without exposing the country to all the calamities of a civil war.[3]

The political situation in France had, however, very much changed. The nobles in the council of state, led by the Duc de Noailles, Louis XV's Polonius, had been opposed to the expedition against England, and were offended at not being consulted. They advocated the more traditional ways of fighting Austria by way of a campaign in Flanders, and were warm partisans of an alliance with Frederick II of Prussia. This reflected the views of the majority of nobles at Versailles. In their endeavours to keep the secretaries of state 'in their place', they had a powerful ally in Louis XV's new mistress, the beautiful and haughty Madame de la Tournelle, who was made mistress of the Robes to Maria Leczinska, Louis XV's queen. When as Secretary of State for the King's Household, Maurepas was asked to draw up the patent making Mme de la Tournelle Duchesse de Châteauroux, he had diverted the whole court and

[1] *Parl. Hist.* xiii 982.
[2] Stuart mss. 257/91 and 95; SP 36/63/146; AEM & D. Ang. 77f. 219.
[3] AEM & D. Ang. 77ff. 234–5; Stuart mss. 258/71; 260/7.

much angered the lady by praising in extravagant terms her great services to *the Queen*. Amelot, who was dismissed in April, was made the scapegoat of the failure of the expedition against England, and the conduct of foreign policy was left to the council. The attention of the other ministers was directed to preparing the campaign in Flanders which the King had decided to lead in person. Everything was brought to a stop by his falling gravely ill and being on the point of death at Metz in August 1744.[1]

Charles Edward had been bitterly disappointed at the abandonment of the expedition against England, was tired of waiting, and humiliated at not being allowed by the French to appear in public. Most of all he feared that the failure of the expedition would be attributed to the ill-luck which had dogged his family for so long. He turned his sights to Scotland, hoping that Louis XV would let him have the Irish regiments and the *Royal Ecossais*, and writing to Sempill:

> I am certain there are many in Scotland willing to follow me though I would go naked and alone among them, and I will try my fortune that way, if I can do nothing better. You'll see by what I write to you how heavy the present disappointment is upon my mind, at the same time I inform you that no mortal will ever find me discouraged, while there remain any means untried.

He was encouraged in this by the Scots in exile who complained that Scotland had been 'neglected' since the French had not bothered to prepare a separate expedition for its relief, and particularly by Lord Marischal, who had been very offended by being summoned to Dunkirk in February and told to show himself in public, as he found out, only to act as a decoy to make the English government think the expedition was meant for Scotland should they learn of it.[2] In the summer Charles Edward received a visit from Murray of Broughton, the Jacobite agent in Scotland, who took the same line. Sempill introduced Murray to the French ministers, and Balhaldy, to whom Murray was said to be related,

---

[1] *Correspondance de Louis XV et du maréchal de Noailles* ii; *Mémoires du maréchal de Noailles* iii 357–8; AECP Allemagne 526f. 108; Add. 32804ff. 59–64; Duc de Broglie, *Histoire de la Politique extérieure de Louis XV* iii 440–1; iv 276; *Lettres de Madame de Tencin au Duc de Richelieu* (1790 ed.) 52, 56; Argenson iv 89.

[2] AEM & D. Ang. 91ff. 311–14; 81f. 93; 82ff. 105–6.

highly commended him to the Prince. In return, Murray, blaming them for everything which had gone wrong, succeeded in discrediting them with Charles Edward.[1] This had very unfortunate results. Sempill and Balhaldy both had a good understanding of English politics and knew the Tory leaders personally. Murray had neither. When he went to London in August (on his own showing) none of James's friends in England would receive him, and he was reduced to seeing only Col. Cecil and to blaming everyone else's management in his company. Consulted through Sempill and Dr Barry about the plan for a landing in Scotland alone, the English Tories expressed their satisfaction at the readiness of the Scots to rise, but they were absolutely opposed to an expedition to Scotland without a simultaneous landing near London. The reasons they gave were that if Charles Edward landed in Scotland, it would take him three or four months to get to London, and meanwhile the Elector of Hanover would have control of the army, the fleet, the public funds, and, as the Prince advanced, would be able to bring over not only English troops from Flanders, but also Dutch, Hanoverian and Hessian troops, while they, with no arms or military experience, would be helpless. Above all they wanted to avoid a civil war in London and the home counties which contained most of the riches of the kingdom. James very much agreed: 'I have been all along against an expedition to Scotland alone, or rather in general against any faint attempt the consequence of which might be more fatal to the cause than the not attempting anything at all'.[2] Murray always denied that he had advised the Prince to come to Scotland, even without any troops, but all the signs are that he did. One of the Scots who took part in the '45 wrote:

> Murray had imposed upon the Prince and hurried him into it, without concerting anything with England. The English had always insisted upon a body of regular troops, not under seven and not above twelve thousand effective men . . . [as] under the Hanoverian government the people had been disarmed and overawed by armies of well disciplined troops.[3]

[1] AEM & D. Ang. 77ff. 248-9; *Murray of Broughton* 70-6; Stuart mss. 258/108; 259/199.
[2] AEM & D. Ang. 85ff. 131-3; 77ff. 248-52; 87f. 109.
[3] Maxwell of Kirkconnel, *Narrative of Charles Prince of Wales's expedition to Scotland in the year 1745* (Maitland Club, 1841) 77-8.

There was indeed a startling contrast in the situation of the Jacobites in Scotland and those in England. Because of the heretable (hereditary) jurisdictions, George II's authority just did not run in large parts of Scotland. The Scottish chiefs had feudal authority over the clans. In theory, the clans had been supposed to hand over their arms under the Disarming Act passed after the '15, but whereas the clans loyal to King George had done so, the Jacobite clans had kept theirs or only handed in old, rusty arms, and had been able to purchase and land others from abroad since. In Scotland there was no Tory party as such, and for over twenty years Argyll and his brother Ilay had governed Scotland by a series of bargains whereby they secured the Jacobite interest in elections in return for keeping forfeited estates in the same family. Nor could forfeited estates be sold on the open market. One man who had purchased a forfeited estate in Scotland after the '15 had his cattle stolen, his servants kidnapped and his house burnt down. Not surprisingly, would-be purchasers were difficult to find. The Scottish chiefs in exile still received income from their former estates. In order to govern Scotland, as the English Government found out in the '45, Argyll and Ilay had appointed crypto-Jacobites to places of trust, who either abetted or connived at the rebellion in 1745.[1] In England, the New Model Army had put an end to the chances of country gentlemen raising their tenants. Judging from the turnout at the royalists' risings during the Protectorate, even Sir George Booth's rising of 1659 which was supported by Presbyterians as well as Cavaliers, one would have had to conclude that there would have been little support for a restoration.[2] English country gentlemen were watched by government spies who reported any sign of disaffection and were rewarded for doing so. The life expectations of a Fraser who defied Lord Lovat would have been short indeed, but by this time tenants of English squires would not always follow them in elections, let alone on a field of battle. Members of prominent English families who rose and were caught in the '15 in Lancashire, Cheshire and Northumberland lost their lives and their estates, and this decimated the numbers of supporters in those counties. English Tories were Jacobites in the sense that their

[1] Ewald, *Life of Charles Edward Stuart* i 123–4; *HC* i 159–60; Ryder diary 1 Jan. 1747.
[2] See D. Underdown, *Royalist Conspiracy*.

Sir John Hynde Cotton, 3rd Bt. (*c.* 1688–1752) Painting by Sir Godfrey Kneller, formerly at Madingley but present whereabouts (1978) unknown. By courtesy of the National Portrait Gallery

John Boyle, 5th Earl of Orrery, later 5th Earl of Cork (1707–62). Engraving by John Faber junior *ad vivum*, 1741. By courtesy of the Ashmolean Museum, Oxford

Sir Watkin Williams Wynn, 3rd Bt. (c. 1693–1749), and Henry Somerset, 3rd Duke of Beaufort (1707–1745), at Newmarket. Painting by John Wootton at Badminton. By kind permission of the Duke of Beaufort; photograph by courtesy of the Courtauld Institute of Art

James, Earl of Barrymore, an Ottway print. By courtesy of the Department of Prints and Engravings, British Museum

'A very Extraordinary Motion', on the Broadbottom Administration, December 1744. George II, leaning on a table, evacuates Lord Hobart, treasurer of the chamber, while the Duke of Newcastle and his brother Henry Pelham prepare to cram Sir John Hynde Cotton down the King's throat, exclaiming 'Push home he must goe down' and 'His Bottom's damn'd Broad'. King George cries out 'Hounsfool me no stomach him!' On the dresser several others (one of them George Lyttelton) lie ready to be forced down the King's throat, while two bystanders remark 'Remember The [treasonable] Healths' and 'Consider your Oaths'. On the left, one of the outgoing ministers shouts 'Damn their Broad Bottom'. By courtesy of the Department of Prints and Drawings of the British Museum (political satire no. 2613)

The '45 medal. Designed by Jacques Rottier de la Tour, goldsmith to Louis XV (*ex. inf.* M. J. Delaubre of the Administration des Monnaies et Médailles, Paris). The obverse is presumably taken from the 1744 medal (see p. 54) since a 4 is clearly visible underneath the 5 of 1745, with a different reverse. By courtesy of the National Portrait Gallery

'The March to Finchley' by William Hogarth. The guards marching towards the camp at Finchley to defend London in December 1745 (wrongly described in the engraving as the march towards Scotland). At the Tottenham Court turnpike in London, soldiers in very irregular array are going through to join the column marching away in the distance to the improvised camp at Finchley. On the right, the King's Head (a portrait of Charles II) is filled with prostitutes at the windows offering their services, with at the window under the sign an enormously fat woman, Mother Douglas, a notable procuress, praying for victory. In the crowd, young women are being indecently assaulted by the military. A pregnant woman clinging to a soldier carries in a basket a portrait of the Duke of Cumberland and a ballad of 'God save our Noble King', while another woman selling opposition newspapers grabs his arm. Behind the drummer, a Frenchman holds a letter directed 'A Monsier Monsier – a Londre' supposed to contain intelligence of a French invasion, and whispers the news into the ear of an Independent Elector of Westminster. Hogarth wished to dedicate the print to George II, who on seeing it exclaimed: 'I hate bainting and boetry too! Neither the one nor the other ever did any good! Does the mean fellow mean to laugh at my guards?' When told it was a burlesque, the King replied: 'What, a bainter burlesque a soldier? He deserves to be picketed for his insolence! Take his trumpery out of my sight', whereupon Hogarth dedicated it to Frederick the Great instead. By courtesy of the Department of Prints and Drawings of the British Museum (political satire no. 2639)

'A Sight of the Banging Bout at Litchfield', September 1747. On the right a
tent with the Hanoverian Horse is advertised to let. Heston Humphrey, an
attorney, is horsewhipping the Duke of Bedford, who exclaims 'don't you know
me?' The bystanders wearing clothes of plaid watch, as a fiddler plays 'The
King shall enjoy his own again' while trampling on 'God save ye King' and
'God save great George our—'. A peer (Lord Gower) says 'I was ye Staffordshire Jacobite'. Behind are horsemen in plaid dress, one of whom is reading
the 'Declaration of ye Hunters', while a man cries out 'No turn Coats'. On the
left, near a starting post, on which is perched a man in plaid waving a flag
with the Pretender's motto 'Pro patria mori' are two plaided horsemen, one
singing 'And a Hunting we will go go will', and the other 'The chiefest Harts
to slay'. A man on foot points to a race with one rider wearing plaid (Charles
Edward) and the other being very fat (the Duke of Cumberland), and shouts
'The H[anoverian] Prince five to one'. By courtesy of the Department of Prints
and Drawings of the British Museum (political satire no. 2863)

'Jaco-Independo-Rebello-Plaido', the Independent Electors of the City of Westminster, February 1747. The scene in front of Westminster Hall is the Westminster election of 1747 when Lord Gower's son, Lord Trentham, was returned
with Admiral Sir Peter Warren against two Tory candidates. One of the Tories,
Sir Thomas Clarges, was steward of the club of the Independent Electors that
year. The devil hovers over, exclaiming 'I have the Fee in my Hands'. On the
left, one of the government supporters cries out 'Give the Devil his Due',
i.e. the Jacobites. Crowds are rushing towards the house shouting 'no Indepen-
dency', 'no Pretender'. On the right the Jacobite house with a flag inscribed
'Morgan's ghost' and an owl saying 'We are all of a Feather'. By courtesy of
the Department of Prints and Drawings of the British Museum (political
satire no. 2856)

leaders, answering for the party, wanted a restoration of the Stuarts in the person of Charles Edward, hoping he would conform to the established church, but they had said again and again that only regular troops could bring it about. With scant regard for logistics, Whig historians have ridiculed them for showing their zeal to the Pretender only by drinking his health in secret. This was so, but after all, *in vino veritas!*

At Westminster, the struggle for power between Carteret, now Lord Granville, and the Pelhams had left everything at a standstill. Granville, who still had the favour of the King, had little following in Parliament, and in November 1744 offered the Tories *carte blanche* in return for their support, but, wrote Ryder, 'they absolutely refused to be concerned with him.' Pitt told Bolingbroke—

> that he had seen Lord Cobham, and had had much treaty with the Grenvilles, who were obliged to follow Lord Cobham, and that he saw the opposition designed to move questions, little, if at all, inferior to high treason; that the best method possible must be used to stop them, and to moderate, but that they must preserve the coalition.

Lord Chancellor Hardwicke thought that 'the body of the Tories' wanted the removal of Granville, but that their support 'can't be attained without bestowing, on some of them, honours, on others lucrative or honourable employments. But it may be attained without letting them into places of great power at Court or of considerable influence in the country'. They were still regarded by the King and most of his ministers as political untouchables who would prove Trojan horses in the Government, but had to be given something as part of a deal with Chesterfield and Cobham. They, on the other hand, wanted to make terms as a party and resist any moves to split them or pick them off in two or threes, leaving the rest helpless. Walpole understood this, telling Ryder the Tories 'would be hardly satisfied' with 'letting them into some places given to the discontented Whigs, leaving the old ones just as they were'. Gower was negotiating on behalf of the whole party, as head of the Loyal Brotherhood, the Tory board, and Chesterfield wrote to Newcastle on 1 December:

> when I had the honour of seeing your Grace last you seemed desirous to know the numbers and names of our necessary people in

6

consequence of which, Lord Cobham, Lord Gower and myself, have prepared such a list which we are ready to give your Grace whenever you please to command us.

The Broadbottom Administration formed in December 1744 included Lord Gower as Privy Seal, Sir John Hynde Cotton as treasurer of the chamber, Sir John Philipps and John Pitt on the board of trade—all places of little importance apart from Gower's. Wynn was said to have refused a peerage as he was 'resolved to live and die Sir Watkin'. Some Tory knights of the shire, it was reported, were offered minor places 'by the mediation of Lord Gower; but that serving for Jacobite counties they could not hazard a new election, and therefore declined the acceptance of them'.[1] Knights of the shire who became placemen usually did lose their seats, as Sir William Pole had found out in Cornwall in 1712 and others since, but this did not mean the party as a whole did not want office. As soon as he was in place, Sir John Cotton, who took the salary but not the oaths, sent through Dr Barry an express to the King of France renewing the pledge he had given, and adding that the Tories in office would make sure even more troops were sent from England to Flanders than last year. Lord Barrymore, at this time, wrote to Newcastle, who did not know that Richard Barry had just returned from France, complaining that his son had been passed over 'in the course of preferment' and that 'several have been made captains that were his juniors'. In fact Newcastle obtained his promotion to the rank of commander. Presumably George II, who reserved army appointments for himself, but did not concern himself with the navy, made no objections. In January 1745 Wynn spoke and voted with the Government for the first time in his life, in favour of sending the army to Flanders, saying 'that he did not doubt that all his friends would do the same, and that the whole nation would be unanimous in it'.[2]

Gower was regarded by the Tories as having taken office on terms which amounted to unconditional surrender, and not meeting the conditions agreed upon.[3] These were, on past form, a real end to

---

[1] Ryder diary Nov. and Dec. 1744; Owen 240–1; *Letters of Lord Chesterfield* ii 541; *HC* i 544; Coxe, *Horatio, Lord Walpole* ii 106.

[2] AEM & D. Ang. 77ff. 49– 50; *HC* i 442; ii 543–5.

[3] Dr William King, *Anecdotes* 45–6.

the proscription, the repeal of the penal laws passed since 1715, stricter place and pension bills, the repeal of the Septennial Act and a free Parliament, measures which, if implemented, would have given them a majority in Parliament and the ability to do as they chose. Bolingbroke, who was infuriated at the failure of most of the party to toe the line, denounced the Tories as a set of men—

> who mean nothing, or who mean confusion. They are made to be 'hewers of wood, and drawers of water'. Such let them remain, since they seem to proscribe every administration alike, which is to proscribe government itself, even when the proscription, they have complained of so long, is taken off.

The proscription had, of course, not been effectively taken off, and the King refused to take in any more Tories. In fact Bolingbroke himself gained nothing from the formation of the Broadbottom he had worked so hard to bring about. He then suggested to Hardwicke a way out might be to put more Tories on the commissions of the peace.[1] This was not because they were more parochial in their outlook, and indeed remodelling the commissions had an often decisive effect on the elections as the Whigs had found in 1690, 1702 and 1710, but because it was regarded as the most harmless bait politically. Newcastle wrote to Chesterfield, who was then on a mission at The Hague, on 26 March 1745:

> The Duke of Beaufort has set himself up, and the Tories have taken him, for the head of their party: in consequence of which they have excluded Lord Gower from a negotiation depending about justices of the peace, put it into the hands of the Duke of Beaufort; and, upon an unsatisfactory answer, given to what really was no proposal, Sir Watkin Williams, Sir John Hynde Cotton, and one hundred and nine more, voted in our last question, about the £100,000, to be given for extraordinary services of the war, against 247, amongst which were all the Whigs, your friends, all Lord Gower's family, and upon the whole, near forty Tories. This affords the best opportunity to Lord Gower, so ill used by them, to separate and detach a number, which, with your Whigs and our old Corps, would form a body not to be resisted. . . . If you write to Lord Gower, for God's sake, preach up firmness towards those who have left him; and moderation and inclination towards those who desire to join with him.

[1] *Marchmont Papers* ii 340; Dickinson 286–7; Add. 32804f. 309; *Letters of Lord Chesterfield* ii 597.

Lord Noel Somerset had succeeded his brother as 4th Duke of
Beaufort, and was one of the chief of the 'remitters', as those who
sent money to the Pretender were called. Horace Walpole reported:

> The new Duke of Beaufort, a most determined and unwavering
> Jacobite, has openly set himself at the head of the party and forced
> them to vote against the Court and to remove Lord Gower. My wise
> cousin Sir John Philipps has resigned his place, and it is believed that
> Sir John Cotton will soon resign.

Chesterfield, answering Newcastle on 2/13 April, wrote:

> I don't much mind the Duke of Beaufort's opposition, which singly
> as his, and a few of the red hot absurd Tories, might rather do good
> than hurt; but then such reasonable satisfaction should be given to
> the others, as to enable Gower to carry off the best, and leave only a
> marked avowed Jacobite faction behind him. Little things, and in my
> mind prudent things in themselves, would I am convinced strip this
> new opposition of Watkin Williams, and Lord Oxford, the only two
> people to be regarded in it. Therefore for God's sake my dear Lord
> do all that is possible, nationally to satisfy the reasonable part of that
> party, and then you may with safety and even with advantage despize
> the rest ... I will write to Gower, whose good intentions I know, but
> I know his distress too; and it is impossible for me to advise him to
> do, that which if I were in his place, I would not do myself. I would
> by no means have him intimidated by an unreasonable party clamour,
> and if he can make a decent schism of the Tory party, I would have
> him stand it, but if he cannot do that, I cannot advise him to stand
> single, a supposed apostate from a party of which he was once the
> head, and which will remain too numerous and possessed of too
> many national pretences at least, to be called Jacobite or factious.

To Gower, Chesterfield said:

> the small band of opposition which I find is forming itself under the
> Duke of Beaufort's banner, would I believe give neither of us much
> trouble were it not for two or three names that I see in that list, I
> mean Lord Oxford, Watkin and Cotton. I confess I am astonished at
> the first and the last. For I make allowances for Watkin's prejudices
> and Welsh popularity. But Lord Oxford's cool good sense and
> Cotton's sagacity, I thought would have hindered them both from
> engaging in a measure that must have the worst consequences, both

with regard to the public, and with regard to the Tory party in particular. I can more easily represent to myself your distress in this situation of your party, than point contrary means of redress of the evil. You little want, and I am less able to give advice. But I should think you ought to stand it out with firmness for some time at least, and with such of the Tories as will adhere to you, which I cannot think will be an insignificant number. And in the meantime work hard to recover Lord Oxford, Watkin, and Cotton, this last will in my mind be willing to be recovered. And Lord Oxford will surely recover himself; but in all events you cannot in my opinion yield to this attack which is directed in a manner personally at you, and be dragged through all the absurdities of such an ignorant hot headed set of people. If our friends in the Administration are wise they will contrive to strengthen your hands, by such concessions as will satisfy the reasonable and greater part of the Tories in the nation, and so brand the others with Jacobitism and faction.

Edward Harley, nephew of the first Lord Oxford, had succeeded as 3rd Earl of Oxford. As a Member of Parliament he had kept a valuable parliamentary diary, had been influential as the head of a Tory board or club to promote a bill to prevent the packing of juries and other reforms, the membership of which overlapped with the Tory Board, the Loyal Brotherhood. Recent research on Tory party organisation helps to explain the reasons for the survival of the party but it does not explain why they were outcasts. The 3rd Earl of Oxford has been said to have been 'unquestionably loyal to the Hanoverian dynasty' and a close friend of Philip Yorke, with no evidence given for these statements, and a search through contemporary sources has failed to reveal any. It is true that Oxford had not been a party to the negotiations with the French since 1743, but Carte who knew him describes him as being devoted to the Pretender's cause.[1] What in fact happened was that 'when it was discovered that Gower was really a friend to the Hanover succession, the Tories discarded him for being their leader, and adopted a determined Jacobite the Duke of Beaufort in his stead'.[2] In the hope of placating the Tories, the Pelhams and

[1] Lord Fitzmaurice, *Life of William, earl of Shelburne* i 49–50; Add. 32804ff. 287–8, 291–2; PRO Granville papers 30/29/1/11; Dr Linda Colley, *Historical Journal* xx (1977) 77–95; *HC* ii 111; Stuart mss. Box 1/299.
[2] *Lyttelton Memoirs* i 238.

Hardwicke, who continued to deal with Gower, included more Tories in the Gloucestershire, Yorkshire, Bedfordshire, Lincolnshire, Hampshire, Cambridgeshire, and Oxfordshire commissions,[1] a process which was only stopped after the battle of Prestonpans. It proved of little assistance to Gower, who far from bringing over a hundred Tories carried only six, three of them his own relations: Baptist and William Leveson Gower, Lord Trentham, Thomas and Charles Gore, John Pitt and (temporarily) George Venables Vernon. He could not bring in John Proby nor Randle Wilbraham whom he had brought into Parliament at Newcastle. Dr King, who knew Gower well, commented that his defection—

> was a great blow to the Tory party, and a singular disappointment to all his friends. For no one had entertained the least jealousy or suspicion of this part of his conduct . . . The Tories considered him as their chief; they placed the greatest confidence in him, and did nothing without his advice and approbation. They even persuaded themselves that he had an excellent judgement and understanding, though his parts were very moderate, and his learning superficial.[2]

While all this was taking place, across the Channel letters from James's friends in England had suddenly stopped. This was done by Lefebure after two letters from Balhaldy to Dr Barry of 7 and 14 January 1745 had been intercepted by the Government and the names of Lord Barrymore and Sir Watkin Williams Wynn correctly decyphered. James wrote to Sempill:

> I am, with reason, very anxious as to what relates to the security of our correspondent of the Post Office, both on his own account, and because of the bad consequences it would be to be deprived of that channel of correspondence . . . The Government may have taken such steps and precautions as may give a just motive of jealousy to the person concerned, and make him think they know more than they really do.

It turned out there had been no treachery but an indiscretion on the part of the banker in Holland through whom the letters were sent; the venue was changed and contact was renewed in June.

---

[1] Add. 35,602ff. 46, 50, 54, 83.
[2] *Anecdotes* 45–8.

In that month Dr Barry sent a message from Wynn and Cotton, who led the Tories in the Commons, joined by Beaufort as the head of the party, to say that almost all the troops were out of England so that 'if the Prince lands in present circumstances with ten battalions or even smaller body of troops there will be no opposition'.[1] As it was 'impossible to get any stranger into England without arousing suspicion', they and their friends offered 'to open themselves' to the Maréchal comte de Belle-Isle, then a prisoner in Windsor Castle but one who was allowed a good deal of latitude there. This offer was not accepted because the French secretaries of state had no wish to give Belle-Isle an important role to play, and because Belle-Isle's wife, though a relation of Charles Edward through his mother, objected that he had given his word to the English Government that he would remain neutral in order to obtain the amount of freedom he enjoyed, and that he could not break it.[2] Instead of this, the Tory leaders sent to France Lord Orrery's cousin Robert Maccarty, 5th Earl of Clancarty [I], chosen because he was a naval officer with practical knowledge of the Essex coast, and also, it must be said, because he had not too much to lose. Clancarty's father had forfeited estates worth £90,000 a year by adhering to James II in Ireland, and had married a daughter of Sunderland. Regarded by Horace Walpole as 'of great parts, but mad and drunken', he had fought to recover his estates in co. Cork in a lawsuit at which the Duchess of Marlborough was 'said to be at the whole expense'. Failing in this, he was given a commission in the Navy, was made governor of Newfoundland in 1733–5, and was given a pension of £1,000 p.a. by the Government. What he wanted was to recover his estates. Arriving in France in August, he brought a message from Beaufort, Lichfield, Orrery, Barrymore, Wynn and Cotton, asking for 10,000 troops and 30,000 arms to be landed near Maldon and pledging themselves to meet them on landing. The 3rd Earl of Lichfield was the son of Gower's predecessor as the head of the Tory Board, and the brother of Hon. Fitzroy Lee, who had offered to join Charles Edward in the spring of 1744. Lichfield's sister and eventual

---

[1] SP 36/65/4 and 10; Browne ii 454, 456, 462; Stuart mss. 263/37 and 265/207.
[2] Stuart mss. 266/33; AEM & D. Ang. 78ff, 46–50. For Belle-Isle's imprisonment in England see SP 78/231; for Madame de Belle-Isle see *Mémoires de Saint-Simon*, ed. Boislisle, xv 154, xxxvi 70–2.

heir had just married Henry Dillon, 11th Viscount Dillon [I], the commander of an Irish regiment in the French service and himself a zealous Jacobite. Sitting in the Commons as Lord Quarendon, Lichfield has been regarded as 'the most promising in point of parts amongst all the young men of the Tory party'. Those still in the concert with them were Sir Henry Slingsby, Sir Robert Abdy, Thomas Bramston and Sir Edward Smith. Carew and St. Aubyn had died; Read had, not surprisingly, been dropped.[1] As it turned out, the moment was well chosen, for the conduct of foreign affairs by the nobles on the council of state had proved disastrous, Madame de Châteauroux was dead, and with the secretaries of state once more in full charge and the *rapprochement* between England and Prussia, French policy was again turning towards a restoration of the Stuarts. But Charles Edward, without consulting his friends in England, the French ministers or his father, had already landed in Scotland.

---

[1] AEM & D. Ang. 77ff. 126–7; 78ff. 46–50; *H. Walpole Corresp.* xix 160; *Orrery Papers* i 132, 190. For the Duchess of Marlborough and the Jacobites, see *HC* ii 66–7. Cokayne, *Complete Peerage* vii 647; AEM & D. Ang. 78ff. 46–50; 54f. 12.

6

England and the '45

If historians, Scottish historians particularly, have never left the '45 in Scotland alone, historians have left the '45 in England very strictly alone, or dismissed it as never a serious threat. The Scottish story is obviously the more attractive proposition: the story of David against Goliath, of Lochiel and other chiefs so moved by the youth and bravery of Charles Edward that they raised their clans contrary to their better judgment and, joining a handful of men, went on to win a kingdom. The English story is much more complex, with heroics conspicuously absent on both sides. It is proposed to examine the statements of Lord George Murray, Lord Elcho and Murray of Broughton, who seem to have expected the Tory gentlemen to raise their clans, that there was little support in England for the Stuarts, that Government forces had overwhelming superiority, and that there was no hope of assistance from France, and to let contemporaries, some of them nearest to the centre of power and to the seat of war, speak for themselves.

Charles Edward left St. Nazaire on 3/14 July on the *Doutelle*, a vessel belonging to Anthony Walshe, a shipowner of Irish extraction, landing at Moidart on 15 July. George II was in Hanover, pursuing ambitious diplomatic schemes in the Empire with Granville (who was out of office since the Broadbottom ministry) without consulting the Pelhams or Hardwicke, and England denuded of troops. It took several weeks for the Duke of Newcastle even to be able to discover that the Prince had already landed and that a substantial number of clans had joined him. Henry Pelham took a Walpolean view of the situation, sending at once for 6,000 Dutch troops, and writing to Argyll (the former Lord Ilay) as early as 20 August: 'I see the contagion spread in all parts . . . For my part, I have long dreaded it, and am as much convinced as my late friend Lord Orford was, that this country will be fought for some time before this year is over.' Granville and Lord Tweeddale, the Secretary of State for Scotland, advised the King that there was no cause for alarm. Although the Pelhams suspected Granville of acting the part of Sunderland to James II, it would seem that Granville regarded the rebellion as a tiresome interruption to his plans for a grand alliance on the Continent. Henry Pelham wrote to Chesterfield on 10 September:

> I heartily wish the troops were arrived both Dutch and English, for though I look upon these Highland rebels as a sort of rabble, yet if there is no force to oppose them, they may come in time to be considerable. We have scarce any regular troops in the country, and between you and I, I don't find that zeal to venture purses and lives that I formerly remember.

The Dutch landed by mid-September and were ordered to Lancashire. It took the total rout of Sir John Cope at Prestonpans on 21 September, which made the rebels masters of Scotland, to alarm George II, who had just returned from Hanover, and to make him agree to recall some of the troops from Flanders and Ireland and to send 8,000 troops under Marshal Wade to Northumberland. Lord Perceval, later 2nd Lord Egmont, a Whig, proposed to Pelham that the Hanoverians and the Hessians should be called over at once, but this was not done. Horatio Walpole told Ryder that 'if the rebels should make a progress, the King hated his son so much that he might be induced to composition with the Pretender, by giving up this Crown and saving Hanover'. Winnington, a Whig who was regarded as one of the ablest men in the Government and came from a Tory family, told Egmont 'he believed certainly the Pretender would succeed', and, until the retreat from Derby, continued to assert that the rebellion would succeed and there would be a restoration. On 28 September the Cabinet was concerned to find that a run on the Bank of England had begun and that the Bank having run out of other species was forced to pay in silver. The Government was unable to raise a loan in the City in the normal way as most people had ceased to pay the land tax. An association of London merchants 'saved the Bank for a time' when they 'subscribed an agreement to take banknotes in payment'. The Bank, Ryder wrote, 'acted imprudently in taking fright so soon', and yet even after being rescued by the merchants, continued, 'paying in silver, which occasioned a decay in credit'. Newcastle wrote to his friend the Duke of Richmond:

> I am very apprehensive, that the Pretender, being in possession of Scotland may encourage France to try to put them in possession of England also ... Everything is done that can be done by an Administration that has no power, and to whom the King, their master, will hardly vouchsafe to say one word about his own business. The greater the danger is, the more angry he grows with those who alone can help him out of it, and if he goes on he may run the risk of losing another kingdom by the rashness and hating of some as he has already done one by the folly and obstinacy of others.

To the Whigs, who, of course, sincerely believed that the Hanoverian succession was the only guarantee for the constitution, the situation was appalling. Charles Yorke, Lord Chancellor Hardwicke's son, commented:

> It is indeed a dreadful and amazing consideration to reflect that the work of so many wise and honest men, and of so many Parliaments of fifty seven years, that a fabric of so much art and cost at the Revolution and its train of consequences, should be in danger of being overwhelmed by the bursting of a cloud, which seemed, at first gathering, no bigger than a man's hand.

The addresses from all parts of England did not give him much comfort, for, as he wrote, 'The Gazettes about the time of the Revolution are filled with very handsome ones to King James!'[1]

Upon the first news of His Royal Highness's arrival, Sempill wrote:

> The City of London, Sir John Hynde Cotton, Lord Barrymore, the Duke of Beaufort, and all the English cry loudly and vehemently for a body of troops to be landed near London, as the most effectual means to support the Prince, and the only method by which a dangerous and ruinous civil war can be avoided.

---

[1] Coxe, *Horatio, Lord Walpole* ii 111; Owen 228–83; *HMC 14th Rep.* ix 131, 132; Northumberland mss., A. Mordaunt to Lady Hertford, 19 Sept. 1745; Ryder diary 14 August, 20, 26, 28 September 1745, 5 January 1746; Add. 47098Bff. 6, 9, 10; Yorke, *Hardwicke* i 417, 458, 462; *HMC* i 115.

They were unable to act without 'a body of troops to support them' but 'would join the Prince if His Highness could force his way to them'. In the City of London 'Alderman Heathcote, and several more, have been with Sir Watkins, to assure him that they will rise in the city of London at the same time. He begs that arms and ammunition be brought with the troops.' Sir John Douglas, a Member of Parliament who was in London at the time, later told Charles Edward that Heathcote had collected £10,000 in the City against his arrival. Lefebure reported that there were then not 'above 10,000 regular troops' in England, but that eight battalions of foot from Flanders were expected at Newcastle, and that the 6,000 Hessians in English pay were bound to be sent for.[1]

Charles Edward had, in fact, never had any intention of doing without French assistance. As soon as he had landed, he wrote to Louis XV, informing him of his arrival and asking him to send arms and troops to Scotland. In order to counteract the use Whig propaganda would make of his appeal to France, he counterattacked vigorously in his proclamation issued from Edinburgh on 11 October:

> The fears of the nation from the powers of France and Spain appear still more vain and groundless. My expedition was undertaken unsupported by either: but, indeed, when I see a foreign force brought by my enemies against me, and when I hear of Dutch, Danes, Hessians and Swiss, the Elector of Hanover's allies, being called over to protect his government against the King's subjects, is it not high time for the King my father to accept also of the assistance of those who are able and who have engaged to support him? But will the world, or any one man of sense in it, infer from thence that he inclines to be a tributary prince rather than an independent monarch? Who has the better chance to be independent of foreign powers? He who, with the aid of his own subjects, can wrest the government out of the hands of an intruder or he who cannot, without assistance from abroad, support his government, though established by all the civil power, and secured by a strong military force, against the undisciplined part of those he has ruled over so many years? Let him, if he pleases, try the experiment; let him send of his foreign hirelings, and put the whole upon the issue of a battle. I will trust to the King my father's subjects, who are, or shall be, engaged in mine and their country's cause.

[1] Stuart mss. 268/5; 269/109; *HC* i 618; Browne iii 446–7, 450–1.

France, who had already sent arms, ammunition, money, officers and a few troops to Scotland, was preparing a larger scale force, and the Pretender's younger son, Henry Duke of York had already arrived in France to lead it. Boyer, Marquis d'Eguilles, the brother of the Marquis d'Argens later French ambassador at the Court of Berlin, arrived by 15 October at Edinburgh as accredited envoy to Charles Edward as regent of Scotland and the ally of France. Lord Elcho's statement that Boyer 'had not the least authority from the Court of France' is simply preposterous. On 13/24 October 1745 France had signed the Treaty of Fontainebleau with the Pretender, by which she ceased to recognise the Elector of Hanover as King of Great Britain; promised to send military assistance to Charles Edward; recognised James VIII as King of Scotland and undertook to recognise him as King of England as soon as this could be shown to be the wish of the nation and a free Parliament. Eguilles wrote to the Marquis d'Argenson, the French foreign minister, that the Prince now wanted troops sent to England, and asked France to find ways of putting pressure on the Dutch to withdraw their troops. As it turned out the Dutch troops sent to England had undertaken, under the terms of the capitulation of Tournai, not to serve against France or her allies, and were forced to withdraw, so that Charles Edward did not find them in Lancashire. He wrote to his father from Edinburgh on 15 October:

> I wish to God I may find my brother landed in England by the time I enter it, which will be about ten days, having with me near 8000 men, and 300 horse at least, with which, as matters stand, I should have one decisive stroke for it, but if the French land, perhaps none.

To the Duc de Richelieu, who was to lead the expedition into England, he wrote later that his main object in entering England was to make a junction with him and his brother in the south, preferably near London.[1]

On 9 October the attorney general and solicitor general had begun to prepare a bill to suspend the Habeas Corpus Act in readiness for the meeting of Parliament on the 17th. Wynn, Cotton,

[1] AEM & D. Ang. 77f. 47; Ewald i 238–9; Ld. Elcho, *An Account of the Affair of Scotland* (1973 ed.) 358; *Murray of Broughton* 436–7; AEM & D. Ang. 87ff. 191; 82ff. 128–9, 189–90; 78ff. 231, 316–7, 439–42; Mahon iii App. p. xxviii; Stuart mss. 269/191.

Barrymore and the rest attended, for if they had not they were liable to arrest on suspicion of treason as well as for being absent from the service of the House. It was reported that the Government had sent instructions to governors of towns, justices, and local officials to watch for signs of disaffection. In Yorkshire, Staffordshire and the northern counties, orders were sent to search the houses and papers of suspected persons and arrest them if needs be. In Flintshire, Newcastle wanted reports not only of those who might favour the Pretender but also of those who cursed King George! Even in London, Wynn and Barrymore were being tailed by Newcastle's spies. Sir John Philipps moved an unsuccessful amendment to the loyal address to pass first a bill 'for securing his Majesty's faithful subjects the perpetual enjoyment of their undoubted right to be freely and fairly represented in Parliament, frequently chosen, and exempted from undue influence of every kind', declaring 'the addresses of the people of England are already become a proverb among our foreign neighbours; and if we go on but a few years as we have done, the addresses of our Parliament will fall under the same reproach.' The suspension of the Habeas Corpus Act moved the same day met, Horace Walpole wrote, 'with obstructions from the Jacobites. By this we may expect what spirit they will show hereafter.' In the Lords Westmorland said the Act had never been suspended under William and Anne except just after the Revolution, but now it was being for ever suspended on 'the least pretence'.[1] All over England, Associations were being formed in defence of the King and the Government and subscriptions to raise additional forces collected. On limited evidence, since these have never been studied systematically, the response of Tories varied according to counties. Horatio Walpole wrote, that many Tories 'for fear of being suspected, joined in the Associations, and a great many in the subscriptions', as did most Roman Catholics. Humphrey Sydenham, a high Tory, complained in Parliament that pressure was being put on Tories to take both subscriptions and Associations under threat of being branded as traitors if they did not. In Oxfordshire, one of the strongest Tory counties in England, the Tories did not take them. In Shropshire, none of the Tory gentlemen appeared at the county meeting or

[1] Ryder diary 9, 18 Oct. 1745; SP 36/76/45 and 152–65; *CJ* xxv 4; *H. Walpole Corresp.* xix 106–7; *Parl. Hist.* xiii 1322, 1353.

took the Association. In Derbyshire, Tories, including Sir Nathaniel Curzon, took the subscriptions. In Yorkshire the Archbishop of York was very active in organising the Association and subscriptions, and it was reported 'the Yorkshire gentlemen have had the greatest meeting that ever was known to shew their zeal for the Government, and several Tories took them, though some of the aldermen of York were suspected as disaffected', rightly since two of them had offered to send the freedom of the city in a gold box to the Duke of York the year before. The Archbishop himself did not take these at their face value, writing to Hardwicke that 'we had very gallant professions of zeal and unanimity but *quid verba audiam cum facta non videam*'. In London, George Heathcote had tried to get the grand jury of Middlesex to present the Associations and subscriptions as illegal (a device used by the Whigs in 1680 to present the Duke of York as a Papist) and he failed by one vote, while in Parliament he and Thomas Carew compared them to the 'benevolences of Charles I's time'. Wynn also subscribed as a precaution. Charles Edward, on his side, declared himself—

traduced, misrepresented and reviled in those fulsome addresses and associations made to and in favour of the Elector of Hanover, by those very bishops of the Church of England, who, for so many years, have contributed their utmost endeavours to abet and support every measure the most unpopular, pernicious, and hurtful, and that the worst of ministers, be he of what party he would, could ever devise for the undoing of these nations.[1]

Lord Perceval wrote that Lord Gower had been to see the King 'and assured him that he had formerly been his enemy and a Jacobite, but he saw the folly of it and that he be no more', and offered to raise a regiment in Staffordshire for him. The Duke of Bedford and several other Whig noblemen followed suit. However, the gesture was somewhat spoilt when, according to Horace Walpole, it was noticed that these 'most disinterested colonels' had filled these

[1] *Parl. Hist.* xiii 1351–2; R. J. Robson, *The Oxfordshire Election of 1754* 2; Chatsworth mss., Lord Herbert to Duke of Devonshire, 10 Oct. 1745; Newcastle to Devonshire, 11 Oct. 1745; Northumberland mss., A. Mordaunt to Lady Hertford, 19 Sept. and 9 Oct. 1745; C. Collier, 'Yorkshire and the Forty Five', *Yorkshire Archaeological Journal* xxxviii 71–95; *Murray of Broughton* 41; P. Thomas, *Jacobitism in Wales* 297; Browne iii 113–14.

regiments with their relations and friends and expected them to have rank in the Army, and this was strongly opposed by 'the Jacobites and Patriots', the last by now were only Cobham's cubs. The commanders of these newly raised regiments were satirised by Sir Charles Hanbury Williams, a Whig, in *The Heroes: A new Ballad* published at this time, in which Gower was advised to reflect:

> And now, dear G . . ., thou man of Pow'r,
> And comprehensive Noodle;
> Tho' you've the Gout, yet as you're stout,
> Why wa'n't you plac'd in Saddle?
> Then you might ride to either Side,
> Chuse which K . . . you'd serve under;
> But, dear Dragoon, charge not too soon,
> For fear of th'other Blunder.[1]

One of the most remarkable features of the '45 is that while Charles Edward was in touch with the French and with his father throughout, he never once managed to establish contact with the Tory leaders. He had not consulted them before landing in Scotland, had established no safe channel of communication, didn't even know where they were. On 22 September, the day after the battle of Prestonpans in late September, he sent a messenger into Northumberland with the following message:

You are thereby authorised to repair forthwith into England, and there to notify my friends, and particularly those in the north and north-west, the wonderful success with which it had hitherto pleased God to favour my endeavours for their deliverance. You are to let them know that it is my full intention, in a few days, to move towards them; and that they will be inexcusable before God and man if they do not do all in their power to assist and support me in such an undertaking. What I demand and expect is, that as many of them as can, shall be ready to join me, and that they should take care to furnish provisions and money, that the country may suffer as little as possible by the march of my troops. Let them know that there is no time for deliberation—now or never is the word. I am resolved to conquer or perish. If this last should happen, let them judge what they and their posterity have to expect.

[1] Add. 47098Bf. 11. *H. Walpole Corresp.* xix 153; Chatsworth mss., Lord Hartington to Devonshire, 5 Nov. 1745.

It never got through as the messenger was arrested. The rebel army crossed into England on 8 November, and three days later he sent the following letter to Lord Barrymore at Marbury in Cheshire, sending it by two messengers:

> This is to acquaint you with the success we have had since our arrival in Scotland, and how far we are advanced without repulse. We are now a numerous army, and are laying siege to Carlisle this day . . . After that we intend to take our route straight to London, and if things answer our expectations we design to be in Cheshire before the 24th inst. Then I hope you and all my friends in the county will be ready to join us. For now is the time or never.

They got to Marbury only to be told that Barrymore was in London, but that his eldest son Lord Buttevant was there to whom they gave the letter. Now Barrymore's relationship with his eldest son was Hanoverian and Buttevant sided with the Government, handing over letter and messengers. Barrymore later repaid him by letting him rot in prison for debt! The Prince wrote a letter which was also intercepted, apparently meant for Wynn at Wynnstay:

> After the success which providence has granted to my arms in Scotland, I thought I could not do better than to enter England, where I have always been assured that I should meet with many friends, equally disposed to exert their loyalty to their native king, and to shake off a foreign yoke under which the nation has so long groaned. I have now put into their hands an opportunity to doing both, by repairing with what strength every man can to my army, from which the enemy industriously keeps at such a distance. The particular character I have heard of you, makes me hope to see you among the first. I am persuaded you will not baulk my expectations, and you need not doubt but I shall always remember to your advantage the example you shall thus have put to your neighbours, and consequently to all England.[1]

Whereas every aspect of the rebellion in Scotland has been covered, and every Jacobite prisoner identified, English response

---

[1] Chatsworth mss.; Ewald i 260, 274–5, 277; *HC* i 441–2; *HMC Egmont diary* iii 317.

to the rebellion has hardly been touched upon. Obviously the amount of sympathy there was in England cannot be known, how can one quantify views which cannot be expressed? To make matters worse, as the situation became tenser, most Whig sources dry up. Newspapers printed only Whig propaganda. Letters from the North and Midlands were held up by the Government, and in the absence of solid news, it was believed in London that 'all Manchester to a man had joined the rebels'. The agent of the Duke of Devonshire in Derbyshire thought that the disaffected would rise only if 'any foreign force should land'. It is true that a small number of Englishmen joined the rebels, but more did join than Elcho and the two Murrays assert. Only two are said to have done so in Northumberland, neither of any consequence; yet a list of the tenants of the Duke of Somerset who joined the rebels, sent by his steward at Alnwick, alone contains over a dozen names, including those of Thomas Forster of Etherstone (son of the Jacobite general of the '15), Edward Blackett, John Clavering, and Sir Nicholas Sherburn, a Roman Catholic, the historic names of Northumberland. An English gentleman called Clifton, who came to France in early January 1746 with a pass from the English Government as his wife was dying there, and whose account of the situation in Cheshire and Derbyshire tallies with that from government sources, said that there were at Derby 1,500 Englishmen with the Prince, and he could have had large numbers in Lancashire especially had he been able to provide them with arms and officers. This agrees with what Lochiel (who was there) later said to Charles Edward:

> Your Royal Highness is not ignorant, that, both before and during the time of your last attempt, your English friends were ready and willing to declare for you, if you could either have furnished them with arms, or brought a body of troops capable to protect them.[1]

The general attitude of Englishmen before Derby, was very much one of wait and see until it was clear who would come out

---

[1] C. S. Terry, *The Forty Five* 78; Northumberland mss. 'a particular account of his Grace's tenants . . . in the rebellion'; A. Mordaunt to Lady Hertford, 3 Dec. 1745; Chatsworth mss., John Griffith to Devonshire, 25 Sept. 1745; Guerre A1/1352/167 and 177; Browne iii 489.

on top, and this is easy to understand in view of the penalty of being caught on the wrong side of a civil war. The Whigs who had been given arms by the Government were not keen to use them. Cumberland was a Whig county, but when the Whig governor wanted to defend Carlisle, the militia absolutely insisted on surrendering, and some of the local aldermen were accused of having carried the keys of the city to offer them to Charles Edward at Brampton. In Lancashire, where the Whigs had made a good showing in the '15, Lord Derby the lord lieutenant disbanded the militia as he could find neither officers nor recruits. The same applied to Cheshire where Lord Cholmondeley reported to Newcastle that as the rebels approached 'I found despair, fear and confusion had seized the minds of everyone so that when the danger came nearer, not a justice was to be found, or gentlemen of estate to do any one act for the safety or protection of it'. The most notorious example was the Derbyshire Blues, the regiment raised by the Duke of Devonshire, who when ordered by the duke to march against the rebels 'to a man refused him'. Similarly when Sir Richard Wrottesley raised a troop of yeomanry and set out to join his father-in-law Lord Gower's regiment, his men would go no farther than the nearest inn, less than a mile from their starting point.[1]

At Preston, which the rebels entered on 26 November, Charles Edward was greeted 'by a great concourse of people and welcomed with the loudest shouts and acclamations of joy'. At Manchester, which local sympathisers contrived to hand over on the 30th, there were illuminations and ringing of bells, and they were joined 'by some young men of the most reputable families in the town, several substantial tradesmen and farmers, and above a hundred common men', 300 altogether who presumably had or were given arms, and were led by Francis Townley a Roman Catholic of an old Lancashire family who had military experience, having served in an Irish regiment in France. No doubt Charles Edward's popularity was enhanced by the fact that he had attended Protestant services ever since landing, and that Lord Elcho told the Lancashire people that the Prince's religion 'was to seek'. Sir Thomas Abney, a Whig judge, wrote to the Duke of Devonshire at this time 'the joy that I

[1] Mounsey 52-96, 204-5; Northumberland mss., A. Mordaunt to Lady Hertford, 10 Dec. 1745; SP 36/40/118; *HC* ii 143-4, 439, 559.

observed on the countenances of too many persons in the several counties I went through on the Oxford circuit gives me great uneasiness'. According to Clifton, the Government was very angry at the welcome the rebels were given in Lancashire, Staffordshire and Nottinghamshire. People's conduct was far from uniform: the treasurer of the Derbyshire subscriptions, Samuel Heathcote, who was Sir Nathaniel Curzon's steward, ended up being taken prisoner to London on a charge of high treason. He had not only tried to prevent the escape of a spy on the rebels sent by the Duke of Cumberland, but had ordered him to be shot through the head if found.[1]

London's reaction to the rebellion has long interested historians, but, as one of them noted, since it never got to London the real feelings of Londoners were never put to the test.[2] Recent work purporting to show that Jacobites in London consisted mainly of Irish Roman Catholics would seem to illustrate rather the usual behaviour of Irishmen in public houses.[3] Pitt later reflected that if the rebels 'had obtained a victory and made themselves masters of London, I question if the spirit of the population would not have taken a different turn'.[4] Some of the most interesting descriptions of London in the first week of December are in French sources; from a London merchant who came to France; from a Captain Nagle, an Irish officer in Lally's regiment, as well as information derived from the smugglers. They all describe London at this time as a ghost town, with the shops and playhouses shut, and noblemen dismissing half their servants. Nagle made his way to see a Lord whose name he left blank (perhaps Orrery, who was in touch with Lally) who told him they were all being watched and lying low in full expectation that Charles Edward would make his way to them or that the French and the Duke of York would land, and they would then take off the mask and that people never suspected

---

[1] James Maxwell of Kirkconnel 70; David Daiches, *Charles Edward Stuart* 106–7; Howell, *State Trials* xviii 371; Eardley Simpson 97; Guerre A1/3152/157; Chatsworth mss., affidavit by E. Birch of 23 Dec. 1745; SP 36/76/93; SP 36/76/339–40.

[2] George Rudé, *Hanoverian London* 155.

[3] N. Rogers, 'Popular disaffection in London during the Forty Five', *London Journal* i 1–26.

[4] Sharpe, *London and the Kingdom* iii 50–6. See also A. A. Mitchell, 'London and the Forty Five', *History Today* Nov. 1965, 719–26.

before would declare for the Prince. Meanwhile, both sides drank the healths of 'the King, the Prince, the Duke' without naming names. Lord Cobham was reported to have said in public of Charles Edward that the young man has not put a foot wrong since he landed, and would be a great man if he were not a Papist. Wynn had been questioned by the Government, but had escaped arrest as the Duke of Bedford had vouched for him.[1] Official sources in England show that a government spy reported that Lefebure had been seeing Jacobites, but this was not followed up by Newcastle. The Pretender's declaration of 23 December 1743 and Charles Edward's proclamations were being printed and distributed in London, and though they were ceremoniously burnt by the hangman at the Royal Exchange, Newcastle was never able to catch more than one of the persons responsible for them.[2] To everyone's surprise the Duke of Norfolk was seen at Court 'to clear himself of his steward being gone over to the rebels' and his visit, though not the reason for it, was put in the *Gazette* 'that the disaffected and Roman Catholics may see it'. Sir Robert Grosvenor, a friend of Wynn and member of the Jacobite Cycle of the White Rose, also went, 'having never been there before and always counted very high', either to reinsure his immense wealth or for a reason similar to the Duke of Norfolk's. Beaufort's man of affairs David Morgan (see below) had already joined Charles Edward, perhaps an illustration of Walpole's prophecy 'if you see them come again, they will begin by their lowest people; their chiefs will not appear till the end'.[3]

The position of Charles Edward and his army at Derby in the first week of December and the decision of whether to march on London must be seen not only in the light of the reaction of people in the North and the Midlands but against the position and strength of the Government forces, the psychological factors operating at the time, and whether there was any serious prospect of assistance from France.

General Wade, who had been at Newcastle was now at Doncaster, several days march away and showed no sign of moving.

---

[1] Guerre A1/3152/167, 170, 171, 174, 189, 196.

[2] SP 36/78/12, 18 and 154.

[3] Northumberland mss., A. Mordaunt to Lady Hertford, 10 Dec. 1745; SP 36/76/274; *H. Walpole Corresp.* xix 118.

A veteran of Steinkirk in 1692, Wade was now in his seventies. Newcastle said that Wade 'was timid, and had always black atoms before his eyes'. A military historian has rightly said that Wade's favourite tactic was 'masterly inertia'. Henry Pelham commented earlier on:

> I dare say the old man will act for the best, and if he can come to a fair field of battle, I should not despair of success. We must hope for the best. I pray God this may be soon decided, for if it is not, all our accounts from abroad open a sad scene. It is pretty certain that France will support the Pretender openly, and I hear from good hands that the Duke of Richelieu and most of their favourite officers are destined for this service. Amidst these general misfortunes, I cannot help mentioning our particular situations at home. The King frightened yet impracticable and some of our new Allies [in Parliament] filled with the most extraordinary notions, and even now stipulating before hand, what we shall or shall not do with regard to foreign affairs, before the rebellion is put an end to.

Finding it impossible to get recruits for the army, the Cabinet asked the law officers to prepare a Pressing Act on the model of that of 1640. A second army of about 6,000 men under the Duke of Cumberland and the Duke of Richmond was sent to try and prevent the rebels getting to London. The newly raised regiments, in addition to these, were regarded as useless, Cumberland writing of Bedford's which was regarded as the best, 'neither men nor officers know what they are about, so how they will do before an enemy God only knows'. Cumberland was confident he could get between the rebels and London. The Duke of Richmond did not share his optimism. In letters to Newcastle marked 'most secret' to be shown 'to nobody but the Chancellor and Mr. Pelham', Richmond complained that Wade was 'quite out of the way'; that the rebels were always too fast; that his army was 'marched to death' and could get no rest not daring to go into cantonment for fear of being attacked at night. At the very time of the retreat from Derby Richmond reported that he feared the rebels would get to London first:

> what in the name of wonder is become of Marshal Wade? . . . the rebels will certainly be two days march ahead of us . . . I make no doubt but this embarkation will go on at Dunkirk. Are we all mad?

that you don't send for ten thousand more forces be they Hessians, Hanoverians, or devils, if they will but fight for us . . . The whole kingdom is still asleep. Our cavalry can't be here before February, and the Pretender may be crowned at Westminster by that time.[1]

The psychological advantage of Charles Edward and his army at this stage was enormous. Horace Walpole, who had treated the rebellion lightly at first began to say, 'sure banditti can never conquer a kingdom. On the other hand, what can't any number of men do that meet with no opposition; they have hitherto taken no place but open towns.' A Whig clergyman who escaped from Carlisle reflected that it seemed as if Heaven 'had made all opposition either to fall before them, or to become ineffectual'. In London, the news that Charles Edward was at Derby came on Black Friday, 6 December, when Philip Yorke wrote to his brother who was with Cumberland's army:

The motion of the rebels to Derby threw us into no small panic here lest they should give you the slip as they had done Mr. Wade and get to London by hasty marches. Our alarm was much increased by the news of a large embarkation at Dunkirk, which was intended for the south and in concert with the Young Pretender to land near the capital. The same terror but in a higher degree (as the strength to resist was less) has spread itself through all parts of the kingdom and to every great town, on every road which it was possible for the rebels to take in on their way to London.[2]

Ever since his first landing in Scotland, Charles Edward had been appealing for French help, but having neither consulted nor concerted anything with them it was not until the middle of October that any serious plans to give it were made and not until mid-November that preparations began in earnest. They were then still planning to send troops to Scotland and the *Royal Ecossais* under Lord John Drummond had already left for Montrose via Ostend when Sir James Stewart arrived in France from the Prince

---

[1] Chatsworth mss., H. Pelham to Devonshire, 19 Nov. 1745; George Wade to Devonshire, Doncaster 8 Dec. 1745; W. T. Waugh, *James Wolfe* 46; Ryder diary 21 Dec. 1745; Add. 32705ff. 360–1, 362, 365, 409, 411, 421–3.

[2] *H. Walpole Corresp.* xix 109–110; Mounsey 125; Add. 35363f. 109; Yorke, *Hardwicke* i 477.

to ask that no more troops be sent to Scotland and all available troops
be sent to England, whereupon the Fitzjames regiment ready to
embark at Ostend was recalled.[1]

In London Cotton and Barrymore sent a message through Dr
Barry and Lefebure asking the French to land troops in Essex as
first arranged in 1744 'on account of its vicinity to London and
the facility of joining them', adding:

> The King's friends entreat in the most earnest and pressing manner
> that the troops be sent without delay there being nothing at present
> to obstruct the expedition for Admiral Vernon has only two frigates
> with him. Lord Barrymore desires he may have some warning in
> order to secure himself and the King's friends.

They asked that spare arms be brought over, and undertook to
meet the Duke of York and the troops on landing. At this stage
they were asked through Lord Clancarty to give assurances under
their own hands, but this once more they refused to do for reasons
explained to the Pretender:

> The sentiments and inclinations of Sir Watkin, Lord Barrymore, and
> their friends, are known to all, they intend they should and even use
> means to manifest them; but they, with great reason, make a vast
> distinction between the owning of their principles, and being engaged
> in any direct or indirect correspondence with Your Majesty and the
> French Court, with an actual design of overturning the present
> government; the owning of their principles exposes them only to the
> hatred of an administration from which they neither expect nor desire
> any favour, but a correspondence of the nature I have mentioned, is
> an overt act of treason according to the present laws, the least sus-
> picion of which would bring certain ruin upon them, and conse-
> quently render them insignificant and useless to Your Majesty's
> cause, whereas they have all along kept it awake, and can by their
> influence and example to determine above two-thirds of the nation
> to act vigorously for it, as soon as they see a probability, nay, even a
> possibility of success.

All letters to the Pretender and to Sempill from England were
signed in cypher only. Instead, Sir John Cotton offered to resign
his place as a pledge of earnestness. He was not asked to do so then,

[1] Marine B3/429/256, 267, 268, 353, 356, 368, 384, 406; Marine B3/426/661;
Guerre A1/3152/16, 22, 23, 24.

but according to Chesterfield Cotton's resignation was to be the sign from England for the embarkation to begin. How Chesterfield learned this can only be surmised. He was then lord lieutenant of Ireland, writing to Newcastle before Derby that the rebellion caused him not the least alarm, and that there was no need to send for more troops from abroad. Ryder noted in his diary that Chesterfield had refused an offer from the Irish House of Commons to raise 6,000 troops to be sent to England.[1]

The refusal to give signatures proved no obstacle since the new Secretary of State for Foreign Affairs René Louis de Voyer, Marquis d'Argenson, had been a warm partisan of a restoration of the Stuarts since 1739. He was the elder brother of the Comte d'Argenson the minister for war, but very different in character. An idealist, who frequented clubs used by the *Philosophes*, he was interested in projects for universal peace and his own philosophical writings were later used by Jean Jacques Rousseau. His schoolfriend Voltaire nicknamed him secretary of state for Plato's republic. In charge of the expedition to England at his own request was Louis François Armand du Plessis, Duc de Richelieu, great grand-nephew of Cardinal Richelieu, and the intimate friend of Louis XV. The Don Juan of eighteenth-century France and the patron of Voltaire, Richelieu was a freethinker who, as governor of Languedoc had stopped the persecution of the Protestants, and was in 1756 to capture Minorca from Admiral Byng. When the English ministers learned of the appointment Ryder noted that Richelieu, a prime favourite at the French court was not going to be sent to *Scotland*.[2] Having taken the decision, Louis XV and his ministers, as a witness at the court of Versailles wrote, worked on nothing and thought of nothing but the expedition to England. It was planned on a bigger scale than the 1744 attempt, with about 12,000 troops altogether, and this time consisted of Irish regiments including those commanded by General Bulkeley, a relation of James 6th Viscount Bulkeley [I] Wynn's friend in Wales; by Viscount Dillon;

---

[1] Stuart mss. 270/51, 105, 142; 271/3; AEM & D. Ang. 77ff. 246–7, 335–6; Walpole, *Memoirs of George II* ii 103; Add. 32804ff. 379–83; Ryder diary 1 Jan. and 6 Mar. 1746.

[2] Argenson ii 264 and passim; Balteau; *Mémoires authentiques du duc de Richelieu*, ed. Boislisle. For Richelieu's administration of Languedoc, see Bibliothèque de Rouen, Collection Leber ms. 3344; Ryder diary Oct. 1745.

Lichfield's brother-in-law, Lord Clare; and included the Duke and Count of Fitzjames, James II's grandsons; as well as the Prince de Turenne and other French noblemen. The military arrangements were placed under Lally, colonel of an Irish regiment, working with Anthony Walshe and Lord Clancarty (now vice-admiral in the French navy) who were organising all naval preparations. Unlike Charles Edward in 1744, Henry Duke of York, who was to be in nominal charge of the landing, was received at Versailles with great ceremony, but Richelieu was not impressed by him, objecting particularly to his 'Italianate devotion' which was having an adverse effect on the Protestant officers in the expedition. The death of Ormonde, who had been once again asked to take part, in late November was particularly regretted by Barrymore 'inasmuch as the Duke's age and rank set him above all jealousies and envy, an advantage no other subject can pretend to'.[1]

The French were well aware that their plans in 1744 had been betrayed to the English Government and, unaware that their own man Bussy was responsible, thought the Tories in England had been indiscreet. So that, while outwardly agreeing with Sir John Cotton's proposal of a descent at Maldon in Essex, they decided that the real places of landing were to be Folkestone, Hythe and Romney, and that Cotton and his friends should not be told until the very last minute. Similarly, to deceive the English Government, elaborate shows of preparation were made at Dunkirk and Ostend, but the real places of embarkation were to be Calais and Boulogne. Since Bussy never gave any more information after the declaration of war with England, the feint worked, and all along the Pelhams believed that the embarkation was preparing at Dunkirk. Walshe used only ships under 30 tons capable of landing in shallow waters to transport the troops, drawing these from Calais, Ambleuteuse, Boulogne, St. Valéry-en-Somme, Dieppe and Fécamp. An escort of warships he thought would be more of a danger than a protection as it would alert the English fleet, and since they could rely on the smugglers to tell them when the coast was clear and to act as pilots. The Marquis d'Argenson worked out that the operation immobilised most of French commercial shipping in the northern ports and cost France about five million

[1] Guerre A1/3152/46, 48, 52, 186 and 225; Marine B3/429/384, 385, 416 and 417; Luynes vii 142–3, 152–3, 156–7; Stuart mss. 271/51; Argenson iv 319–20.

livres. The Council of State thought that since England and France were now at war, there was no need to draw up a manifesto to distribute on landing, but Richelieu disagreed, writing:

> If our object was to subjugate the English and to conquer England, there would be no need for a manifesto since we are at war, but as we are counting less on the force of our arms and the number of our troops than on the party which will support us among the nation, it seems to be of the highest importance to explain clearly to the English in which spirit we are come, and that we arrive less to fight than to succour them.

Thereupon, he and the Marquis d'Argenson commissioned Voltaire to write it and had it printed in English and French. This declared that the Duc de Richelieu was landing at the head of French troops at the request of persons of great consideration in England; that they would be withdrawn as soon as the legitimate king was restored; and that Prince Charles Edward's only object was to maintain the laws and liberties and to secure the happiness of his subjects. Bussy, who was consulted when the declaration was drawn, made every possible objection to the policy of restoring the Stuarts, presumably because he knew he faced certain discovery if it succeeded. The Marquis d'Argenson, who had formed a warm friendship for Charles Edward, whom he regarded as 'a hero and a man of sense', used Voltaire's pen at this time to mount a full-scale public relations campaign on his behalf in Europe. The Duke of York sent his brother the following letter which reached him at Manchester:

> The Marquis d'Argenson in a conference with me a few days ago told me I might send immediately to advise you in his name and his brother's [the Comte d'Argenson] that the King of France was absolutely resolved upon the expedition into England *qu'il y avoit mis le bon*, and that you might count upon it being ready the 20th of December new style [9 December o.s.].[1]

[1] A1/3152/62; AEM & D. Ang. 77f. 224; 78ff. 213, 224-5, 381, 389; Marine B3/426/677 and 687; 82ff. 166-70, 173-9; Voltaire, *Oeuvres Complètes*, ed. Beuchot, xxxviii 543; L. Bongie, 'Voltaire's English, high treason and a manifesto for Bonnie Prince Charles', *Studies on Voltaire and the eighteenth century* clxxi (1977) 7-29; Argenson iv 316-20; Ewald i 278-9.

On his own initiative, the Duke of York wrote to Sir Watkin
Williams Wynn in London, suggesting that he and his friends
should assist the French landing by seizing a seaport. When
James heard of this some time later, he wrote to the Duke:

> I suppose you took all proper precautions that your letter to Sir
> Watkins Williams might come safely to his hands; but I don't see how
> it is possible for our friends in England to order what you propose to
> them, for how can they, without arms, without regular troops, with-
> out enfin, any support, pretend to rise in arms, and much less to
> seize on any seaport, while the government have so many regular
> troops in this island, and at present, even a considerable body near
> London. I have often blamed the indolence and timidity of our
> friends in England; but, in the present moment, I own I think they
> would act imprudently and even rashly not to lie quiet still.

Richelieu, who had not been consulted, could not see how unarmed
civilians could be expected to capture a seaport, and if they could,
it would be no help to him as it would pinpoint the place of landing.
He was much more sympathetic to the difficulties of James's friends
in England than the Comte de Saxe had been, telling Bulkeley
who was blaming their 'timidity' that people could not be bold
when surrounded by regular troops. All he asked of them, he said,
was that they should join him when he landed. There were delays,
partly because the locks of the canals on which equipment was
being taken to Calais and Boulogne froze, and partly because
French army and navy officials insisted on their six months' supply
of everything, despite Walshe's objection that this was far too
much. The date on which the expedition was to sail was the night
of 14/25 December 1745.[1]

Thus the rebels could count on massive reinforcements if they
marched South—provided these reinforcements could get across
the Channel. The admiral to whom the task of preventing the
French landing had been entrusted was Admiral Edward Vernon,
an able commander, and one of the few admirals of his time
who showed any real concern for the welfare of his men. His
effectiveness, however, was diminished by the fact that he was

[1] Marine B3/429/456, 457, 458 and 470; Guerre A1/3152/167, 174, 177, 195,
204, 205; Browne iii 456-7; Argenson iv 318 (writing many years later
his chronology is inexact); Stuart mss. 271/150.

continually at odds with the Lords of the Admiralty, and that both were at this time repeatedly at cross-purposes. It was one of the many ironies of the situation that he was confiding his difficulties with the Admiralty to Sir John Philipps, a Jacobite closely associated with Wynn and those inviting the French invasion. With only a limited force at his disposal, some of his ships too large for narrow seas, and the ten Dutch ships seconded to him withdrawn by Holland under pressure from France, he was asked by the Admiralty to blockade Dunkirk and Ostend, as well as to protect the Downs and the coasts of Kent, Sussex, and East Anglia. He considered a close blockade of enemy ports impracticable: 'For my part, I have always looked upon pretending to block up the port of Dunkirk from their privateers getting out in the winter time to be a little better than the labour of the wise men of Gotham for hedging in the cuckoo.' It would have been no use if he had, since Dunkirk was not the real port of embarkation. Moreover, Vernon believed the French designed to land in Suffolk, and concentrated his resources on a squadron to cover the mouth of the Thames and the coasts of Norfolk and Suffolk, but there again the French did not intend to land there. Quite rightly, he complained that the French had the advantage of good intelligence 'from their friends and spies the smugglers' and that 'there is not the least thing done or ordered but the enemy immediately knows it by their means'. As things were, therefore, the French expedition had a good chance of getting through.[1]

On 5 December the leaders of the rebel army called a council of war at Derby to decide whether to march on London with about 6,000 men. David Morgan, a barrister who acted as legal adviser to the 3rd and 4th Dukes of Beaufort, and was a leading member of the Association of Independent Electors of Westminster, had joined them at Preston. He advised them:

> It would be an easy matter to march forward for London, for there were not above 3000 soldiers between them and London and most of them dragoons besides a few undisciplined troops that were raised by Lord Gower and Lord Cholmondeley who would make but little opposition.

[1] *H. Walpole Corresp.* xix 168; *HMC 14th Rep.* ix 138–9; *Vernon Papers* (Navy Records Society) 439, 540–4, 550, 555, 560, 568, 571 and 575.

Apart from the Guards who were few in number, the defenders of
London had a comic opera quality, illustrated in Hogarth's *The
March to Finchley*, and Pelham himself did not think London
could be defended. Charles Edward told Lord George Murray and
the others that his objective all along had been London; that they
could get there before Cumberland; that he was sure he would be
made as welcome there as he had been in Edinburgh; and that he
had letters to show that the French under the Duke of York were
about to land so that they would be reinforced. Boyer, the French
envoy, told them 'he was confident the French would land and
offered to be shot if they did not land in a fortnight's time'.
Nothing succeeds like success, and at this point when everything
was going their way and for reasons never made entirely clear,
Charles Edward met with a blank wall of obstinacy from most of
the leaders of his army, who forced him to retreat. Apart from the
Duke of Perth and Sir William Gordon, the rest of the council
absolutely refused to believe that a French expedition was about to
come to their help, and objected, more reasonably, that few
Englishmen of note had joined them. The real reason for their
decision to retreat, however, was a narrow kind of Scottish
nationalism. All along they had complained that Charles Edward
was 'occupied with England' to the exclusion of Scotland the land
of his ancestors, and some of them even told him 'they had taken
arms and risked their fortunes and their hopes, merely to seat him
on the throne of Scotland; but that they wished to have nothing to
do with England.' The Chevalier Johnstone, a-d-c to Lord George
Murray, even thought it would have been a good thing for the Prince
to have fomented a 'national war' between England and Scotland!
In his declaration, Charles Edward had promised to dissolve the
Union, but he had no desire to be King of Scotland only, nor
could he have been for how could an independent Scotland have
been defended from King George and his allies? By forcing the
retreat, Lord George Murray and the others threw away the best
chance there had been of a restoration of the Stuarts, threw away
all that the bravery of the Highlanders and their own military skill
had achieved. The '45 was a gamble from the beginning, but they
threw in their hand when they held most of the trump cards. Nor
was this decision made under pressure from the clans, who had
been reluctant to cross into England at first but were now in good

spirits. They showed great indignation at being made to turn back; 'if we had been beaten,' wrote one of the rebels, 'the grief could not have been greater.' After quarrelling with Lord George Murray, Charles Edward declared:

> After this, I know that I have an army that I cannot command any farther than the chief officers please, and, therefore, if you are all resolved upon it, I must yield; but I take God to witness that it is with the greatest reluctance, and that I wash my hands of the fatal consequences which I foresee, but cannot help.

The retreat began the next day, and by 20 December they were back in Scotland. A good many of the English went home, a few like Morgan being denounced and caught as having been with the rebels. A substantial number garrisoned Carlisle and were taken when the Duke of Cumberland took it with Dutch troops (who had remained in England and began to act as soon as the rebels retreated), and other Englishmen marched to Scotland, to Culloden and inevitable doom. This time there were no deals in Scotland but terrible retribution and barbarous repression of the innocent as well as the guilty, and the heretable jurisdictions were abolished. Lord George Murray and Lord Elcho, assisted by Murray of Broughton, sought to evade responsibility for the consequences of the retreat. They blamed Charles Edward, the English, the French, everyone in fact except the lords of the council at Derby, and their statements have been accepted by historians all too uncritically.[1] Two days after the retreat, a messenger arrived in Derby from Barrymore and Wynn to say they would join in the capital or each in their own counties. Presumably the disarray in London was so great they felt free to act at last.[2]

The retreat from Derby came as an incredible relief to the English Government, who resumed the initiative at once. On 19 December the King sent a message to Parliament that:

[1] H. M. Vaughan 'Welsh Jacobitism', *Cymmrodorion Society* 1920-1, 29; Howell, *State Trials* xviii 371-91; SP 36/77/71; Lord Elcho, 302-5, 339-40; *Murray of Broughton* p. xxiii, 248, 432, 434; Yorke, *Hardwicke* i 477-8; Chevalier de Johnstone *Memoir of the Forty-five* (1820 ed.) 34-41, 45, 73; James Maxwell 73; Mounsey 152-3; SP 36/78/262; SP 36/80/160.
[2] *HC* i 442-3.

His Majesty having received undoubted intelligence, that preparations are making at Dunkirk, and other parts of France, which are
now in great forwardness, for invading this kingdom with a considerable number of forces, in support of the rebellion carrying on
here, in favour of the Pretender to his Crown; and some French
troops are actually landed in Scotland ... His Majesty having the last
summer taken into his service 6000 Hessian troops ... has judged it
necessary to direct the said Hessians to be brought into these
kingdoms.

Wynn and Heathcote took the unprecedented step of dividing
the House against the loyal address. In the debate, Gower and
his few followers spoke for the Hessians. Sir John Cotton and
his son were absent, 'kept away' by Gower according to one
source. Lord Cornbury declared his loyalty to the Crown but
objected to the use of foreign troops against his countrymen.
The Hessians came over within ten days, as well as additional
forces from Flanders all sent north after the rebels, and Wade was
replaced by 'Hangman Hawley'.[1]

The retreat to Scotland was the last thing the French had been
led to expect. On 14/25 December Richelieu, who was ready to
go, had not received the appointed signal from England and had
lost touch with Charles Edward. Officers from Lally's regiment
were sent over via the smugglers, reporting a great build up of
forces round London and the South East. Richelieu then consulted Bulkeley on the possibility of a landing in Wales, but the
reply was 'circumstances are sadly changed since the Prince of
Wales had marched back to Scotland'. On 18/29 December, two
of Vernon's privateers attacked and damaged two of the French
munition ships outside Calais. Richelieu looked on this as a
'minor setback', but Vernon had captured one of them and by
questioning the prisoners prised out of them the fact that the
embarkation was to go from Boulogne and Calais and from then
on English ships patrolled outside these two ports. At the end
of the month the enormous build-up of forces against his brother
led the Duke of York to ask the French to abandon the idea of an
expedition to England and to send all available help to Scotland.
Richelieu was even prepared to go there himself. James's friends

[1] *CJ* xxv 23; *Parl. Hist.* xiii 1392–3; Ld. Ilchester, *Life of Lord Holland* i 121.
HC ii 164–5.

in England made the same request early in January. At this time, Vernon who had for some time been asking to be relieved of his command was 'taken at his word', and an admiral working in harmony with the Admiralty succeeded in preventing the departure of any sizeable force. Whereas they could have hoped to slip across the Channel, an expedition to Scotland needed an escort of warships to defend it, and the Brest fleet was not ready to set out till April, so that they were reduced to send help to Scotland in single ships, some of which were taken and some of which arrived too late.[1]

[1] Guerre AI/3152/100, 103, 106, 146, 150, 152, 195 and 206; Marine B3/429/471 and 472; AEM & D. Ang. 78ff. 225, 402–3, 415; 85f. 159; *Vernon Papers* 578; Ryder diary 30 Dec. 1745 and 6 March 1746.

7

The Tory Backlash

Murray of Broughton, who had acted as Charles Edward's secretary during the rebellion, was captured after Culloden, and unlike the other Jacobite prisoners turned King's evidence to save his own life. Not only did he give evidence against the Scots with him in the rebellion, but he told the Government what he did not know of his own knowledge but only at second hand through Lord Traquair (whom he got excepted out of the Act of Indemnity) of the talks with Butler in 1743, naming Barrymore, Cotton, Wynn, Lord Orrery and Dr Barry and mentioning 'many persons in the City well affected to the Pretender' not identified by him, adding that they had continued to deal with the French in the relation to the Pretender's affairs in the years 1744–5. Either because Traquair did not tell him or for other reasons, Murray never mentioned Beaufort. The Cabinet at a meeting in February 1747 considered 'whether it might not be proper to communicate to the world by the help of the secret committee the information they had' concerning those named by Murray, but decided, as Lord Chancellor Hardwicke wrote, that 'satisfied with having brought the leaders of the rebellion to the block, and having the rest at their mercy, did not choose to push inquiries further'. In any case, not having two witnesses against them they could not have proceeded at law but only in Parliament by way of bill of attainder. True to form, the only person they arrested was Dr Barry, the underling. However, at the trial of Lord Lovat, one of the lords of the Association who had sent his clan out under his eldest son the Master of Fraser fairly late on in the rebellion and who was arrested and executed on Murray's evidence, the Government allowed the names of Barrymore, Wynn and Cotton to come out when the last two were present in the House. Thomas Prowse, a Tory Member who was not a Jacobite, objected that they should be allowed to speak in their own defence, but the Speaker replied 'that he believed the parties concerned would not choose it'. Nor did they![1]

Most of the Tory peers refused to attend the trials of the rebel lords. When, a Whig reported, Lord Chancellor Hardwicke told the 3rd Earl of Oxford he must attend,

> the other said he would not. The Chancellor with some warmth answered that the Lords would force him and being (asked) how, said by fine as they had done in the year 1715 and would be very severe. The other replied he would stand it all and go out of town, and I imagine all the other Tories will do the like.

Lord Foley, Horace Walpole said, 'withdrew as too well a wisher'. Most of the Tory peers writing to Hardwicke to be excused gave reasons of health, the only ones allowed and with a physician's certificate, but it is noticeable that whereas the Whig lords who would not attend prefaced their request with 'my loyalty to the Crown is too well known' or some such expression, not one of the Tory lords did so.[2] Beaufort, who had his windows broken for not illuminating his house in celebration of Culloden, apparently intended to attend Lovat's trial, in which Lovat named his brother the 3rd Duke as one of the people concerned on the English side. Lord Balmerino, one of the Scots, asked to be represented by Randle Wilbraham, a former protégé of Lord Gower, and 'a very able lawyer in the House of Commons, who, the Chancellor said privately, he was sure would be as soon hanged as plead such a cause', but he did. Richard Clayton, a lawyer returned as Member for Wigan by Lord Barrymore in 1747, acted as counsel for David Morgan who had been caught on an informer's evidence after the retreat from Derby. A complaint was made that John Williams, master of an inn where the witnesses against Lord Lovat were kept, had been abused and 'cruelly beat' at a meeting of the Independent Electors of Westminster at Vintners Hall, a meeting at which Sir John Cotton was present, but the Government took no action.

[1] *Murray of Broughton* 424, 445, 456–7; Ryder diary February 1747; *HC* ii 371; *H. Walpole Corresp.* xix 381.

[2] *HMC Polwarth* v 179; *H. Walpole Corresp.* xix 284; Add. 35588ff. 115, 253, 262, 264, 266, 270, 272, 282, 285; Add. 35589ff. 180, 185, 200.

Times were becoming more humane, and there was considerable public sympathy for the prisoners. Hogath in his *Four Stages of Cruelty* exposed practices regarded as normal in former ages. As strong a Whig as Horace Walpole was touched: 'The first appearance of the prisoners shocked me! Their behaviour melted me!' The spectacle of James Dawson, a young undergraduate from St. John's Cambridge, being half hanged, disembowelled, drawn, and quartered killed his sweetheart of shock, and produced public revulsion. Abroad, Voltaire denounced the barbarity of these executions as he was to expose those of Damiens, a madman who tried to murder Louis XV, and of Callas, a French Huguenot.[1]

There was considerable sympathy in England with the plight of the Scots. When it was proposed to offer the freedom of the City of London to Cumberland as the victor of Culloden, someone interjected 'Let it be the butchers', and that was that. In the past English Tories had been as suspicious of the Scots as the rest of England, but now they adopted the plaid as their emblem, a thing inconceivable a few years before. In May 1747 Ryder noted that by appearing 'publicly in body in Warwickshire, Leicestershire and Staffordshire with Scots plaids, waistcoats or other parts of their clothes of plaid', the Jacobites had shown 'they mean a signal to France of their readiness'. The principal targets of the Tory backlash were Lord Gower, who complained of being 'persecuted by the gout and Jacobitism', and the Duke of Bedford. Tory candidates were put up against all Lord Gower's candidates in Staffordshire. At the county election in 1747, Gower wrote to Newcastle that he found the voters in Lichfield—

insolent to a degree that you cannot easily conceive, and seem to me to be animated by the same Jacobite spirit that the mobs at Manchester and Ashbourn were, and can be quelled by no other means; I hope therefore you will order immediately some troops into that town or I think none of our friends can with safety attend the sessions, for they have threatened to pull down the gaol, if any of their accomplices are committed.

[1] *HMC 12th Rep. ix* 98; Badminton mss., Beaufort to Anne, Lady Coventry, Bath 21 December 1746; Howell, *State Trials* xviii. 335; Ryder diary 24 March 1747. *HC* ii 538, 545; Browne iii 337–9; Voltaire, *Siècle de Louis XV* (1826 ed.) i 267–72.

A friend of Gower's at Stafford, who had his house pulled down by the rioters, complained 'this popular rage and rebellious spirit has continued to show itself during the whole course of the county election'. These riots were said to have been stirred up by Sir James Harrington, an agent of Charles Edward's, presumably on his orders. Gower, whose interest in Staffordshire had been paramount, had lost most of it, and Pelham remarked that he owed what successes he did have 'almost entirely to the Whigs'.[1] At the Lichfield races that summer, Sir Watkin Williams Wynn organised Tory subscriptions in support of the expenses of Sir Walter Bagot, re-elected knight of the shire for Staffordshire, against the petition of Gower's candidate, Sir Richard Wrottesley, who had been defeated. But it was much more than that. Not only did Staffordshire Tories turn up in force, but supporters were summoned 'from all parts of the kingdom'. In came 'the Burton mob, most of them in plaid waistcoats, plaid ribbon round their hats and some of them white cockades [the Stuart emblem]' led by Sir Charles Sedley, Member for Nottingham, and Sir Thomas Gresley, who succeeded Richard Leveson Gower as Member for Lichfield in 1753. 'About the same time came another party of the Birmingham people, most of them in the same dress, with Sir Lister Holte [M.P. Lichfield 1741], and some of the Warwickshire gentlemen. Sir Walter Bagot came in alone.' The Warwickshire contingent were said to have 'drunk the Pretender's health publicly in the streets, singing treasonable songs'. The Duke of Bedford was horsewhipped on the racecourse, and Gower's son, Lord Trentham, cudgelled. These events were recorded in the public prints, notably in *A sight of the Banging Bout at Lichfield*, and were said to have taken place to the tune of 'the King shall enjoy his own again'. Years later, Junius was reminding Bedford of 'those ridiculous scenes, by which in your earlier days you thought it an honour to be distinguished—the recorded stripes, the public infamy, your own sufferings'. A friend of Gower's wrote: 'You cannot conceive what noise the Lichfield hunting meeting makes in town, where people make no ceremony of treating the company as Jacobites . . .

---

[1] *H. Walpole Corresp.* xix 288; Ryder diary 16 May 1747; Woburn mss., Lord Gower to the Duke of Bedford, 3 Aug. 1747; Lord Anson to the Duke of Bedford, 21 June 1747; Add. 32712ff. 111, 117, 288; Stuart mss. 301/5; Chatsworth mss., Henry Pelham to Lord Hartington, June 1747.

His Majesty told me . . . he must and ought to consider that company as his declared enemies.' The persistence of Tory resentment against Gower was such that Dr Johnson, a Lichfield man, speaking of his dictionary, told Boswell: 'You know, Sir, Lord Gower forsook the old Jacobite interest. When I came to the word *Renegado*, after telling it meant "any one who deserts to the enemy, a revolter", I added "sometimes we say a Gower", but the printer struck it out.' A similar demonstration occurred at the Newton races in 1748, when Sir Thomas Egerton, the local Member of Parliament, and other members of the hunt were reported in the London press to have proclaimed the Pretender as James III wearing 'white cockades' and 'plaid waistcoats', and to have gone 'riding about to drink and to force others to drink treasonable healths'.[1]

The wearing of the plaid was even more prevalent in London. Alderman Benn, who had been present at the talks with Butler in 1743, and as lord mayor in 1747 had sent to Charles Edward in France a message of sympathy and support, had himself and fellow aldermen painted wearing plaid waistcoats. Nowhere was it more universal than among the Independent Electors of Westminster, satirised as *Jaco-Independo-Rebello-Plaido* in a public print. At the anniversary dinner of the Independent Electors in Vintners Hall in 1747, with the Earl of Lichfield, Lord Orrery, George Heathcote and Thomas Carew presiding as stewards, the *Gentleman's Magazine* reported:

> The following healths were drunk. The King (each man having a glass of water on the left hand, and waving the glass of wine over the water). The Prince, the Duke. Prosperity to the independent electors of Westminster. Prosperity to the city of London and the trade thereof. The Lord Mayor of London [Benn]. Success to the arms of Great Britain by sea and land . . . That the spirit of independency may diffuse itself throughout the nation . . . that the naturalization bill be kicked out of the House and the foreigners out of the kingdom.

The culmination of the campaign against Gower came at the Westminster by-election of 1749–50, stage-managed by Alexander

[1] Add. 32717f. 42; Lichfield mss. Hinton to Lord Anson 26 September 1747; *HC* i 317; ii 7, 321, 494; *Catalogue of Prints and Drawings in the British Museum, satires 1734–50.* No. 2863; *Letters of Junius* (1791 ed.) 103; *Boswell's Johnson*, ed. E. B. Hill, i 296.

Murray, who was influential amongst the Independent Electors and had been active at the 1747 Westminster election. Alexander Murray was an agent of Charles Edward's and never moved a step except upon his instructions. Unfortunately for us, the Prince's notes to Murray in the Stuart papers tell us where he was to go but not what he was to do, since Charles Edward did not believe in putting anything down in writing. Then, Horace Walpole wrote, 'the resentment of the Jacobites against Lord Gower for deserting their principles . . . appeared in the strongest colours'. Another Whig commented:

> There never was any election carried on with so much violence on both sides. The scandal and dirt flung upon Lord Gower's family and the Duke of Bedford's is shocking, and is enough to terrify anybody, and make them have some regard, great how they are how they exasperate an English mob.

Gower was put forward for the post of President of the Council but Pelham turned him down as 'broke in spirit and constitution'. Government supporters attacked the Independent Electors for—

> the earnestness with which they opposed all subscriptions or levies for suppressing the late rebellion: their suspected correspondencies, and the indecent (i.e. treasonable) healths so often proposed and so publicly drunk in their meetings and assemblies.

The retort was 'whose foot was in the stirrup in 1715?'—an allusion to Gower having gone to join the rebellion when Forster was defeated. The first petition of the Independent Electors against Lord Trentham's election drawn up by Alexander Murray said to be 'absolutely treason', was toned down by Sir John Cotton, who defended Murray's conduct at the scrutiny. Imprisoned in Newgate for contempt of the House of Commons, Murray was released by the sheriffs of London as soon as Parliament was prorogued, and he was taken through the streets of London in triumph 'with a standard before him whereon was inscribed "Murray and Liberty!" ' The printer of *The Case of Alexander Murray*, defending Murray and attacking the House of Commons as unrepresentative of the people, was acquitted by a Middlesex jury and given a public ovation on his release. The previous instance of an English jury deciding on a point of law as well as on a point of fact was the case of the Seven Bishops under James II.[1]

The Tory backlash took yet another form. In February 1748 there was a riot in Oxford with people in the streets shouting for King James. The vice-chancellor took no action, but the Government caught two undergraduates who were condemned to two years imprisonment for treason. Gower and Bedford 'pressed extremely for the trial of the vice-chancellor' too. Gower, Horace Walpole wrote,

> asked the attorney general his opinion, who told him the evidence did not appear strong enough. Lord Gower said, 'Mr. Attorney, you seem to be very lukewarm for your party'. He replied, 'My Lord, I never was lukewarm for my party, *nor ever was but of one party*'.

At the opening of the Radcliffe Library in 1749, with the Duke of Beaufort, Lord Oxford, Sir Walter Wagstaffe Bagot, and Sir Watkin Williams Wynn presiding as Radcliffe trustees, Dr King deplored the corruption of manners and the decay of the universities under the Hanoverians, punctuating his oration with the refrain *'redeat ille genius Britanniae'* which was universally interpreted as meaning the Young Pretender. The ministry began to consider action against Oxford, 'the sanctuary of disaffection', and were reported to be bringing in legislation to vest in the King the nomination of the chancellor of the university with a view of replacing the present chancellor Lord Arran (Ormonde's brother) by the Duke of Cumberland. The news, Carte wrote, brought all the Tories to town, 'which nothing else would'. Their numbers in Parliament had been decimated at the 1747 election in the aftermath of the rebellion, and they sought the help of Frederick, Prince of Wales, leader of the Whig opposition, who had been courting them without success since 1747 with offers to 'take away all proscriptions from any set of men whatever who are friends to the constitution' and other Tory points. Horace Walpole reported:

[1] Stuart mss. 288/172; Beaven ii 128, 292; *Catalogue of Prints and Drawings* No. 2856; *Gentleman's Magazine* 1747, 150; 1751, 283; *Malmesbury Letters* i 75. For Alexander Murray, see Andrew Lang, *Pickle the Spy*; Stuart mss. 269/191 and 288/172; *Westminster Elections 1741–51*; Walpole, *Memoirs of George II* i 13–17, 19–22, 25–31; *Parl. Hist.* xiv 893–4, 978, 1064–5; Howell, *State Trials* xviii 1203–30; *HC* i 77; ii 122.

This menace gave occasion to a meeting and union between the Prince's party and the Jacobites, which Lord Egmont has been labouring all the winter. They met at the St. Alban Tavern [the headquarters of the Loyal Brotherhood] near Pall Mall . . . 112 lords and commoners. The Duke of Beaufort opened the assembly with a panegyric on the stand that had been made this winter against so corrupt an Administration, and hoped it would continue, and desired harmony. Lord Egmont seconded this strongly . . . Lord Oxford spoke next, and then Potter with great humour and to the great abashment of the Jacobites, said he was very glad to see this union and from thence hoped, that if another attack like the last rebellion should be made on the royal family, they would all stand by them. No reply was made to this.

Carte wrote that they had agreed to 'a sort of coalition with Prince Frederick's party to stand by the University of Oxford, to join in opposing all unconstitutional points, to be under no obligation to visit Prince Frederick's court nor unite in other points'. Carte's patron, Sir John Cotton, however, who was much more a politician than the others, did sometimes go to Frederick's court. There was a meeting of the Cabinet to consider 'the reformation of the University of Oxford'. The solicitor general thought this 'might create a flame in the nation' and since Prince Frederick was defending the University could 'overthrow the present ministry'. Ryder, the attorney general, did not think 'materials in point of disloyalty could be found in evidence sufficient to charge the University', and it was agreed to drop the bill.[1] In its death throes, Jacobitism was bolder than it had been since the passing of the Riot Act in 1715, but the opportunity had gone for ever.

When Charles Edward returned to France after his escape and long wanderings through the Isles, he was welcomed as a hero. When he appeared in the royal box at the opera, the whole audience rose to clap. He was befriended by Montesquieu. He took his pick of the great ladies at Court who were in love with him. When Lord Cornbury went over to Paris, old loyalties were too

[1] *H. Walpole Corresp.* xx 6, 50, 137; *Gentleman's Magazine* 1749, 164–5; A. D. Godley, *Oxford in the Eighteenth Century* 257–8; *Bodleian Quarterly Record* i (1915) 165–72; Stuart mss. Box 1/299; *HC* i 75–6; Ryder diary 25 May 1749.

strong for him, and on his own admission he committed 'twenty extravagancies' in the Prince's company. But it did not last. Charles's friend the Marquis d'Argenson was disgraced for his too zealous championship of him and for involving France in diplomatic difficulties in trying to move heaven and earth at all European Courts to save the Jacobite prisoners. Although Maurice of Saxony defeated the Duke of Cumberland at Laffeldt, under the influence of Louis XV's new mistress Madame de Pompadour France concluded the peace of Aix-la-Chapelle in 1748 on terms which made *bête comme la paix* a French proverb. Charles Edward obstinately refused to leave France, or at least not to appear in public, and was arrested at the Paris opera. He had made himself popular with the French mob too, and there were riots in Paris after his arrest. Argenson, who was scandalised at his Government seizing like a criminal 'the son of the legitimate King of England', advised him never to go back to Rome. The English Government, resentful at not being able to keep him under observation, was sending spies all over Europe to try and track him down, as if he had been the Scarlet Pimpernel. Most of the time he was living privately in France with his uncle the Duc de Bouillon or elsewhere. Pelham wrote to Newcastle:

> If this young gentleman should declare himself a Protestant, and another [Frederick, Prince of Wales] should not act suitable to the great and good examples he has had before him, the Lord knows how matters may end.

Balhaldy, who was in London in the autumn of 1749, wrote to the Pretender that notwithstanding all the demonstrations in Staffordshire and elsewhere, the party was 'dispirited, frightened out of their wits at what had happened and without any trust or confidence in one another'. Charles Edward came over to London with Col. Brett in September 1750 without the Government finding out! He had a meeting with about fifty of his supporters, including the Duke of Beaufort and Lord Westmorland, and was received into the Anglican Church in Marylebone. He inspected the defences of the Tower of London and said one of the gates 'might be beaten down with a petard', but there was little to be done without an army. In 1752 there was a prospect of assistance from Prussia, Heathcote being one of the chief managers, but Frederick II was playing the Jacobite card only to bring pressure on the English Government.[1]

During the Seven Years War, Choiseul, the French foreign minister, formed a plan for a descent on Scotland on 1759. He did not consult the Pretender, although he had an inconclusive meeting with Charles Edward in France. Although he seriously considered a Stuart restoration, he could not have effected it in any case since the French fleet was annihilated by Admiral Hawke at Quiberon Bay. Under generals chosen by Madame de Pompadour, France went on to lose most of the battles of the Seven Years War. By this time most of the Tories realised that the cause they had supported for over forty years was hopeless. Charles Edward knew this too, and he had become an alcoholic, which led his last few supporters to abandon him. 'Jacobitism,' Horace Walpole wrote, 'the concealed mother' of Toryism was dead. The Tories could identify with the policies of the elder Pitt, and his use of sea-power, and could feel a genuine pride at England's victories. The accession of George III completed the task of national reconciliation. Once again, Tory peers were lords lieutenants of their counties and held places at Court. Once again, careers of every kind were open to Tories. By treating all Tories as his enemies, George I had made them Jacobites, and by continuing the same policy George II had kept them Jacobites. For the most part, the Whigs were very well pleased as it gave them a monopoly of office, but when it would have been politically more convenient to take the Tories in than keep them out—in 1721 and in 1742–4—they dared not risk sharing real political power with men they knew to be disaffected. The death of Jacobitism solved the problem of the proscription, and enabled George III to be the king of all his people.[2]

[1] Barbier ii 499, iv 45, 49, 57; Cornbury to Speaker Onslow 27 Jan. 1751, Royal Archives. There is in the Stuart papers a whole box of love letters from French ladies to the Prince; Argenson iv 308–25, 322–7; Andrew Lang, *Pickle the Spy* 178, 190, 213; Coxe, *Pelham* i 462; Stuart mss. 301/5; letter from Lord Stanhope to *The Times* 29 Dec. 1864; *HC* i 77.

[2] *Recueil des Instructions données aux ambassadeurs et ministres de France*, Angleterre, 1698–1791, ed. Vaucher, 370–1; *ex inf.* Professor Claude Nordmann; *HC* i 77–8; J. C. D. Clark, 'The decline of party', *English Historical Review* xciii (1978) 499–527; John Brooke, *George III* (1972 ed.) 25–207.

Appendix I

List of lords and country gentlemen in each county given to Butler in 1743

This list has been transcribed from the original (AEM & D. Ang. 76ff. 203–207). A copy (AEM & D. Ang. 82ff. 49–57) taken by a French Foreign Office clerk is imperfect as he could not cope with English names. Balhaldy sent a fair copy to James, the Old Pretender (Stuart mss. 253/51). Except where otherwise stated the information given in the notes is taken from Cokayne *Complete Baronetage* and *Complete Peerage* or from *The History of Parliament; the House of Commons 1715–1754* ed. Romney Sedgwick.

It is a list of persons expected to declare for a restoration, or more probably to declare for a free Parliament (as in 1660) to effect a restoration, in the event of a successful attempt by the French to restore the Stuarts. The majority are Tory peers or Tory M.P.s, or Opposition Whigs connected with the Whig lords who appear to have been a party to the bargain made with the Pretender to secure the fall of Walpole. A fair number are people in debt who would be expected to support a change of régime in exchange for rewards. Many are Roman Catholics, who though relatively few in numbers, held very large estates. Roman Catholics had not been active Jacobites since 1717 when at the request of the Duke of Norfolk they were allowed by the Pope to take the oaths to George I in order to avoid further penal taxation (Stuart mss. 206/2; Martin Haile, *James Edward Stuart, the Old Chevalier*, 232–4, 462–3), but they would naturally have welcomed a restoration. Another category is Roman Catholics who had conformed in order to get a career and might be expected to return to their former loyalties. Anglicans, who formed the bulk of Jacobites after 1717, with the exception of a few nonjurors, took the oaths under the assumption that oaths taken under duress were not binding, as the Cavaliers had done in the Civil Wars.

Septembre 1743. Etat des seigneurs ou gentilhommes qui ont le plus de crédit dans les differentes Provinces d'Angleterre et sur lesquels on peut compter.

Province de Bedford

Cette Province est entierement devouée au Roy legitime; le Duc de Bedford, le plus riche d'entre les sujets d'Angleterre en fond de terres, y a beaucoup de credit, et après ce duc, M. Charles Leigh qui a cinq mille livres sterling de rentes; M. Samuel Ongley qui en a six mille; le Chevalier Jean Chester qui en a cinq mille, le Chevalier Roger Bourgoyne qui en a quatre mille, et le Chevalier Boteler Chernock qui a pareillement quatre mille livres sterling de rentes, sont ceux auxquels les peuples de cette Province sont attachés.[1]

Province de Berks

Cette Province est sous la conduite de Mylords Craven, Willoughby de Brook, Stawell, Abingdon, et des Sieurs Howard Packer, Peniston Powney, Jean Blograve, et Guillaume Strode, gentilhommes dont le moins riche jouït de quatre mille livres sterling de rentes.[2]

Province de Buckingham

Cette Province est menée par le Duc de Bedford, les Mylords Chesterfield, Orrery, Dormer, Masham et Bathurst, et par les Sieurs Greeville, Lowndes, Denton, Greenville, Marshal, Gore, Selby, et Fleetwood, tous gentilhommes qui y ont des terres considerables.[3]

Province de Cheshire

Cette Province suivra les mouvemens de Mylords Barrymore, Warrington et Mollineux, et du Chevalier Robert Grosvenor qui a vingt deux mille livres sterling de rentes, du Sieur Jean Crew, qui en a douze mille, et des Sieurs Charles Cholmondeley, Pierre Warburton, et les Messieurs de Leigh, tous gentilhommes très riches.[4]

Province de Cornouailles

Cette Province, distinguée par le grand nombre de mineurs qui s'y trouvent, a toujours eté attachée à son roi naturel; les Mylords Arundel de Trerice, Arundel de Wardour, et de Falmouth; les Chevaliers Guillaume Carew, Jean St. Aubin, et Guillaume Morris; les Sieurs Trelawney, Penton, Cooke, Lydell, Foster, Cotton, et Nugent, sont les plus accredités d'entre la noblesse qui y est nombreuse, brave et tres zelée.[5]

Province de Cambridge

l'Université de Cambridge, opposée à celle d'Oxford, a gâté une grande partie de cette Province, mais le Chevalier Jean Cotton, qui y a de gros biens, est en etat de la partager avec la Cour d'Hannover.[6]

Province de Cumberland

Cette Province est la plus pauvre et la plus corrompue de toute l'Angleterre; la plupart des terres y etoient autrefois du domaine de la couronne, et ont ete alienées depuis la Revolution à des gens qui craignent de les perdre par le rétablissement du Roi légitime; il n'y a dans toute la province que le Baron de Hilton et le Chevalier Haggerston sur lesquels on puisse compter avec assurance, quoiqu'il y ait plusieurs mécontens.[7]

Province de Derby

Le Duc de Rutland et Mylord Chesterfield, le Chevalier Nathaniel Curson, et Monsieur Jean Stanhope menent toute cette Province: le Chevalier Curson qui y possede douze mille livres sterling de rentes a dix mille mineurs sous ses ordres.[8]

Province de Devon

Cette Province est sous la conduite du Duc de Bedford, des Lords Clinton et Clifford, du Chevalier Courtenay qui y a dix mille livres sterling par an, du Sieur Fortescue qui y a six mille, du Chevalier Northcote qui en a cinq mille, et des Sieurs Sydenham et Littleton qui y ont aussi des terres considerables.[9]

Province de Dorset

Cette Province est menée par Mylord Dierhurst, par le Sieur George Chaffin, qui y possede quatre mille livres sterling de rentes, par le Sieur Pleydell qui en a cinq mille et par les Sieurs Brown, Richards et Pitts.[10]

Province de Durham

Cette petite Province a beaucoup de noblesse qui est generalement bien disposée; Mylord Falconberg, le Sieur Bowes qui y a dix mille livres sterling de revenu, et le Sieur Tempest sont à la tête de cette noblesse.[11]

Province d'Essex

Cette Province est sour la conduitte des Mylords Suffolk, Waldegrave, Petre, et Masham, des Chevaliers Abdy, Smith, et Long, des Sieurs Bramston, Smith, Grey, et Saville, tous gentilhommes de gros biens et d'un merite reconnu.[12]

Province de Gloucester

Cette Province est sous la conduite du Duc de Beaufort, des Mylords

Gainsborough, et Bathurst, des Sieurs Chester, Berkley, Benjamin Bathurst, Master, et Gage, gentilhommes dont le moindre a trois mille livres sterling de rentes.[13]

Province de Hereford
Cette Province est sous la conduite du Duc de Beaufort, des Mylords Oxford et Foley, des Sieurs Thomas Foley, Cornwall, Winford, Cope Hopton, de Monsieur Robert Harley, et les Messieurs Lowes. Le moins riche de ces gentilhommes a quatre mille livres sterling par an.[14]

Province de Hertford
Le Duc de Bridgewater, les Mylords Exeter et Stanhope, les Sieurs Gore, Houblon, et Stanley sont les conducteurs de cette Province qui est tres riche et bien peuplée.[15]

Province de Huntingdon
Les Mylords Sandwich et Rockingham, les Sieurs Mitchel et Fellows président dans cette Province, qui n'est point d'une grande étendue.[16]

Province de Kent
Cette Province, l'une des plus riches et des mieux peuplées de l'Angleterre, qui s'étend sur la côte depuis Douvres jusqu'aux portes de Londres, est entierement sous la conduite des Mylords Westmorland, Thanet, Stanhope, Rockingham, Aylesford, Teynham, Guernsey, des Chevaliers Dering, Hales, et Dashwood, des Sieurs Dorill, Twisden, et Watson, gentilhommes qui y ont de gros biens.[17]

Province de Lancastre
Cette Province d'une grande étendue et ou il y a grand nombre de très anciennes maisons est absolument attachée au Roi legitime, sous la conduite des Mylords Derby, Barrymore, Petre, Chesterfield, Molineux, Strange, et des Sieurs Shuttleworth, Curzon, Fenwick, Fazakerly, Master, Lister, etc.[18]

Province de Leicester
Cette Province est menée par le Duc de Rutland, les Mylords Huntingdon et Stamford, le Chevalier Cave, les Sieurs Smith, Wigley et Wright.[19]

Province de Lincoln
Cette province suit les mouvements des Mylords Bristol et Haversham, des Sieurs Vyner, Wichcote, Mitchell et Proby.[20]

Province de Middlesex

Les gens de campagne, dans cette riche Province où la ville de Londres est située, ont toujours eu de bons sentimens; ils sont presque tous sous la conduite des Ducs de Somerset, de Beaufort, et de Bedford, de Mylord Burlington, et des Chevaliers Newdigate et Smithson, seigneurs ou gentilhommes qui y ont des fonds de terre tres considerables.[21]

Province de Monmouth

Cette Province est entierement soumise au Duc de Beaufort et à Mylord Noel Sommerset son frère.[22]

Province de Norfolk

La noblesse de cette Province est generalement attachee au Roy naturel, mais les dépenses excessives du Chevalier Walpole ont corrompu une grande partie du peuple. Le Duc de Norfolk, Mylord Andover, les Chevaliers Jerningham et Andrews, et le Sieur Woodhouse soutiennent le bon partie contre celui de Walpole.[23]

Province de Northampton

Cette Province est sous la conduite des Mylords Thanet et Rockingham, du Chevalier Edouard Isham, des Sieurs Cartwright, Parker, Shirley et Wortley: ce dernier jouit de vingt mille livres sterling de rentes.[24]

Province de Northumberland

Cette Province limitrophe de l'Ecosse abonde en maisons anciennes qui n'ont jamais eté perverties; presque toute la noblesse est unie avec les Mylords Derwentwater et Widrington, le Chevalier Swinburne, les Sieurs Fenwick et Blacket: ce dernier a sous ses ordres plusieurs milliers de ceux qui travaillent dans les mines de charbon de terre, qui se transporte par mer à Londres.[25]

Province de Nottingham

Cette Province est menee par le Duc de Norfolk, les Mylords Chesterfield, Middleton, et Trevor, les Sieurs Levinz et Warren.[26]

Province d'Oxford

Cette Province, fameuse par l'université qui a constamment soutenu les principes de l'obeïssance passive, a une noblesse très nombreuse et très zélée; les Mylords Abingdon et Litchfield, le Chevalier Dashwood, le Docteur Butler, les Sieurs Rowney, Herbert, Dawkins, et Moore sont les plus distingués par leurs talens et leur credit.[27]

Province de Rutland

Les paysans de cette petite Province sont presque tous sous les ordres des Mylords Gainsborough et Westmorland, et du Sieur Jacques Noel. Les villes y sont entierement gatées. [28]

Province de Shropshire

Cette Province est presque unanimement Jacobite; elle est sous la conduite des Chevaliers Astley et Corbet, des Messieurs de la Maison de Kynaston et du Sieur Lister. [29]

Province de Somerset

Cette Province d'un étendue considerable renferme une noblesse generalement zelée pour le Roy le gitime; le Duc de Beaufort, les Mylords Orrery, Clifford, et Stawell, le Chevalier Chapman, les Sieurs Portman, Prouze, Houblon, Buck, Carey, Dodington et Harvey y ont le plus de biens et de credit. [30]

Province de Southampton

Cette Province plus riche qu'étendue est generalement gatée; néanmoins les Mylords Shaftsbury et Dormer, le Chevalier Barington, et les Sieurs Delmé et Gibbon, tous zélés Jacobites, y ont beaucoup de credit. [31]

Province de Stafford

Cette Province situee à peu pres au milieu de l'Angleterre, et l'une des plus riches qu'il y ait, est unanimement attachée au Roy legitime; les Mylords Shrewsbury, Berkshire, Audley, Stourton, Gower, Ward, Stamford, Leigh, Chetwind, les Chevaliers Wagstaffe Baggot, Lister Holt, Guillaume Fowler, Guillaume Woosley, Guillaume Ridgley, les Sieurs Lewison Gore, Baptist Gore, Venables Vernon, et Wilbraham, le Colonel Lane et plusieurs autres qui y possedent des terres trés considerables, sont d'une fidelité à toute épreuve. C'étoit aux courses de chevaux qui se sont faites à Litchfield, ville de cette Province que Monsieur Butler a eu le plaisir de voir une assemblée de plus de trois cent seigneurs ou gentilhommes, dont le moins riche a près de quatre mille livres sterling par an, qui ont tous declaré qu'ils sont prêts à suivre les mouvemens de Mylord Barrymore pour parvenir au retablissement de leur Roi naturel. [32]

Province de Suffolk

Cette Province est menée par les Mylords Suffolk et Bristol, par le Chevalier Cordel Firebrace, qui y jouït de six mille livres sterling par an, par le Sieur Affleck, qui en possede quatre mille, et par le Chevalier Thomas Hanmer qui en a dix mille. [33]

Province de Surrey

La plûpart des terres de cette Province ont eté acquises par des agioteurs et autres partisans du Gouvernement, ce qui fait que les ministres y emportent tout: il y a cependant des seigneurs d'un grand merite qui y ont des terres, entre autres Mylord Butler de Weston frère du Duc d'Ormond, les Mylords Aylesford, St. Jean, et Montjoy, et les Sieurs Thrale, Newland, Harvey, Scawen, et Woodroffe sont aussi des gentil-hommes incorruptibles.[34]

Province de Sussex

Le Gouvernement a beaucoup de partisans dans cette Province qui est une des plus considerables du Royaume, mais les plus anciennes maisons et ceux qui sont les plus riches en fonds de terres sont invariablement attaches au Roy legitime; entre autres nous sommes assurés des Ducs de Norfolk et de Somerset qui y font souvent leur residence, des Mylords Derby, Montacute, Thanet et Caryll, des Chevaliers Goring, Fag et Peachy, des Sieurs Campion, Kemp, Webster, et Richard Caryll, qui y ont tous de gros biens.[35]

Province de Warwick

Cette Province qui est au centre du Royaume a toujours eté des mieux disposée; elle est menée par les Mylords Westmorland, Denbigh, Northampton, Aylesford, Hereford, Willoughby de Brook, Brook, Craven, Middleton; par les Chevaliers Throgmorton et Mordaunt; par les Sieurs Edouard Digby, Sheldon, Carrington, Berkley, Grove, Farmer, Perkins, et autres, dont plusieurs ont au moins dix mille livres sterling de rentes.[36]

Province de Westmorland

Cette Province est la moins bien cultivée d'Angleterre; l'aliénation des domaines du Roy y a corrompu environ la moitié des habitans: Le Chevalier Musgrave est le seul homme de condition auquel nous nous fions dans ces cantons.[37]

Province de Wilts

Cette Province, quoique peu etendue est très bien cultivée et tres riche; il y a une nombreuse noblesse dont la plûpart sont des personnes affidées; Le Duc de Somerset, les Mylords Berkshire, Arundel de Wardour, Craven, et St. Jean; les Chevaliers Robert Long, Jacob Bouverie, Edouard Seymour, Edouard Turner, les Sieurs Popham, Greenville. Pitt, Thursby, Neale, et Crawley y sont très distingués tant par leurs gros biens que par l'ardeur de leur zèle.[38]

Province de Worcester

La ville de Worcester tient encoure du levain de Cromwell, mais la Province est très bien disposée; elle suit les mouvemens des Mylords Shrewsbury, Coventry, et Foley; des Sieurs Lechemere, Pitt, et Foley, tous gentilhommes très riches.[39]

Province de York

Cette Province, la plus grande de l'Angleterre, est un peu gatée du coté de Hull, mais la noblesse est generalement attachée a son souverain legitime, et les gens de campagne y sont presque tous prêts à suivre le Duc de Norfolk, les Mylords Aylesbury, Shrewsbury, Burlington, Carlisle, Gower, Langdale, Abingdon; des Chevaliers Miles Stapleton et Henry Slingsby; des Sieurs George Fox, Aislaby, Berkley et Charles Pelham, gentilhommes dont le moindre a quatre mille livres sterling en fond de terre.[40]

Principauté de Galles

Les douze Provinces de la Principauté de Galles sont entierement soumises aux Ducs de Beaufort et de Powis, au Mylord Bulkely, au Chevalier Watkin Williams et a ceux qui sont unis avec ces seigneurs, qui sont tous engagés a se tenir prêts à monter à cheval au premier signal que Mylord Barrymore leur donnera.[41]

La ville de Londres et de Westminster

[The first part has been omitted as it duplicates the account of the City of London given in Appendix II. The text then goes on:]

Il est visible par ce detail qu'on peut juger sainement du penchant et des sentimens des citoyens de Londres par les choix qu'ils font de leur mayors, sheriffs et membres du Parlement: choix qui sont éclatants et dont l'observation ne peut échapper à personne; mais pour mettre la disposition de cette grande ville dans une evidence entière, l'on a examiné les principes et la conduite de chacun de deux cent trente six, qui composent actuellement le commun conseil, et l'on a trouvé qu'il y en a actuellement cent quatre vingt six qui sont jacobites zélés: On a donne une liste a Monsieur Butler en luy indiquant les moyens de la verifier par lui même, ce qu'il a pris la peine a faire avec une exactitude scrupuleuse et a eu le plaisir d'être temoin des voeux qu'ils font pour le retablissement de leur Roy legitime et de l'ardeur avec laquelle ils aspirent après le secours du Roy tres Chretien pour y parvenir.

Il seroit inutile d'entrer dans le detail des autres grandes villes du royaume dont la plupart suivent l'example et les mouvements de celle de Londres dans les conjonctures importantes. C'est ainsi que dans le tems des dernières elections des membres du Parlement, elles adopterent presque unanimement les instructions que la ville de Londres a juge a propos de donner à ses députés. Mais la conduite de la ville de Westminster, qui touche à Londres et dans laquelle le Roy fait séjour est tres digne de remarque. Cette ville a droit de choisir deux membres du Parlement, et comme ce choix devoit se faire sous les yeux de la cour et de tous les ministres étrangers qui y étoient, Walpole mit en usage toute sorte de pratiques, et eut enfin recours à la violence pour faire tomber le choix sur deux de ses creatures. Les habitants indignés de ce procéde se réunisent avec une ardeur incroyable, et firent choix de deux hommes dont l'un est jacobite zelé et l'autre un mécontent que Walpole s'etoit vante d'exclure de toute seance au Parlement.[42] Les habitans ont prouve dans cette occasion, que tous les tresors dont ce ministre avoit la disposition etoient incapables de les corrompre. Monsieur Butler a entendu de la bouche de celui qui a mene toute l'opposition de Westminster a la cour presente ne provient que de leur zèle pour leur Roy legitime et naturel.

FOOTNOTES TO APPENDIX I

Bedford

[1] Bedford, 4th Duke of (1710–1771). (See pp. 44–5, and under Bucks, Devon and Middlesex.

Leigh, Hon. Charles (*c*. 1685–1749), of Leighton Buzzard, Beds. M.P. Warwick 13 Dec. 1710–1713, Higham Ferrers 12 Mar. 1714–1722, Bedfordshire 1722–1727, 16 Feb. 1733–1734. Tory.

Ongley, Samuel (1697–1747), of Old Warden, Beds. M.P. New Shoreham 29 Jan. 1729–1734, Bedford 1734–15 June 1747. Tory.

Chester, Sir John, 6th Bt. (1693–1748), of Chicheley, Bucks and Lidlington, Beds. M.P. Bedfordshire 1741–1747. Tory.

Burgoyne, Sir Roger, 6th Bt. (1710–1780), of Sutton, Beds. M.P. Bedfordshire 26 Feb. 1735–1747. A Whig who went into opposition in 1739 and came back to the Government side in Dec. 1744.

Chernock, Sir Boteler, 4th Bt. (1696–1756), of Holcot, Beds. M.P. Bedford 24 Nov. 1740–1747. Tory.

Berks

[2] Craven, Fulwar, 4th Baron (d. 1764). (See under Warwickshire and Wilts.) Tory.

Willoughby de Broke, Richard Verney, 13th Lord (1693–1752). (See under Warwickshire.) Tory.

Stawell, Edward, 4th Baron (1685–1755). (See under Somerset.) A Tory and a poor lord. (See Holmes, *British Politics*, 391–2.)

Abingdon, Willoughby Bertie, 3rd Earl of (1692–1760). (See under

Oxfordshire and Yorkshire.) M.P. Westbury 28 March–1 June 1715. Tory. Refused Association in 1745.

Packer, Winchcomb Howard (1702–1746), of Donnington and Shellingford, Berks. M.P. Berkshire 5 May 1731–21 Aug. 1746. Tory.

Powney, Peniston (*c.* 1699–1757) of Ives Place, Bucks. M.P. Berkshire 5 Dec. 1739–8 Mar. 1757. Tory.

Blagrave, John (1713–1787), of Southcot, nr. Reading, Berks. M.P. Reading 6 Dec. 1739–1747. Tory.

Strode, William (*c.* 1712–1755), of Ponsbourne, Herts and Mapledurham, Oxon. M.P. Reading 26 Nov. 1740–17 Feb. 1741, 1741–1747, 1754–29 Apr. 1755. Tory.

Buckingham

[3] Chesterfield, Philip Dormer Stanhope, 4th Earl of (1694–1773). (See pp. 27–8 and under Derbyshire, Lancs and Notts.) M.P. St. Germans 3 May 1715–1722, Lostwithiel 1722–May 1723.

Orrery, John Boyle, 5th Earl of [1] (1707–1762). (See pp. 42, 46 and under Somerset.)

Dormer, Charles, 6th Baron (d. 1761). (See under Hampshire.) Roman Catholic priest. Arrested on suspicion of favouring Charles Edward in 1745, he is said to have secured his release by claiming his peerage (Kirk, 65).

Masham, Samuel, 1st Baron (d. 1758). (See under Essex.) M.P. Ilchester 1710–1711, New Windsor May–Dec. 1711. Tory. Husband of Queen Anne's favourite.

Bathurst, Allen, 1st Baron (1684–1775). (See pp. 12, 44 and under Glos.) M.P. Cirencester 1705–1712. Tory.

Greville, Fulke (1717–*c.* 1805), of Wilbury, Wilts. M.P. Monmouth 1747–1754. Tory and a relation of the Duke of Beaufort. His family had lands in the county.

Lowndes, Richard (*c.* 1707–1775), of Winslow, Bucks. M.P. Buckinghamshire 1741–1774. Tory.

Denton, George (*c.* 1703–1757), of Wardington, Oxon and Hillesden, Bucks. M.P. Buckingham 20 Feb. 1728–1747. Opposition Whig connected with Cobham.

Grenville, George (1712–1770). M.P. Buckingham 1741–13 Nov. 1770. Opposition Whig and one of the Cobham cubs.

Marshall, Henry (1688–1754), of St. Mary at Hill, London and Theddle-thorpe, Lincs. M.P. Amersham 1734–2 Feb. 1754. Tory. Alderman and lord mayor of London. Supported London address upon the rebellion in 1745.

Gore, Thomas (*c.* 1694–1777), of the Inner Temple and Dunstan Park, Berks. (See p. 76.) M.P. Cricklade 1722–1727, Amersham 17 Feb. 1735–1746. Portsmouth 3 Mar. 1746–1747, Bedford 1747–1754, Cricklade 1754–1768, Tory connected with Gower.

Selby, Thomas James (d. 1772), of Whaddon Hall, Bucks. Tory and a friend of Lowndes (Lipscomb, iii. 497).

Fleetwood, John (*c.* 1685–1745), Missenden, Bucks. M.P. Buckinghamshire 1713–1722. Tory. Died before the rebellion.

Cheshire

[4] Barry, James, 4th Earl of Barrymore [1] (1667–1748). (See pp 42, 60–1 and under Lancs.) M.P. Stockbridge 1710–1713, 30 Apr. 1714–1715, Wigan 1715–1727, 1734–1747.

Warrington, George Booth, 2nd Earl of (1675–1758). Whig. A poor lord (Namier, *Structure of Politics*, 222, 223). He was reported to have armed his tenants in October 1745 but took no active part against the rebels (Jarvis ii 16).

Molyneux, Caryll, 6th Visct. (1683–1745). (See under Lancs.) Roman Catholic with large estates in and around Liverpool (See G. Molineux, *Molineux Family* and Rev. E. Horley, *Sefton*).

Grosvenor, Sir Robert, 6th Bt. (1695–1755), of Eaton Hall, Cheshire. (See pp. 20, 91.) M.P. Chester 24 Jan. 1733–1 Aug. 1755. Tory. Took subscriptions in 1745 (Jarvis ii 16).

Crewe, John (1681–1749), of Madeley, Staffs, and Crewe Hall, Cheshire. M.P. Newcastle-under-Lyme 1703–1705, Cheshire 1705–1710, 1722–1727. Tory. He stood bail for £15,000 for Lord Barrymore in 1744 (Northumberland mss., Lady Hertford to Lord Beauchamp, 2 Apr. 1744).

Cholmondeley, Charles (1685–1756), of Vale Royal, Cheshire. M.P. Cheshire 1710–1715, 1722–30 March 1756. Tory. He was closely connected with Lord Barrymore (Ormerod i 557).

Warburton, Peter (1708–1774), of Turner's Hill, Herts. Tory. He succeeded his uncle Sir George Warburton, 3rd Bt., M.P. as 4th Bt. and at Warburton and Arley, Cheshire 29 June 1743 (Ormerod i 575).

Legh, Peter (1669–1744), of Lyme, Cheshire. M.P. Newton 1685–1687. Nonjuror and proprietor of the borough of Wigan. Like Barrymore and Cholmondeley he decided against joining the '15 after the arrest of the West Country Jacobites (Ormerod i 557). (See Lady Newton.)

Legh, Peter (1707–1792), of Bank Hall, Cheshire. Nephew of the above and M.P. Newton 15 Dec. 1743–1774. Tory.

Cornwall

[5] Arundel, John, 4th Baron Arundel of Trerice (1701–1768). Roman Catholic.

Arundell, Henry, 6th Baron Arundell of Wardour (1694–1746). (See under Wilts.) Wealthy Roman Catholic.

Boscawen, Hugh, 2nd Visct. Falmouth (1707–1782). M.P. Truro 1727–1734. Opposition Whig who went over to the Government in 1744.

Carew, Sir William, 5th Bt. (1689–1744), of Antony, Cornwall. (See pp. 41, 43.) M.P. Saltash 17 Jan. 1711–1713, Cornwall 1713–8 Mar. 1744. Tory.

St. Aubyn, Sir John, 3rd Bt. (*c.* 1702–1744), of Clowance, and St. Michael's Mount, Cornwall. (See pp. 43, 47.) M.P. Cornwall 1722–15 Aug. 1744. Tory.

Morice, Sir William, 3rd Bt. (*c.* 1707–1750), of Werrington, Devon. M.P. Newport 1727–1734, Launceston 1734–17 Jan. 1750. Tory.

Trelawny, John (1691–1756), of Trelawne, nr. Looe, Cornwall. M.P. West Looe 20 Apr. 1713–1715, Liskeard 1715–1722, West Looe 1722–1727, East Looe 1727–1734. Tory under Queen Anne who went over to the Whigs under the Hanoverians. He was in financial trouble.

Penton, Henry (*c*. 1705–1762), of Eastgate House, Winchester, Hants. M.P. Tregony 1734–1747, Winchester 1747–1761. Whig and Government supporter. Very little is known about his connections.

Cooke, George (*c*. 1705–1768), of Bellamond or Bellackets in Harefield, Mdx. M.P. Tregony 28 Jan. 1742–1747, Middlesex 8 Mar. 1750–5 June 1768. Returned for Tregony by 2nd Visct. Falmouth. Called 'a pompous Jacobite' by Horace Walpole.

Liddell, Richard (*c*. 1694–1746), of Wakehurst Place, Sussex. M.P. Bossiney 12 May–11 Dec. 1741, 18 Mar. 1742–22 June 1746. Opposition Whig connected with Chesterfield who chose him as his chief secretary when lord lieutenant of Ireland.

Foster, Thomas (*c*. 1720–1765), of Elim, Jamaica, and Egham House, Surrey. M.P. Bossiney 12 May–11 Dec. 1741, 18 Mar. 1742–1747, Dorchester 1761–20 Oct. 1765. Opposition Whig.

Cotton, John Hynde (*c*. 1717–1795). M.P. St. Germans 1741–1747, Marlborough 18 Feb. 1752–1761, Cambridgeshire 22 Mar. 1764–1780. Tory. Son of Sir John Hynde Cotton.

Nugent, Robert (1709–1788), of Gosfield, Essex. M.P. St. Mawes 1741–1754, Bristol 1754–1774, St. Mawes 1774–June 1784. Irish Roman Catholic who conformed and became a protégé of Chesterfield.

Cambridge

[6] Cotton, Sir John Hynde, 3rd Bt. (*c*. 1688–1752), of Madingley Hall, Cambs. (See pp. 39–42.) M.P. Cambridge 1708–1722, Cambridgeshire 1722–1727, Cambridge 1727–1741, Marlborough 1741–4 Feb. 1752.

Cumberland

[7] Hylton, John (1699–1746), of Hylton Castle, co. Dur. One of small group of ancient families holding feudal baronies. M.P. Carlisle 1727–1741, 26 Jan. 1742–25 Sept. 1746. Tory. Stood bail for a rebel in 1746 (Mounsey 179–80).

Haggerston, Sir Carnaby, 3rd Bt. (*c*. 1700–1756), of Haggerston Castle, Northumb. Roman Catholic (*Northumberland Co. History* ii 263, 265).

Derby

[8] Rutland, John Manners, 3rd Duke of (1696–1779). (See under Leicestershire.) M.P. Rutland 21 Jan. 1719–22 Feb. 1721. Opposition Whig. Raised a regiment of foot against rebellion in 1745. Henry Pelham described him on 19 Nov. 1745 as 'frightened for his money' (to Duke of Devonshire, Chatsworth mss.), not active against rebellion until after retreat from Derby.

Curzon, Sir Nathaniel, 4th Bt. (*c*. 1676–1758), of Kedleston, Derbs. M.P. Derby 25 Apr. 1713–1715, Clitheroe 1722–1727, Derbyshire 1727–1754. Tory. His attitude to the rebels while he was at Kedleston in December 1745 was equivocal (Simpson 276–7).

Stanhope, Hon. John (1705–1748), of Blackheath, Kent. M.P. Nottingham 1727–1734, Derby 13 March 1736–14 Dec. 1748. Opposition Whig and brother of Chesterfield.

Devon

⁹ Clinton, Hugh Fortescue, 1st Baron (1696–1751). Opposition Whig. Went to France with Lord Barrymore in 1740 (Stuart mss. 222/109A).

Clifford, Hugh, 4th Baron (1726–1783). (See under Somerset.) Grandson of Charles II's lord treasurer. Roman Catholic who became brother-in-law of 3rd Earl of Lichfield.

Courtenay, Sir William, 3rd Bt. (1710–1762), of Powderham Castle, Devon. M.P. Honiton 1734–1741, Devon 1741–6 May 1762. Tory.

Fortescue, Theophilus (*c.* 1707–1746), of Castle Hill, Filleigh, nr. Barnstaple, Devon. M.P. Barnstaple 1727–1741, Devon 1741–13 Mar. 1746. Opposition Whig and younger brother of Lord Clinton.

Northcote, Sir Henry, 5th Bt. (1710–1743), of Hayne and the Pynes, nr. Exeter, Devon. M.P. Exeter 11 Mar. 1735–24 May 1743. Tory.

Sydenham, Humphrey (1694–1757), of Combe, nr. Dulverton, Somerset and Nutcombe, Devon. M.P. Exeter 1741–1754. Tory.

Lyttelton, George (1709–1773), of Hagley Hall, Worcs. M.P. Okehampton 28 Mar. 1735–18 Nov. 1756. Opposition Whig and a Cobham cub.

Dorset

¹⁰ Deerhurst, Thomas Henry Coventry, Visct. (1721–1744). M.P. Bridport 2 Apr. 1742–20 May 1744. Opposition Whig.

Chaffin, George (1689–1766), of Chettle, Dorset. M.P. Dorset 1713–1754. Tory.

Pleydell, Edmund Morton (*c.* 1693–1754), of Milborne St. Andrew, Dorset. M.P. Dorchester 1722–13 Feb. 1723, Dorset 1727–1747. Tory.

Browne, John (1696–1750), of Forston in Charminster, Devon. M.P. Dorchester 1727–25 Apr. 1750. Tory.

Richards, George (d. 1746), of Long Bredy, nr. Bridport, Dorset. M.P. Bridport 1741–25 Nov. 1746. Opposition Whig.

Pitt, George (aft. 1691–1745), of Shroton, Dorset and Strathfieldsaye, Hants. M.P. Wareham 18 Apr. 1715–1722, Dorset 25 Jan.–5 Aug. 1727. Tory.

Durham

¹¹ Fauconberg, Thomas Belasyse, 4th Visct. (1699–1774). Roman Catholic who conformed. Whig.

Bowes, George (1701–1760), of Streatlam Castle, co. Dur. M.P. co. Durham 1727–17 Sept. 1760. Opposition Whig. Active in raising forces against rebels in 1745.

Tempest, John (1710–1776), of Sherburn, nr. Durham. M.P. Durham 23 Apr. 1742–1768. Tory.

Essex

¹² Suffolk, Henry Howard, 10th Earl of (1707–1745). (See under Suffolk.) M.P. Bere Alston 2 Mar. 1728–28 Sept. 1733. Opposition Whig.

Waldegrave, James, 2nd Earl (1715–1763). Of a Jacobite Roman Catholic family. Conformed and served as ambassador at Paris 1730–1740. Friend of Cobham, *Lyttelton Memoirs* i 203).

Petre, Robert Edward, 9th Baron (1742–1801). (See under Lancs.) An infant whose vast estates were administered by his mother Lady Petre. His house at Walmesley was searched for arms in 1745 (Aveling 262).

Abdy, Sir Robert, 3rd Bt. (1688–1748), of Albyns, Essex. (See pp. 38, 42.) M.P. Essex 1727–27 Aug. 1748. Tory.

Smith, Sir Edward, 3rd Bt. (1686–1744), of Hill Hall, Essex. (See pp. 43, 78.)

Long, Sir Robert, 6th Bt. (*c.* 1705–1767), of Draycot Cerne, Wilts. (See under Wilts.) M.P. Wootton Bassett 1734–1741, Wiltshire 1741–1767. Tory. Acquired large Essex estates by marriage.

Bramston, Thomas (*c.* 1690–1765), of Skreens, nr. Maldon, Essex. (See pp. 43, 54). M.P. Maldon 28 Jan. 1712–1734, Essex 1734–1747. Tory.

Smith, Hugh (*c.* 1673–1745), of South Weald, Essex. Tory whose daughter married a younger son of Lord Barrymore (Morant i 119).

Gray, Charles (1696–1782), of Holly Trees, Colchester. (See p. 43.) M.P. Colchester 26 Feb. 1742–13 Mar. 1755, 1761–1780. Tory.

Savill, Samuel (*c.* 1700–1763), of Colchester and Stisted Hall, Essex. (See p. 43.) M.P. Colchester 26 Feb. 1742–1747. Tory.

Gloucester

[13] Beaufort, Henry Somerset, 3rd Duke of (1707–1745). (See pp. 38, 46 and under Herefordshire, Middlesex, Monmouthshire, Somerset, Wales.) Tory.

Gainsborough, Baptist Noel, 4th Earl of (1708–1751). (See under Rutland.) Tory.

Chester, Thomas (1696–1763), of Almondsbury and Knole nr. Bristol. M.P. Gloucester 1727–16 Feb. 1728, Gloucestershire 1734–1 Oct. 1763. Tory.

Berkeley, Norborne (*c.* 1717–1770), of Stoke Gifford, Glos. M.P. Gloucestershire 1741–Apr. 1763. Tory and brother-in-law of Lord Noel Somerset.

Bathurst, Hon. Benjamin (1711–1767), of Siddington, nr. Cirencester, Glos. M.P. Gloucestershire 1734–1741, Cirencester 1754–1761. Tory and son of Lord Bathurst.

Master, Thomas (1690–1770), of the Abbey, Cirencester, Glos. M.P. Cirencester 23 Jan. 1712–1747. Tory.

Gage, Thomas (*c.* 1695–1754), of High Meadow, Glos. M.P. Minehead 11 Apr.–23 May 1717, Tewkesbury 25 Oct. 1721–1754. Roman Catholic who conformed. Opposition Whig.

Hereford

[14] Oxford, Edward Harley, 3rd Earl of (*c.* 1699–1755). (See pp. 74–5.) M.P. Herefordshire 1727–16 June 1741. Tory.

Foley, Thomas, 2nd Baron (*c.* 1703–1776). (See under Worcs and p. 105.) Tory.

Foley, Thomas (*c.* 1695–1749), of Stoke Edith Court, Herefs. M.P. Hereford 1734–1741, Herefordshire 6 Jan. 1742–1747. Tory.

Cornewall, Velters (*c.* 1697–1768), of Moccas Court, Herefs. M.P. Herefordshire 1722–3 Apr. 1768. Tory.

Winford, Thomas Geers (*c.* 1697–1753), of Bridge Sollers nr. Hereford. M.P. Hereford 1727–1734, 1741–1747, Worcester 1747–11 Feb. 1748. Tory.

Cope, Edward Hopton (*c.* 1708–1754), of Canon Frome, nr. Hereford. M.P. Hereford 1741–1747. Tory.

Harley, Robert (*c.* 1706–1774). M.P. Leominster 1734–1741, 29 Mar. 1742–1747, Droitwich 1754–15 Mar. 1774. Tory.

Lowes, Messrs. Probably members of the family of Lowe of All Saints, Hereford.

Hertford
[15] Bridgwater, Scroop Egerton, 1st Duke of (1681–1745). Brother-in-law of Duke of Bedford. Opposition Whig connected with Chesterfield (*Lyttelton Memoirs* i 11).

Exeter, Brownlow Cecil, 8th Earl of (1701–1754). M.P. Stamford 24 Mar.–9 Apr. 1722. Tory.

Stanhope, Philip Stanhope, 2nd Earl (1714–1786). (See under Kent.) Opposition Whig and kinsman of Chesterfield.

Gore, Charles (*c.* 1711–1768), of Tring, Herts. (See p. 76.) M.P. Cricklade 21 Nov. 1739–1741, Hertfordshire 1741–1761, Tiverton 14 May 1762–1768. Tory.

Houblon, Jacob (1710–1770), of Hallingbury, Essex. (See under Somerset.) M.P. Colchester 20 Mar. 1735–1741, Hertfordshire 1741–1747, 1761–1768. Tory and son-in-law of Sir John Hynde Cotton.

Stanley, Hans (1721–1780), of Paultons, nr. Romsey, Hants. M.P. St. Albans 11 Feb. 1743–1747, Southampton 1754–12 Jan. 1780. Opposition Whig.

Huntingdon
[16] Sandwich, John Montagu, 4th Earl of (1718–1792). Whig; grandson of Jacobite Lady Sandwich.

Rockingham, Lewis Watson, 2nd Earl of (1714–1745). (See under Kent and Northants.) Opposition Whig.

Mitchell, William (*c.* 1703–1745), of Hemingford Grey, Hunts. M.P. Huntingdonshire 1741–15 Sept. 1745. Whig of Scottish origin, usually Government supporter.

Fellowes, Coulson (1696–1769), of Ramsey Abbey, Hunts. M.P. Huntingdonshire 1741–1761. Opposition Whig connected with Sandwich.

Kent
[17] Westmorland, John Fane, 7th Earl of (1686–1762). (See under Rutland and Warwickshire and pp. 46, 58). M.P. Hythe 1708–27 Jan. 1711, Kent 28 Sept. 1715–1722, Buckingham 1 Mar. 1727–1734. Tory.

Thanet, Sackville Tufton, 7th Earl of (1688–1753). (See under Northants and Sussex.) M.P. Appleby 1722–30 July 1739. In September 1745 gave assurances of loyalty to George II, but tried to persuade him to call a free Parliament (Add. 47098B f. 11 and *Marchmont Papers* ii 124). Tory.

Aylesford, Heneage Finch, 2nd Earl of (*c.* 1683–1757). (See under Surrey and Warwks.) M.P. Maidstone 3 Nov. 1704–1705, Surrey 1710–22 July 1719. Tory.

Teynham, Henry Roper, 10th Baron (1708–1781). Roman Catholic.

Guernsey, Heneage Finch, Lord (1715–1777). M.P. Leicestershire 20 Dec. 1739–1741, Maidstone 1741–1747, 1754–29 June 1757. Tory; son of Lord Aylesford.

Dering, Sir Edward, 5th Bt. (1705–1762), of Surrenden Dering, Kent. M.P. Kent 2 Apr. 1733–1754. Tory.

Hales, Sir Thomas, 2nd Bt. (1666–1748), of Bekesbourne, nr. Canterbury, Kent. M.P. Kent 1701–1705, Canterbury 1715–1734, 11 Apr. 1735–1741, 23 Jan. 1746–1747. Whig belonging to a junior branch of a Jacobite family.

Dashwood, Sir Francis, 2nd Bt. (1708–1781), of West Wycombe, Bucks. M.P. New Romney 1741–1761, Weymouth and Melcombe Regis 1761–19 Apr. 1763. Opposition Whig; nephew of Lord Westmorland.

Darell, John (d. 1761), of Scotney Castle and Calehill, Kent (Hasted, *Kent*, ii 318) Roman Catholic.

Twisden, Mr. Probably one of brothers of Sir Roger Twisden, 5th Bt. of Bradbourne, Kent (see Sir J. R. Twisden, *Twisden Family*).

Watson, Hon. Thomas (1715–1746). M.P. Canterbury 1741–4 Dec. 1745. Opposition Whig and brother of 3rd Earl of Rockingham.

Lancaster

[18] Derby, Edward Stanley, 11th Earl of (1689–1776). (See p. 89 and under Sussex.) M.P. Lancashire 1727–13 Apr. 1736. Opposition Whig.

Strange, James Stanley, Lord (1717–1771). M.P. Lancashire 1741–1 June 1771. Eldest son of Lord Derby. Independent Whig 'of a party by himself', usually voting with the Tories. Referred to the Stuarts as 'that rascally family', yet sat in on meetings of Independent Electors of Westminster while treasonable healths were being drunk (*Gentleman's Magazine* 1747, p. 150).

Shuttleworth, Richard (1683–1748), of Gawthorpe Hall, Lancs. M.P. Lancashire 1705–22 Dec. 1749. Regarded as 'one of the strongest Jacobites in all England'. Stood bail for £15,000 for Lord Barrymore in 1744 (Northumberland mss., Lady Hertford to Lord Beauchamp, 2 April 1744).

Curzon, William (*c.* 1681–1749), of the Inner Temple. (See under Derbyshire.) M.P. Clitheroe 1734–1747. Tory; brother of Sir Nathaniel Curzon.

Fenwick, Robert (1688–1750), of Burrow Hall, Lancs. M.P. Lancaster 1734–1747. Independent Whig; had Jacobite kinsmen.

Fazakerley, Nicholas (*c.* 1685–1767), of Prescot, Lands. (See p. 67.) M.P. Preston 24 Jan. 1732–Feb. 1767. Tory.

Master, Legh (*c.* 1694–1750), of New Hall, Ashton in Makerfield, Lancs. M.P. Newton 1727–1747. Tory nephew of Peter Legh of Lyme.

Lister, Thomas (1688–1745), of Gisburn Park, nr. Clitheroe. M.P. Clitheroe 23 Apr. 1713 until his death 15 May 1745. Tory.

Leicester

[19] Huntingdon, Theophilus Hastings, 9th Earl of (1696–1746). Tory

Stamford, Harry Grey, 4th Earl of (1715–1768). (See under Staffs.) M.P. Leicestershire 16 Feb. 1738–4 Nov. 1739. Opposition Whig.

Cave, Sir Thomas, 5th Bt. (1712–1778), of Stanford Hall, Leics. M.P. Leicestershire 1741–1747, 25 Mar. 1762–1774. Tory.

Smith, Edward (*c.* 1704–1762), of Edmondthorpe, Leics. M.P. Leicestershire 1734–15 Feb. 1762. Tory.

Wigley, James (1700–1765), of Scraptoft Hall, nr. Leicester. M.P. Leicester 27 Apr. 1737–21 June 1765. Tory.

Wrighte, George (*c.* 1706–1766), of Gayhurst, Bucks and Brooksby Hall, nr. Leicester. M.P. Leicester 1727–27 Jan. 1766. Tory.

Lincoln

[20] Bristol, John Hervey, 1st Earl of (1665–1751). (See under Suffolk.) Father of Lord Hervey, the diarist, who was then in Opposition and connected with Cobham.

Haversham, Maurice Thompson, 2nd Baron (1675–1745). M.P. Bletchingley 1695–1698, Gatton 1698–1705. Opposition Whig.

Vyner, Robert (*c.* 1685–1777), of Gautby, Lincs. M.P. Great Grimsby 1710–1713, Lincolnshire 12 Feb. 1724–1761. Opposition Whig.

Whichcot, Thomas (*c.* 1700–1776), of Harpswell, Lincs. M.P. Lincolnshire 20 Feb, 1740–1774. Independent Whig who went over to Government in Jan. 1744.

Michell, John (1710–1766), of Boston, Lincs. M.P. Boston 1741–1754, 1761–30 Nov. 1766. Tory.

Proby, John (*c.* 1698–1762), of Elton Hall, Hunts. (See pp. 29, 76.) M.P. Huntingdonshire 27 Oct. 1722–1727, Stamford 1734–1747. Tory.

Middlesex

[21] Somerset, Charles Seymour, 6th Duke of (1662–1748). (See under Surrey and Wilts.) Opposition Whig.

Burlington, Richard Boyle, 3rd Earl of (1694–1753). (See under Yorkshire.) Opposition Whig; cousin of Lord Orrery.

Newdigate, Sir Roger, 5th Bt. (1719–1806), of Arbury, Warwickshire and Harefield, Middlesex. M.P. Middlesex 5 Aug. 1742–1747. Oxford University 31 Jan. 1751–1780. Tory. Refused Association.

Smithson, Sir Hugh, 4th Bt. (1715–1786), of Stanwick, Yorks and Tottenham, Middlesex. M.P. Middlesex 15 May 1740–7 Feb. 1750. Tory.

Monmouth

[22] Somerset, Lord Charles Noel (1709–1756). (See pp. 74, 77.) M.P. Monmouthshire 17 May 1731–1734, Monmouth 1734–24 Feb. 1745. Tory.

Norfolk

[23] Norfolk, Edward Howard, 9th Duke of (1688–1777). (See p. 91 and under Notts, Sussex, Yorks.) Roman Catholic implicated in the '15. His house at Worksop, Notts was searched for arms in 1745 (Chatsworth mss., Duke of Newcastle to Duke of Devonshire, 21 Nov. 1745.)

Andover, William Howard, Visct. (1714–1756). (See p. 25.) Son of 11th Earl of Suffolk. M.P. Castle Rising 16 Apr. 1737–1747. Tory.

Jerningham, Sir George, 5th Bt. (1680–1774), of Costessey, Norfolk. Roman Catholic.

Andrews, Sir Francis, 4th Bt. (d. 1759), of Denton, Norfolk. Roman Catholic.
Wodehouse, Armine (*c.* 1714-1777), of Kimberley Hall, Norfolk. M.P.
Norfolk 23 Mar. 1737-1768. Tory.

Northampton
[24] Isham, Edmund, 6th Bt. (1690-1772), of Lamport Hall, Northants. M.P.
Northamptonshire 31 Mar. 1737-15 Dec. 1772. Tory.
Cartwright, Thomas (1671-1748), of Aynho, Northants. M.P. Northampton-
shire 1695-1698, 1701-10 Mar. 1748. Tory.
Parker, Armstead (*c.* 1699-1777), of Burghberry Manor, Peterborough,
Northants. M.P. Peterborough 29 Jan. 1734-1741, 3 May 1742-1747, 1761-
1768. Tory.
Shirley, Hon. Sewallis (1709-1765). M.P. Brackley 22 Mar. 1742-1754,
Callington 1754-1761. Opposition Whig returned by Duke of Bridgwater.
Wortley Montagu, Edward (1678-1761), of Wortley, Yorks. M.P. Huntingdon
1705-1713, Westminster 1715-1722, Huntingdon 1722-1734, Peterborough
1734-1761. Opposition Whig. Husband of Lady Mary Wortley Montagu.

Northumberland
[25] Derwentwater, Charles Radcliffe, but for attainder 5th Earl of (1693-1746).
Taken on way from France to join rebellion in Scotland, and executed 11 Dec.
1746. Roman Catholic.
Widdrington, Henry Francis, but for attainder 5th Baron (1701-1774). Son
of one of the leaders of the '15. Roman Catholic.
Swinburne, Sir John, 3rd Bt. (1698-1745), of Capheaton, Northumb. Roman
Catholic.
Fenwick, John (1698-1747), of Stanton, Brinkburn and Bywell, Northumb.
M.P. Northumberland 1741-19 Dec. 1747. Tory.
Blackett, Sir Walter, 2nd Bt. (1707-1777), of Wallington Hall, Northumb.
M.P. Newcastle-upon-Tyne 1734-14 Feb. 1777. Tory.

Nottingham
[26] Middleton, Francis Willoughby, 2nd Baron (1692-1758). (See under
Warwickshire.) M.P. Nottinghamshire 1713-1722, Tamworth 1722-1727.
Wealthy Tory.
Trevor, Thomas, 2nd Baron (1692-1753). Son of Tory peer. Opposition
Whig.
Levinz, William (*c.* 1713-1765), of Grove and Bilby, Notts. M.P. Notting-
hamshire 1734-1747. Tory.
Warren, Borlase (1677-1747), of Stapleford, Notts. M.P. Nottingham 1713-
1715, 1727-15 May 1747. Tory.

Oxford
[27] Lichfield, George Henry Lee, 3rd Earl of (1718-1772). (See pp. 77-8.)
M.P. Oxfordshire 27 Feb. 1740-15 Feb. 1743. Tory. Lord of Bedchamber to
George III.
Dashwood, Sir James, 2nd Bt. (1715-1779), of Kirtlington Park, Oxon. M.P.

Oxfordshire 30 Jan. 1740–1754, 1761–1768. Tory. Refused association in 1745.

Butler, Edward (*c.* 1686–1745), of Burleigh Park, Leics. M.P. Oxford University 31 Mar. 1737–29 Oct. 1745. Tory. Died before rebellion.

Rowney, Thomas (*c.* 1693–1759), of Dean Farm, Oxon. M.P. Oxford 1722–27 Oct. 1759. Tory.

Herbert, Philip (1716–1749), of Tythorp, Bucks. M.P. Oxford 3 Dec. 1740–1749. Tory.

Dawkins, James (*c.* 1696–1766), of Over Norton, Oxon. M.P. New Woodstock 1734–1747. Tory returned by Duchess of Marlborough.

Moore, William (1699–1746), of Polesden Lacey, Surrey. M.P. Banbury 25 Nov. 1740–26 Oct. 1746. Opposition Whig. Son of Bolingbroke's friend Arthur Moore.

Rutland

28 Noel, Hon. James (1711–1752), of Exton, Rutland. M.P. Rutland 1734–17 June 1752. Tory. Son of Lord Gainsborough.

Shropshire

29 Astley, Sir John, 2nd Bt. (1687–1771), of Patshull, Staffs. M.P. Shrewsbury 1727–1734, Shropshire 1734–29 Dec. 1771. Tory. Went to see Charles Edward in France in 1752 in connection with Prussian Plot.

Corbet, Sir Richard, 4th Bt. (1696–1774), of Longnor, Salop. M.P. Shrewsbury 9 Apr. 1723–1727, 1734–1754. Whig.

Kynaston, Edward (1709–1772), of Garth, Mont. and Hardwick, Salop. M.P. Bishop's Castle 1734–1741 and Montgomeryshire 1747–18 May 1772. Tory and friend of Sir Watkin Williams Wynn. Other Kynastons were presumably his kinsmen rather than William Kynaston M.P. Shrewsbury 1734–24 Feb. 1749 who was a government Whig.

Lyster, Richard (*c.* 1692–1766), of Rowton Castle, Salop. M.P. Shrewsbury 1722–9 Apr. 1723, 1727–1734, Shropshire 11 Dec. 1740–13 Aug. 1766. Tory.

Somerset

30 Chapman, Sir John, 2nd Bt. (*c.* 1710–1781), of Cockenhatch, Barkway, Herts. M.P. Taunton 1741–1747. Opposition Whig.

Portman, Henry William (*c.* 1709–1761), of Orchard Portman, Somerset. M.P. Taunton 1734–1741, Somerset 1741–1747. Tory.

Prowse, Thomas (*c.* 1707–1767), of Compton Bishop, Somerset. (See p. 104.) M.P. Somerset 26 Nov. 1740–1 Jan. 1767. Moderate Tory.

Buck, John (1703–1745), of Bideford, Devon. M.P. Taunton 1741 until his death 3 April 1745.

Carew, Thomas (1702–1766), of Crowcombe, nr. Minehead, Somerset. (See pp. 32, 85.) M.P. Minehead 9 Feb. 1739–1747. Tory. Opposed subscriptions.

Dodington, George Bubb (*c.* 1691–1762), of Eastbury, Dorset. (See pp. 26–7.) M.P. Winchelsea 1715–1722, Bridgwater 1722–1754, Weymouth and Melcombe Regis 1754–1761. Leading Opposition Whig.

Harvey, Michael (1694–1748), of Coombe, Surrey and Clifton Maybank, nr.

Milborne Port, Somerset. M.P. Milborne Port 10 June–6 July 1717, 1722–1741, 2 Feb. 1742–1747. Tory.

Southampton

[31] Shaftesbury, Anthony Ashley Cooper, 4th Earl of (1711–1771). Opposition Whig. Son-in-law of Lord Gainsborough; his wife was a Roman Catholic convert (Aveling, 260).

Barrington, Sir John, 7th Bt. (d. 1776), of Swainstown, I. of W. M.P. Newtown I. of W. 25 Apr. 1729–1734, 1741–Nov. 1775. Opposition Whig.

Delmé, Peter (1710–1770), of Quarley, nr. Andover, Hants. M.P. Ludgershall 1734–1741, Southampton 1741–1754. Opposition Whig.

Gibbon, Edward (1707–1770), of Putney, Surrey. (See p. 40.) M.P. Petersfield 1734–1741, Southampton 1741–1747. Tory.

Stafford

[32] Shrewsbury, George Talbot, 14th Earl of (1719–1787). (See under Worcestershire and Yorkshire.) Roman Catholic.

Berkshire, Henry Howard, 5th Earl of (1687–1757). (See under Wilts.) Tory. Succeeded his cousin as 11th Earl of Suffolk 22 Apr. 1745. During the '45 received a protection from Charles Edward dated Kendal 24 Nov. 1745 (*HMC 10th Rep.* iv 346).

Audley, James Touchet, 17th Lord (1723–1769). Roman Catholic.

Stourton, Charles, 11th Baron (1702–1753). R. C. A poor lord (Aveling 262).

Gower, John Leveson, 1st Baron (1694–1754). (See pp. 44, 99 and under Yorks.).

Ward, John, 6th Baron (1704–1774), of Sedgley Park, Staffs. M.P. Newcastle-under-Lyme 1727–1734. Tory.

Leigh, Thomas, 4th Baron (1713–1749). Tory.

Chetwynd, John, 2nd Visct. [1] (1680–1767), of Ingestre Hall, Staffs. M.P. St. Mawes 1715–1722, Stockbridge 1722–1734, Stafford 31 Jan. 1738–1747. Opposition Whig. Friend of Bolingbroke (Add. 35558ff. 3, 7); associated with Lord Gower in Staffordshire.

Bagot, Sir Walter Wagstaffe, 5th Bt. (1702–1768), of Blithfield, Staffs. (See p. 107). M.P. Newcastle-under-Lyme 20 Nov. 1724–1727, Staffordshire 1727–1734, Oxford University 16 Dec. 1762–20 Jan. 1768. Tory.

Holte, Sir Lister, 5th Bt. (1720–1770), of Aston, Warwks. (See p. 107.) M.P. Lichfield 1741–1747. Tory.

Fowler, Sir William, 3rd Bt. (c. 1716–1746), of Harnage Grange, Salop. Tory.

Wolseley, Sir William, 5th Bt. (1697–1769), of Wolseley, Staffs. (Howard, *Vis. England and Wales*, Notes xiv 31). Probably Tory.

Ridgley, Sir William, prob. a member of Ridgley or Rugeley family of Stafford.

Leveson-Gower, Messrs. (See p. 76.) Hon. William (c. 1696–1756). M.P. Staffordshire 29 Dec. 1720–13 Dec. 1756. Tory, and Hon. Baptist (c. 1703–1782). M.P. Newcastle-under-Lyme 1727–1761. Tory. Lord Gower's brothers.

Venables Vernon, George (1710–1780), of Sudbury, Derbyshire and Kinderton, Cheshire. See p. 76. M.P. Lichfield 20 May 1731–1747, Derby 1754–Apr. 1762. Tory.

Wilbraham, Randle (*c.* 1695–1770), of Rode Hall, nr. Congleton, Cheshire. (See pp. 76, 105.) M.P. Newcastle-under-Lyme 26 Nov. 1740–1747. Appleby 1747–1754, Newton 1754–1768. Tory.

Lane, Col. John (1669–1748), of King's Bromley, Staffs. Grandson of Col. John Lane who saved Charles II after the battle of Worcester (Burke, *Commoners* i 174). Tory.

Suffolk

33 Firebrace, Sir Cordell, 3rd Bt. (1712–1759), of Long Melford, Suffolk. M.P. Suffolk 5 Mar. 1735–28 Mar. 1759. Tory.

Affleck, John (1710–1776), of Dalham Hall, Suffolk. M.P. Suffolk 23 Mar. 1743–1761, Amersham 4 Dec. 1767–1768. Tory.

Hanmer, Sir Thomas, 4th Bt. (1677–1746), of Mildenhall, Suffolk. M.P. Thetford 19 Mar. 1701–1702, Flintshire 1702–1705, Thetford 1705–1708, Suffolk 1708–1727. Former Hanoverian Tory, who retired from political life after the accession of George II.

Surrey

34 Butler, Charles, 1st Baron Butler of Weston (1671–1758). Better known as Earl of Arran [1]. (See pp. 12, 110.) Tory.

St. John, John, 11th Baron St. John de Bletso (d. 1757). Tory.

Mountjoy, Herbert Windsor, 2nd Baron (1707–1758). M.P. Cardiff Boroughs 1734–8 June 1738. Tory.

Thrale, Ralph (*c.* 1698–1758), of Streatham, Surrey. M.P. Southwark 1741–1747. Opposition Whig. Father-in-law of Dr Johnson's friend Mrs Thrale.

Newland, George (*c.* 1692–1749), of Gatton, Surrey. M.P. Gatton 16 May 1738–22 Oct. 1749. Tory.

Hervey, John (1696–1746), of East Betchworth, Reigate, Surrey. M.P. Reigate 16 Feb. 1739–1741, Wallingford 1754–30 July 1764. Whig.

Scawen, Thomas (d. 1774), of Carshalton, Surrey. M.P. Surrey 12 Apr. 1727–1741. Opposition Whig.

Woodroffe, George (d. 1779), of Albury and Farnham, Surrey. Stood unsuccessfully for Surrey in March 1742 (Manning and Bray, *Surrey* iii 175–6). Tory.

Sussex

35 Montacute, Anthony Browne, 6th Visct. Montacute or Montagu (1686–1767). Roman Catholic.

Caryll, John Baptist (1716–1788), of Ladyholt, Surrey. (See pp. 43, 55–6.) Roman Catholic.

Goring, Sir Charles, 5th Bt. (1706–1769), of Highden, and Wiston, Sussex. His father was one of the leaders of the Atterbury Plot, and his younger brother Henry became a member of Charles Edward's household in 1746. Tory.

Fagg, Sir William, 5th Bt. (d. 1791) of Mystole, nr. Canterbury, Kent. A relation of the Gorings.

Peachey, Sir John, 2nd Bt. (*c.* 1680–1744), of West Dean, Sussex. M.P. Midhurst 3 Feb. 1738–9 April 1744. Opposition Whig.

Campion, Henry (d. 1761), of Danny Place, in Hurstpierpoint, Sussex. M.P. East Grinstead 1708–1710, Sussex 1713–1715. Active Jacobite in 1715 (see *HMC Stuart* i and vi).

Kemp, Anthony (*c.* 1663–1753), of Slindon, Sussex. Probably Tory.

Webster, Whisler (d. 1779), of Battle Abbey, Sussex. M.P. East Grinstead 1741–1761. Opposition Whig.

Caryll, Richard, second son of Pope's friend John Caryll. Became a Jesuit (see H. Erskine-Hill 62, 93).

Warwick

[36] Denbigh, William Feilding, 5th Earl of (1697–1755). Tory. Lived in France 'in the middle of a fine vineyard three miles from Lyons'.

Northampton, James Compton, 5th Earl of (1687–1754). M.P. Warwickshire 1710–1711. Tory.

Hereford, Price Devereux, 10th Visct. (1694–1748). M.P. Montgomeryshire 9 Jan. 1719–3 Oct. 1740. Tory. Friend of Sir Watkin Williams Wynn.

Brooke, Francis Greville, 8th Baron Brooke (1719–1773). Tory.

Throgmorton, Sir Robert, 4th Bt. (1702–1791), of Coughton Court, Warwks. Roman Catholic.

Mordaunt, Sir Charles, 6th Bt. (*c.* 1697–1778), of Walton D'Eiville, nr. Kineton, Warwks. M.P. Warwickshire 6 Feb. 1734–1774. Wealthy Tory.

Digby, Hon. Edward (*c.* 1693–1746), of Wandsworth, Surrey. M.P. Warwickshire 11 May 1726–2 Oct. 1746. Moderate Tory.

Sheldon, William (1715–1779), of Beoley, Worcs and Studley, Warwks. Roman Catholic (Nash, *Worcs* i 54).

Carrington, probably Francis, owner of the manor of Drayton in Stratford-on-Avon (*VCH, Warwks* iii 266n.).

Berkley, probably Thomas, of Spetchley, Worcs who was related to the Darells of Kent (Nash, *Worcs* ii 358; Burke, *Commoners* i 471).

Grove, William (1702–1767), of Honiley, Warwks. M.P. Coventry 1741–1761. Tory.

Farmer, John (*c.* 1700–1764), lord of the manor of Oldbury (VCH, *Warwks* iv 122).

Perkins, John (1711–1744), of Orton-on-the-Hill, Leics and Witherley, Warwks. Related to Sir William Perkins executed as a Jacobite in 1696 (Nichols, *Leics* iv 454).

Westmorland

[37] Musgrave, Sir Philip, 6th Bt. (*c.* 1712–1795), of Edenhall, Cumberland. M.P. Westmorland 1741–1747. Tory.

Wilts

[38] St. John, John, 2nd Visct. (1702–1748). M.P. Wootton Bassett 1727–1734. Tory. Half-brother of Bolingbroke. His mother was French and he was educated in France.

Bouverie, Sir Jacob, 3rd Bt. (*c.* 1694–1761), of Longford Castle, Wilts. M.P. Salisbury 1741–1747. Tory.

Seymour, Sir Edward, 6th Bt. (1695–1757), of Maiden Bradley, Wilts. M.P. Salisbury 1741–1747. Tory.

Turner, Sir Edward, 2nd Bt. (1719–1766), of Ambrosden, Oxon. M.P. Great Bedwyn 1741–1747, Oxfordshire 23 Apr. 1755–1761, Penryn 1761–21 Oct. 1766. Tory.

Popham, Edward (c. 1711–1772), of Littlecote, Wilts. M.P. Great Bedwyn 5 Apr. 1738–1741, Wiltshire 1741–14 July 1772. Tory.

Grenville, James (1715–1783). M.P. Old Sarum 5 Jan. 1742–May 1747, Bridport 1747–1754, Buckingham 1754–1768, Horsham 1768–Mar. 1770. Opposition Whig, one of the Cobham cubs.

Pitt, William (1708–1778), of Hayes, Kent. (See p. 90.) M.P. Old Sarum 18 Feb. 1735–1747, Seaford 1747–1754, Aldborough 1754–Dec. 1756, Buckingham 7–11 Dec. 1756, Okehampton 11 Dec. 1756–July 1757, Bath 9 July 1757–4 Aug. 1766. Opposition Whig and a Cobham cub. Later 1st Earl of Chatham.

Thursby, John Harvey (c. 1711–1764), of Abingdon Abbey, Northants. M.P. Wootton Bassett 1741–1747, Stamford 1754–1761. Tory.

Neale, Robert (1706–1776), of Corsham, Wilts. M.P. Wootton Bassett 1741–1754. Whig and Government supporter. Badly in debt.

Crawley, John (1703–1767), of Stockwood Park, Beds. M.P. Marlborough 28 Feb. 1737–1747. Tory.

Worcester

[39] Coventry, William, 5th Earl of (c. 1676–1751). M.P. Bridport 1708–27 Oct. 1719. Opposition Whig.

Lechmere, Edmund (1710–1805), of Hanley Castle, Worcs. M.P. Worcestershire 1734–1747. Tory.

Pytts, Edmund (c. 1696–1753), of Kyre, nr. Tenbury, Worcs. M.P. Worcestershire 1741–24 Nov. 1753. Tory.

Foley, Thomas (1716–1777), of Stoke Edith Court, Herefs. M.P. Droitwich 1741–1747, 9–16 Dec. 1747, 1754–1768, Herefordshire 1768–10 May 1776. Tory.

York

[40] Carlisle, Henry Howard, 4th Earl of (1693–1758). (p. 32) M.P. Morpeth 1715–1738. Opposition Whig.

Langdale, Marmaduke, 4th Lord (d. 1771). Roman Catholic.

Stapylton, Sir Miles, 4th Bt. (c. 1708–1752), of Myton, Yorks. M.P. Yorkshire 1734–Apr. 1750. Tory. Took subscriptions in 1745 (Chatsworth mss., Will Hewett to Duke of Devonshire, 27 Sept. 1745).

Slingsby, Sir Henry, 5th Bt. (c. 1693–1763), of Scriven, nr. Knaresborough. (See pp. 43, 47.) M.P. Knaresborough 17 May 1714–1715, 1722–18 Jan. 1763. Tory.

Fox, George (c. 1696–1773), of Bramham Park, Yorks. M.P. Hindon 1734–1741, York 21 July 1742–1761. Tory. Took subscriptions in 1745 (Chatsworth mss., Will Hewett to Duke of Devonshire, 27 Sept. 1745).

Aislabie, William (c. 1699–1781), of Studley Royal, nr. Ripon, Yorks. M.P. Ripon 1 Apr. 1721–17 May 1781. Opposition Whig, who went over to Government in 1744.

Berkeley, Hon. George (*c.* 1692–1746), of Marble Hill, Twickenham, Mdx. M.P. Dover 20 Dec. 1720–1734, Hedon 1734–1741, 4 Mar. 1742–29 Oct. 1746. Opposition Whig.

Pelham, Charles (*c.* 1679–1763), of Brocklesby, Lincs. M.P. Great Grimsby 1722–1727, Beverley 2 Feb. 1738–1754. Tory.

Wales
[41] Powis, William Herbert, 2nd Marquess of (*c.* 1665–1745). Duke of Powis in Jacobite peerage. Arrested as a Jacobite suspect 1696, 1715 and 1722. Roman Catholic who conformed. Died 22 Oct. 1745.

Bulkeley, James, 6th Visct. [I] (1717–1752), of Baron Hill, Anglesey. M.P. Beaumaris 20 April 1739–23 April 1752. Tory and friend of Sir Watkin Williams Wynn.

Wynn, Sir Watkin Williams, 3rd Bt. (*c.* 1693–1749), of Wynnstay, Denbighshire. (See pp. 41–2.) M.P. Denbighshire 30 June 1716–1741, Montgomeryshire 1741–23 Feb. 1742, Denbighshire 23 Feb. 1742–20 Sept. 1749. Tory.

City of London and Westminster
[42] At the Westminster election of May 1741, when the Government saw that its candidates were about to be defeated, troops were called in to close the poll. In one of the crucial divisions before the fall of Walpole the Westminster election was declared void. At the ensuing by-election on 31 December 1741 the Independent Electors of Westminster secured the return of Edward Vernon, an Opposition Whig and a popular hero (see pp. 98–9), and of Charles Edwin, a Tory (*HC* i 285–6).

Appendix II

List of the Corporation of London given to Butler 1743

After private talks with Robert Willimot, Robert Westley, George Heathcote, Edward Gibbon, William Benn and Daniel Lambert (see pp. 40–1), Butler was given the following list of the corporation of London and an account of its constitution (AEM & D. Ang. 85f. 106) Balhaldy took a copy with some minor variants which he sent to the Pretender (Stuart mss. 254/154). Those marked with an asterisk took the subscriptions and or the Association (see p. 84–5) in September–October 1745 (from information kindly supplied by Dr. Nicholas Rogers).

J = Jacobite
P = Patriot
H = Hanoverian
W = Whig

A list of the names of the lord mayor, aldermen, recorder and sheriffs of the City of London together with the deputies and common councilmen of the several wards for the year 1743 as they are returned by the ward mote inquests in their respective indentures.

The Rt. Honourable Robert Willimot Esq. Lord Mayor J.P.*	Lime Street
Sir John Eyles Bart. H.W. Seldom or scarce ever attends. Post Master General	Bridge Without
Sir Robert Baylis Knt. H.W. Attends. Commissioner of the customs*	Bread Street
Sir William Billers Knt. H.W. Generally attends. Director of the East India Company	Cordwainer
Sir Edward Bellamy W. Seldom attends, old and very infirm*	Billingsgate

Sir John Thompson Knt. H.W. Seldom attends   Candlewick
  because infirm*
Sir John Barnard Knt. Turned H. Seldom   Dowgate
  attends*
Micajah Perry Esq., H.W. Dying of a dropsy.   Aldgate
  Not able ever to attend
Sir John Salter Knt. H.W. Director of the East Cornhill
  India Company
Daniel Lambert Esq. J.P.*   Tower
George Heathcote Esq. P. Against the Court   Walbrook
Sir Harcourt Master Knt. H.W. Court pensioner   Coleman Street
Sir George Champion Knt. Renegado. Bribed   Bridge Within
  for which famous*
Sir Joseph Hankey Knt. W.*   Langhorn
Robert Westley Esq., J.P. Next the chair   Queenhithe
Henry Marshal Esq. J.P.*   Farringdon Within
William Baker Esq., W. Director of the East   Bassisshaw
  India Company*
George Arnold Esq. W.*   Cheap
Richard Hoare Esq., J.P.*   Farringdon Without
William Benn Esq. J.P.*   Aldersgate
Robert Ladbrooke Esq. J.P.*   Castle Baynard
William Calvert Esq. J.P.   Portsoken
Walter Barnard Esq. J.P.   Broad Street
Samuel Pennant Esq. P. Against the Court   Bishopsgate
Edward Gibbon Esq. J.P.   Vintry
John Blachford J.P.*   Cripplegate Within
                                                   and Without

Simon Urlin, Serjeant-at-law. Recorder W.
  Against the Court (indifferent)
William Benn Esq. J.P. sheriff
Charles Eggleton sheriff, of no consequence
John Bosworth Esq. chamberlain J.P.
Thomas Garrard Esq., common serjeant,
  indifferent
Miles Man Esq., town clerk J.P.

The names of the deputies and common councilmen of the several
  wards

Aldersgate 8   Richard Bayley J.P.
Major John Snart deputy J.P.   John Underwood J.P.
Joseph Rose J.P.   Samuel Ballard deputy J.P.*

Robert Henshaw J.P.
Richard Reily J.P.*
Nathaniel Maccascree J.P.

Aldgate 6
Thomas Stanford deputy P.
Christopher Fullagar J.P.*
Thomas Harrison H.W.*
John Hall J.P.
Thomas Sharp J.P.
William Pond J.P.

Bassisshaw 4
William Coulhurst deputy H.W.*
Francis Cooper H.W.*
Samuel Fludyer H.W.*
Samuel Ellis H.W.*

Billingsgate 10
Edmund Stevens deputy P.
William Parker J.P.
Samuel Harris H.W.
Edward Robinson J.P.
Henry Cowling H.W.
Robert Peck H.W.
Thomas Crozier H.W.
Robert Rossiter H.
George Woods J.P.
Thomas Winterbottom H.

Bishopsgate 14
James Dunsie deputy J.P.
George Wylde J.P.*
Daniel Davies J.P.
Thomas Long J.P.
Samuel Vickers J.P.
William Munday J.P.
William Poole J.P.
Francis Cockayne J.P.
Peter Roberts J.P.
Robert Fawdery J.P.
John Holland deputy J.P.*
Henry Wily J.P.

John Forty J.P.*
William Hookham J.P.

Breadstreet 12
Robert Cady deputy H.W.*
John Sedgwick H.W.*
William Wooley H.W.*
Anthony Plank H.W.
John Todd H.W.*
Richard Witts H.W.*
James Budgette H.W.*
Thomas Morris H.W.*
Thomas Smith H.W.*
Heneage Robinson J.P.*
Anthony Lucas J.P.
John Ogilvie H.W.

Bridge 15
Richard Clay deputy J.P.*
Cornelius Herbert J.P.
Thomas Durnford J.P.*
James Hodges J.P.*
Michael Methens J.P.
Benjamin Tyson J.P.
Ambrose Hammond J.P.*
William White J.P.
John Cooper J.P.
Christopher Taylor J.P.*
Stephen Cooper J.P.
James Heywood J.P.*
Joseph Gonson J.P.*
George Baskerville J.P.*
Thomas Pritchard J.P.

Broadstreet 10
John Clarke deputy J.P.*
Ralph Wilson J.P.
Thomas Eden J.P.
Hugh Knowlings J.P.
John Low J.P.
Timothy Helmsley J.P.*
Robert Bishop Esq. J.P.
John Mitford J.P.

Broadstreet 10—cont.
William Whitaker J.P.*
William Chapman J.P.

Candlewick 8
Samuel Osborne deputy H.W.*
William Arnold H.W.
Peter Thomas Esq. H.W.
Edward Yeates H.W.
John Blacksley H.W.
Thomas Mallett H.W.*
George Hoare H.W.*
Arthur Lane H.W.

Castlebaynard 10
William Hunt deputy J.P.
Benjamin Crook J.P.*
Nathaniel Nash J.P.*
John Willis J.P.
Robert Territt J.P.
Thomas Powell J.P.
John Winder J.P.*
William Giles J.P.*
William Lord J.P.
John Cordwell J.P.*

Cheap 12
Thomas Wright deputy W.
Samuel Sedgwick wavers*
Robert Waite J.P.
Edward Southhouse J.P.
George Verney J.P.
Waller Hayter J.P.
Theodore Cock H.W.
Leonard Read H.W.*
Frederick Stanton H.W.
Windmill Compton wavers
John Skinner wavers
Thomas Smith H.W.*

Coleman Street 6
Thomas Wilkinson deputy H.W.
Edward Roberts H.W.

Robert Lovick Esq. H.W.
John Lloyd H.W.*
Thomas Gibson Esq. H.W.
Wm. Hayter H.W.*

Cordwainer 8
John Daye deputy J.P.*
George Smith J.P.
Percival Pott J.P.*
Francis Grissel J.P.*
Josiah Colebrooke J.P.*
Henry Spencer J.P.*
William Reynolds J.P.*
Richard Blunt J.P.*

Cornhill 6
George Townsend J.P.
William Meadows J.P.
John Young J.P.*
James Walton J.P.*
Francis Ellis J.P.
Bourchier Cleeve J.P.

Cripplegate Within 8
Thomas Elton deputy J.P.*
Richard Molineux J.P.
Thomas Nichol J.P.
William Sims J.P.
Robert Elliot J.P.
Thomas Scott J.P.
Charles Hartley J.P.
James Mount J.P.*

Cripplegate Without 4
Richard Farington deputy J.P.
William Cooper J.P.
John Wallington J.P.
Thomas Bourne J.P.

Dowgate 8
Thomas Curryer deputy J.P.*
Peter Hambley J.P.*

William Ford J.P.
Richard Swithin J.P.*
Thomas Rhodes J.P.
William Stephenson J.P.*
Samuel Stretton J.P.
Christopher Robinson J.P.*

Faringdon Within 17
Richard Sclater deputy J.P.*
Richard Skinner J.P.
Robert Stringer J.P.*
James Price J.P.
Michael Martindale J.P.*
Jenner Swaine J.P.
Thomas Hodges J.P.*
John Humphreys J.P.
Giles Mills J.P.
Thomas Fawson J.P.
Henry Sisson J.P.
Richard Holland J.P.
John Reeve J.P.
Samuel Scawell J.P.*
John Blackhall J.P.
Robert Willes J.P.
Richard Grainger J.P.

Faringdon Without 16
St. Sepulchres
Robert Gammon J.P.*
Cadwallader Coker J.P.*
Charles Taylor Ballard J.P.
Edward Walmesley J.P.
John King J.P.*
Christopher Myngs J.P.*

St. Andrew Holborn
Thomas Nash deputy J.P.
Christopher Horsenail J.P.*

St. Dunstan West
John Child deputy J.P.
William Hart J.P.
Samuel Cranmer J.P.*

St. Brides
Philip Robinson J.P.
Samuel Rutter J.P.*
George Grainger J.P.*

St. Martin's Ludgate
Richard Nutt J.P.
George Burton J.P.

Langborn 10
Thomas Oyles deputy dead
William Pepys H.W.
Edward Neale H.W.
Thomas Minors H.W.
Henry Lawton H.W.
Robert Wilson J.P.*
Edward Ironside J.P.
John Barker J.P.
John Townsend J.P.
Thomas Rawlinson H.W.

Limestreet 4
Giles Vincent deputy J.P.*
Samuel Southouse J.P.*
John Fleetwood J.P.
George Mason J.P.

Portsoken 5
Robert Pyecroft deputy J.P.
John McKellan J.P.*
Richard Bridgman J.P.
William Myers J.P.
Crispe Gascoyne Esq. J.P.

Queenhithe 6
Joseph Ayliffe deputy J.P.
Robert Allsop J.P.
George Nelson J.P.
Edward Davis J.P.
Charles Bland J.P.
Thomas Northey J.P.

Tower 12
Samuel Tatem deputy J.P.*

Tower 12—cont.
William Cleaver J.P.
James Phillips J.P.
William Prowting J.P.*
John Sellar J.P.
Thomas Green J.P.
Robert Booth Esq. J.P.
John Woodbridge J.P.
Jonathan Granger J.P.
Daniel Lambert J.P.*
Henry Seale J.P.
Richard Romman J.P.*

Vintry 9
Thomas Gregg deputy H.W.*
James Kelham J.P.
William Beddel H.W.*

William Mills H.W.*
Thomas Parker H.W.
Martin Wardell H.W.*
William Hoggard H.W.
Marsh Dickenson H.W.
Thomas Rous Esq. H.W.[1]

Walbrook 8
William Wilkins deputy H.W.
Robert Peirce Esq, J.P.
Col. Richard Martin J.P.
William Farmer J.P.
James Ennis J.P.*
Francis Flower Esq. J.P.
Basil Brown J.P.*
William Arnold J.P.

Total 236

The city of London is governed by twenty six aldermen one of which is lord mayor and presides universally in the City, the serjeant-at-law, two hundred and thirty six common councilmen, twenty six whereof are deputies of the aldermen, a recorder, two sheriffs, a chamberlain, a city common serjeant, and town clerk.

This number of twenty six aldermen arises from the division of the city in twenty six districts or divisions, by the citizens called wards. Each ward chooses its own aldermen, whose office is for life and such a regular number of common councilmen as they have a right to, who may be all changed or continued every Michaelmas by the ward, save the alderman's deputy of the ward named by the alderman and ward.

When this body meets, which is as often as the lord mayor pleases besides their regular day of meeting, the court is named the lord mayor, aldermen and common council of the city, and they have many principal powers, privileges and immunities for the government of the City in general, powers in whatever regards the policy of the city or conduct of the citizens, save so far as particular corporations have charters given from the Crown, with special privileges for the policy of their corporation; in their court of assistants, as they name them, the members of these corporations are odd of eighty; each of which have their chart of assistance with different privileges and exemptions as favoured by the King granted of these charters.

I have observed that each ward has the sole right of choosing its own

[1] Will be changed as Gibbon is alderman.

alderman; this is done in a court held by the lord mayor for that effect within the ward wherein each freeman of the ward has a voice, by which it happens that the inclinations and temper of the ward is known by the choice of their alderman, but much better by the choice they make of their common councilmen, because the alderman for the ward, once chosen, is for life, and often for fifty years past, has dissembled till once named, that he came out of their power; whereas the common councilmen are once a year at their mercy.

Tho every freeman in each ward have the power or privilege of choosing their own alderman, yet the whole freemen of the City have not a voice in naming the mayor, nor any of them unless he be entered and of a particular corporation or company; the body of freemen entered in this manner are named the livery of the city; twelve companies whereof are designed the greater companies and the number of the whole is computed betwixt eight and nine thousand. This livery has the right of presenting two each year qualified for being lord mayor; one of which the body of aldermen must name mayor. In this the livery seldom offer any other for mayor, but the senior alderman, commonly designed next in the chair, and who is highly affronted when disappointed as being marked out by the City as infamous, which seldom happens save in such extraordinary cases as Champion's.[1] The livery has likeways the power of naming their sheriffs, with this they often divert themselves at the expense of the rich men they judge will not officiate, they having it in their choice to accept or pay what they name a fine to some hundred pounds sterling, but in this sometimes they are bit, the person named accepting contrary to what they judged and that they become burdened with a sheriff to vex them. It has the privilege also of choosing the City's representatives in Parliament from this flows the first figure the City has made by its representatives in Parliament.

Notwithstanding the presumption of learning the certain temper of the citizens by the choice of their aldermen, yet this has been for a long time a very uncertain mark, because the administration uses, with all the power, interest and even money of the Crown and by all manner of art to divert and corrupt the natural bent of the people. When it happened that the body of the city or ward was on their guard, as it sometimes was, it disappointed all their art, power and influence, by the force of a very great majority, they always showed at least for twenty eight years past, when heedful, to make that majority exert itself. But even then, the City or ward was often frustrated by the alderman it had forced on the administration by his changing sides. It was not so easy a matter to corrupt the common councilmen, because the purchase would have been very

---

[1] George Champion, passed over as lord mayor for voting against the Spanish Convention in 1739 (*HC* i 541).

expensive, so often repeated; the corruption could last but one year; the corrupted then returned under the power and consequently the disgrace of their fellow citizens, and for this reason the majority of common councilmen has for twenty-eight years past been of the side of nature, justice and the true interest of the community.

This will make it appear a paradox, how it came about that for some time every question was carried on against the opinion of the majority of the city court. But the paradox ceases when it is informed that the majority of the aldermen have a negative in any question where the common councilmen, and they divide,[1] which tho the majority of aldermen seldom made use of because extremely disagreeable to the body of the city, yet they sometimes have made use of it and have it always in their power, for this reason the majority of common councilmen became careless of attendance, while there was a great majority of aldermen against them which gave an opportunity to the other party, to carry whatever they had in mind, and made the majority of common councilmen very careful not to push anything against the bent of their aldermen, who by this negative and other powers inherent in the body of aldermen over the city and in each particular alderman over his ward, have great weight and influence in bringing about what they have a mind to; by this it happens that the body of aldermen were enabled to supply the place of any of their number that died which are of a kidney with themselves and administration, or the administration purchased him when chosen against its interest. But the City in the case of their renegade Champion has noted that desertion with such marks of infamy and disgrace, that hardly any other will ever dare to follow his example. It flows from this spirit of honour, virtue and resentment, that the city now makes such a leading figure in the kingdom, and has got so far the better of a poisoned body of aldermen supported and assisted by all the power, authority and money of the Crown, as to have supplied the room of any that deceased with one of the same genius within the City till they have got a majority of aldermen of their side, and that the Administration has given over making any opposition to it, or meddling in the City's affairs because the Administration find that opposition only serves to augment the zeal and application of the City.

It will then appear a question not very difficult to answer, how a body of people living in a society governed by a lord mayor and a majority of aldermen, against thirteen aldermen some of what are indifferent which side prevail, and the greatest part so superannuat and infirm, as not to be able to attend, and this majority of aldermen joined and supported by a

---

[1] For the circumstances of the Act of Parliament imposing the aldermen's veto over the decisions of the court of common council, see *HC* i 280.

hundred and fifty three common council men J.P. of the same mind and disposition with the people and about thirty more Patriot for the people against fifty H.W. some of which waver and will be changed as their aldermen die, who in the mean time seldom attend, because when present in their courts serve only for cyphers, especially when those such as Calvert, Benn, deputy Dunzie and others, I demand how will they do when it is put in their power to act naturally and according to their inclinations.

But if even yet it should be doubted that doubt cannot remain when informed that the City have chosen the most zealous and distinguished Patriots governors of their public hospitals, and its advisers in affairs of moment with Sir John Hynde Cotton, Sir Watkin Williams Wynn, the Earl of Lichfield, Sir William Carew, Sir John St. Aubyn, Sir Robert Abdy, Mr. Bramston and others of the same kidney.

Chronology

1739

January   Spanish Convention
October   Declaration of war between England and Spain

1740

March   Jacobite emissary sent to England to sound Tories on prospects of a restoration

1741

13 Feb.   Motion for removal of Sir Robert Walpole defeated
April   General election, 286 Government Whigs, 136 Tories and 131 Opposition Whigs returned
August   Lord Chesterfield goes to see Duke of Ormonde at Avignon
16/27 Sept.   Pretender's letter instructing the Tories to bring down Walpole
December   Meeting of 1741 Parliament

1742

11 Feb.   Resignation of Walpole, formation of Carteret administration
12 Feb.   Meeting of Opposition at Fountain Tavern in the Strand
18 Feb.   Duke of Argyll takes the Tories to Court
10 March   Resignation of Argyll
10 Dec.   Division on taking Hanoverian troops into English pay

1743

16 June   Battle of Dettingen, George II defeats French
Aug.–Oct.   French emissary sounds Tories on prospects of a restoration

November   Preparations for French expedition to restore Stuarts begin

1744

10 Jan.   Division on continuing Hanoverian troops in English pay
14 Feb.   English Government learns secret of invasion from a French secret agent
15 Feb.   King's message to Parliament on French invasion
22 Feb./5 March   French embarkation begins at Dunkirk
24 Feb.   French fleet off Dungeness
24-26 Feb.   Storms damage English and French fleets
28 Feb./11 March   French expedition abandoned
20/31 March   France declares war on England
December   Fall of Carteret, formation of Pelham ministry in so-called Broadbottom Administration

1745

May   Battle of Fontenoy, Maurice of Saxony defeats Duke of Cumberland
23 July   Charles Edward lands in Scotland
16 Sept.   Jacobite army enters Edinburgh
21 Sept.   Defeat of Sir John Cope at Prestonpans
October   Parliament meets at Westminster
8 Nov.   Charles Edward crosses into England
17 Nov.   Carlisle surrenders
26 Nov.   Jacobite army takes Preston
29 Nov.   Charles Edward enters Manchester
4 Dec.   Jacobite army in Derby
6 Dec.   Black Friday in London
6 Dec.   Retreat from Derby
14/25 Dec.   Date set for French landing to join Charles Edward near London
19 Dec.   King's message to Parliament on threatened French invasion, Hessian troops sent for
20 Dec.   Jacobite army crosses back into Scotland

1746

17 Jan.   Defeat of General Hawley at Falkirk
11 April   Division on continuing Hanoverian troops into English pay

16 April   Battle of Culloden, Cumberland defeats Jacobite army
August   Trial of rebel Lords
29 Sept./10 Oct.   Charles Edward back in France
October   Maurice of Saxony defeats General Ligonier at Roucoux

1747

January   Trial of Lord Lovat
June–July   General election, 338 Government Whigs, 117 Tories, 97 opposition Whigs returned
July   Maurice of Saxony defeats Cumberland at Laffeldt

1748

18 Oct.   Treaty of Aix-la-Chapelle, peace made between England and France

Bibliography

1. GUIDE TO MANUSCRIPT SOURCES USED

ENGLAND

ROYAL ARCHIVES, WINDSOR CASTLE
Stuart mss.

BRITISH LIBRARY
Additional mss.
  9129–9224 William Coxe's transcripts
  32712–32805 Newcastle papers
  35337–35602 Hardwicke papers
  47098B   Egmont papers

PUBLIC RECORD OFFICE
State Papers
Series 36 Domestic, George II
Series 44 Domestic, entry books
Series 78 Foreign (France)

Granville Mss 30/29/1

OTHER COLLECTIONS
Ryder diary transcript made available to the History of Parliament Trust by the Earl of Harrowby and the Treasurer and Masters of the Bench of Lincoln's Inn, transcribed from the original shorthand by Mr K. L. Perrin.
Blenheim Mss. Sunderland papers
Badminton Mss. Beaufort papers
Chatsworth Mss. Devonshire papers
Alnwick Mss. Northumberland papers
Bank of England. Morice papers
Lichfield Mss. Anson papers (transcripts in possession of the History of Parliament Trust)
Borlase Mss. Letters from Sir John St. Aubyn to William Borlase in Morrab Library by courtesy of A. Pool of Pool, Purchas & Le Grice, Solicitors, Penzance

Digby Mss. formerly in possession of Miss Fiona Digby, transcripts communicated by Howard Erskine-Hill

FRANCE

Paris
QUAI D'ORSAY (Archives du Ministère des Affaires étrangères)
Correspondance Politique, Angleterre
Mémoires et Documents, Angleterre
Correspondance Politique, Bavière

CHATEAU DE VINCENNES (Archives du Ministère de la Défense Nationale)
Guerre série AI

ARCHIVES NATIONALES (Archives du Ministère de la Marine)
Marine séries B2 and B3

Rouen
BIBLIOTHEQUE DE ROUEN
Collection Leber Richelieu papers

2. PRINTED WORKS CITED

Argenson, Marquis d', *Journal et Mémoires*, ed. E. J. B. Rathéry, 9 vols, Paris 1859–67.

Aveling, J. C., *The Handle and the Axe*, 1976.

Balteau, J., *Dictionnaire de Biographie française*, Paris 1933–76.

Barbier, E. J. F., *Journal Historique et anecdotique du règne de Louis XV*, ed. A. de Villegille, 4 vols, Paris 1847–56.

Beaven, A. B., *The Aldermen of London*, 2 vols, 1908–13.

Bennett, G. V., *The Tory Crisis in Church and State 1688–1730, The career of Francis Atterbury, Bishop of Rochester*, Oxford 1975.

Bodleian Quarterly Record, anon., 'The opening of the Radcliffe Library in 1749' i (1915), pp. 165–72.

Bongie, Laurence, 'Voltaire's English, high treason and a manifesto for Bonnie Prince Charles', *Studies on Voltaire and the eighteenth century* clxxi (1977), pp. 7–29.

Boswell, James, *Life of Johnson*, ed. G. B. Hill, rev. L. F. Powell. 6 vols, Oxford 1934–50.

Boyer, Abel, *The Political State of Great Britain*, 60 vols, 1711–40.

Broglie, J. V. A., duc de, *Histoire de la Politique étrangère de Louis XV*, 10 vols, Paris 1883–95.

Brooke, John, *George III*, 1974.

Brosses, Charles de, *L'Italie il y a cent ans, ou Lettres écrites d'Italie à quelques amis en 1739 et 1740*, ed. M. R. Columb, 2 vols, Paris 1836.

Browne, James, *A History of the Highlands and of the Highlands Clans*, 4 vols, Glasgow 1832–3.

Browning, Andrew, *Thomas Osborne, Earl of Danby and Duke of Leeds*, 3 vols, Glasgow 1944–51.

Broxap, Henry, *The Later Non-Jurors*, Cambridge 1924.

Burke, John, *A History of the Commoners of Great Britain and Ireland*, 4 vols, 1833–8.

Carson, Edward, *The Ancient and Rightful Customs*, 1972.

Charnock, John, *Biographia Navalis*, 6 vols, 1794–8.

Chesterfield, Philip D. Stanhope, 4th Earl of, *Letters of Lord Chesterfield*, ed. B. Dobrée, 6 vols, 1932.

Clark, J. C. D. 'The decline of party, 1740–1760', *English Historical Review*, xciii (1978) pp. 499–527.

Cobbett, William, *The Parliamentary History of England*, 36 vols, 1806–1820.

Cokayne, G. E., *Complete Baronetage*, 6 vols, 1900–1909, *Complete Peerage*, 14 vols, 1910–59.

Colin, J. L. A., *Louis XV et les Jacobites, le projet du débarquement en Angleterre de 1743–1744*, Paris 1901.

Colley, Linda, 'The Loyal Brotherhood and the Cocoa Tree: The London Organization of the Tory party 1727–1760', *The Historical Journal* xx (1977), pp. 77–95.

Collier, Cedric, 'Yorkshire and the Forty-Five', *The Yorkshire Archaeological Journal*, xxxviii (1952–5), pp. 71–95.

Journals of the House of Commons, 1803 ed.

Conduct of, *The Conduct of the late and present ministry compared; with an impartial review of public transactions since the resignation of the Right Honourable the Earl of Orford, and the causes that immediately effected the same*, 1742.

Cox, Marjorie, 'Sir Roger Bradshaigh, 3rd Bart., and the electoral management of Wigan', *Bulletin of John Rylands Library*, xxxvii (1954–5), pp. 120–64.

Coxe, William, *Memoirs of the life and administration of Sir Robert Walpole, Earl of Orford*, 3 vols, 1798.

Memoirs of Horatio, Lord Walpole, 2 vols, 1820.

Memoirs of the administration of the Rt. Hon. Henry Pelham, 2 vols, 1829.

Cruickshanks, Eveline, '101, Secret Agent', *History Today*, April 1969, pp. 273–6.

'The Tories and the succession to the Crown in the 1714 Parliament', *Bulletin of the Institute of Historical Research*, xlvi (1973), pp. 176–85.

Daiches, David, *Charles Edward Stuart*, 1975.

Dalton, Charles, *English Army Lists and Commissions Registers 1661–1714*, 6 vols, 1892–1904.

Dean, C. G. T., *The Royal Hospital, Chelsea*, 1950.

Dickinson, H. T., *Bolingbroke*, 1970.

Elcho, Lord, *Short Account of the Affairs of Scotland in 1744, 1745, & 1746*, Edinburgh 1973.

Ellis, K., *The Post Office in the Eighteenth Century*, 1958.

Erskine-Hill, Howard, *The Social Milieu of Alexander Pope*, 1975.

Ewald, Alexander Charles, *The Life and Times of Prince Charles Stuart*, 2 vols, 1875.

Fitzmaurice, Lord, *Life of William, Earl of Shelburne*, 2 vols, 1912.

Frederick II, *Oeuvres complètes*, 17 vols, Berlin 1790.

Foord, Archibald S., *His Majesty's Opposition 1714–1830*, Oxford 1964.

Fritz, Paul S., *The English Ministers and Jacobitism between the Rebellions of 1715 and 1745*, Toronto 1975.

Gentleman's Magazine, *The Gentleman's Magazine and Historical Chronicle*, 1730–51.

Gibbon, Edward, *Memoirs of my own Life*, ed. G. A. Bonnard, 1966.

Godley, A. D., *Oxford in the Eighteenth Century*, 1908.

Goldie, Mark, 'Edmund Bohun and *Jus Gentium* in the Revolution Debate 1689–93', *The Historical Journal*, xx (1977), pp. 569–86.

Gyllenborg, *Letters which passed between Count Gyllenborg, the Barons Görtz, Sparre and others*, 1717.

Haile, Martin, *James Francis Edward, the Old Chevalier*, 1917.

Hasted, Edward, *The history and topographical survey of the county of Kent*, 4 vols, Canterbury 1778–99.

Hay, D., Linebaugh, P. and Thompson, E.P., eds., *Albion's Fatal Tree*, 1977.

Hervey, John, Lord, *Some Materials towards Memoirs of the Reign of George II*, ed. Romney Sedgwick, 3 vols, 1931.

Hill, B. W., *The Growth of Parliamentary Parties 1689–1742*, 1976.

Historical Manuscripts Commission

    First Report (Richmond mss.), 1870.

    Tenth Report, Appendix iv (Bagot mss.), 1885.

    Twelfth Report, Appendix ix (Beaufort mss.), 1891.

    Fourteenth Report, Appendix ix (Trevor mss.), 1895.

    Fifteenth Report, Appendix vii (Puleston mss.), 1898.

    Fifty-sixth Report, Stuart Papers i, 1902, vi, 1916.

    Sixty-third Report, Diary of Viscount Percival, afterwards 1st Earl of Egmont 1730–47, 1920–3.

    Sixty-seventh Report, Polwarth mss. v, 1961.

Holmes, Geoffrey, *British Politics in the Age of Anne*, 1967.
The Trial of Doctor Sacheverell, 1973.
Horley, Rev. E., *Sefton*, 1893.
Horwitz, Henry, *Parliament, Policy and Politics in the reign of William III*, Manchester 1977.
Houblon, Alice, Lady, *The Houblon Family*, 1907.
Howard, Joseph J., *Visitation of England and Wales*, 32 vols, 1893–1921.
Howell, T. B., *A Complete Collection of State Trials*, 34 vols, 1816–28.
Hunt, N. C., *Two Early Political Associations, the Quakers and the Dissenting Deputies in the Age of Sir Robert Walpole*, Oxford 1961.
Ilchester, Lord, *Henry Fox, First Lord Holland*, 2 vols, 1920.
Jarvis, Rupert C., *Collected Papers on the Jacobite Risings*, Manchester 1972.
Johnstone, Chevalier de, *A Memoir of the Forty-five*, 1820.
Jones, G. H., *The Main Stream of Jacobitism*, Harvard 1954.
Jones, J. R., *The Revolution of 1688 in England*, 1972.
Junius, *Letters of Junius*, 1791.
Kenyon, J. P., *Revolution Principles, the Politics of Party 1689–1720*, 1977.
Kettle, Anne J., 'The Lichfield Races', *Lichfield and S. Staffordshire Archaeological and Historic Society*, vi (1964–6), pp. 39–44.
King, William, *Political and Literary Anecdotes*, 1819.
Kirk, Rev. John, *Biographies of English Catholics in the Eighteenth Century*, 1909.
Lacour-Gayet, G., *La Marine militaire de la France sous le règne de Louis XV*, Paris 1910.
Lang, Andrew, *Pickle the Spy*, 1897.
Lipscomb, George, *The History and Antiquities of the County of Buckingham*, 4 vols, 1847–51.
Luynes, Philippe d'Albert, duc de, *Mémoires du duc de Luynes sur la cour de Louis XV*, ed. L. Dussieux et E. Soulié, 17 vols, Paris 1860–6.
Lodge, John, *The Peerage of Ireland*, revised by Mervyn Archdall, 7 vols, Dublin 1789.
Lyttelton, George, *Memoirs and Correspondence of George Lord Lyttelton*, ed. R. J. Phillimore, 1845.
A Letter to the Tories, 1747 [by G. Lyttelton].
Mahon, Lord, *History of England from the Peace of Utrecht*, 7 vols, 1858.
Letter to *The Times*, 29 Dec. 1864 [as Lord Stanhope].
Malmesbury, *A Series of Letters of the First Earl of Malmesbury, His Family and his Friends from 1748 to 1820*, 2 vols, 1870.
Manchester, Duke of, *Court and Society from Elizabeth to Anne*, 2 vols, 1864.

Manning, O. and Bray, W., *The History and Antiquities of the County of Surrey*, 4 vols, 1804–14.

Marion, M., *Histoire Financière de la France depuis 1715*, 6 vols, Paris 1927–31.

Marchmont, Earls of, *A Selection from the Papers of the Earls of Marchmont*, ed. Sir G. H. Rose, 3 vols, 1831.

Maxwell of Kirkconnel, James, *Narrative of Charles Prince of Wales's expedition to Scotland in the year 1745*, Edinburgh 1841.

Mitchell, A. A., 'London and the Forty Five', *History Today*, Nov. 1965, pp. 719–26.

Molineux, G., *Memoir of the Molineux Family*, 1882.

Morant, Philip, *The history and antiquities of the county of Essex*, 2 vols, 1768.

Mounsey, G. G., *Carlisle in 1745*, 1846.

Murray, John, *Memorials of John Murray of Broughton*, ed. R. F. Bell, (Scottish History Society, xxvii) Edinburgh 1898.

Namier, Sir Lewis, *The Structure of Politics at the Accession of George III*, rev. ed. 1957.

    Crossroads of Power, 1963.

Nash, T. R., *Collections for the history of Worcestershire*, 2 vols, Oxford 1894–5.

Newton, Lady, *The House of Lyme*, 1917.

    Lyme Letters 1660–1760, 1925.

Nichols, John, *The History and antiquities of the county of Leicester*, 4 vols, 1795–1815.

Nichols, John, *Literary Anecdotes of the Eighteenth Century*, 9 vols, 1812–1815.

Noailles, Adrien Maurice, duc de, *Mémoires politiques et militaires*, ed. Millot, 3 vols, Paris 1825.

    Correspondance de Louis XV et du maréchal de Noailles, ed. C. Rousset, 2 vols, Paris 1865.

Northumberland County History Committee, *A History of Northumberland*, 15 vols, 1893–1940.

Ormerod, George, *The History of the County Palatine of Chester*, 3 vols, 1882.

Orrery, Earls of, *The Orrery Papers*, ed. E. C. Boyle, Countess of Cork and Orrery, 2 vols, 1903.

Owen, John B., *The Rise of the Pelhams*, 1957.

Pauli, R., 'Actenstücke zur Thronbesteigung des Welfenhauses in England', *Zeitschrift des Historischer Vereins für Niedersachen*, Leipzig 1883.

[Perceval, Lord, by], *Faction Detected by the evidence of Facts:*

containing an impartial view of parties at home, and affairs abroad,
1742.

Piccioni, Camille, *Les Premiers Commis des Affaires étrangères au xviie et au xviiie siècles*, Paris 1928.

Quarterly Review, anon, 'William Borlase, St. Aubyn and Pope', cxxxix (1875), pp. 367–95.

Richelieu, L. F. A. du Plessis, duc de, *Mémoires authentiques du maréchal de Richelieu*, ed. A. de Boislisle, Paris 1918.

Richmond, H. W., *The Navy in the War of 1739–48*, 3 vols, Cambridge 1920.

Roberts, John Askew, *Wynnstay and the Wynns*, 1876.

Robinson, John, *The Delaval Papers*, Newcastle-upon-Tyne 1890.

Robson, R. J., *The Oxfordshire Election of 1754*, Oxford 1949.

Rogers, N., 'Popular disaffection in London during the Forty Five', *London Journal*, i 1–26.

'Popular Protest in early Hanoverian London', *Past and Present*, lxxix (1978), pp. 70–100.

Rudé, George, *Hanoverian London*, 1971.

Saint-Simon, Louis de Rouvroy, duc de, *Mémoires complètes*, ed. A. de Boilisle, 41 vols, Paris 1923–30.

Sautai, Maurice Théodore, *Les Préliminaries de la Guerre de la Succession d'Autriche*, Paris 1907.

Les Débuts de la Guerre de la Succession d'Autriche, Paris 1909.

Sedgwick, Romney, ed. *The History of Parliament; the House of Commons 1715–1754*, 2 vols, 1970.

Sharpe, R., *London and the Kingdom*, 3 vols, 1894–5.

Simpson, Llewellyn Eardley, *Derby and the Forty-five*, 1933.

Speck, W. A., *Tory & Whig. The Struggle in the Constituencies 1701–15*, 1970.

Tencin, Pierre et Alexandrine Guérin de, *Correspondance du cardinal de Tencin, ministre d'état et de madame de Tencin sa soeur avec la duc de Richelieu*, ed. B. de Laborde, Paris 1790 (in Bibliothèque Nationale).

Terry, Charles Sandford, ed., *The Forty-five. A narrative of the last Jacobite rising by several contemporary hands*, Cambridge 1922.

Thompson, E. P., *Whigs and Hunters. The Origin of the Black Act*, 1975.

Thomas, P. D. G., 'Jacobitism in Wales', *The Welsh History Review*, i (1962), pp. 279–300.

'Wynnstay versus Chirk Castle: Parliamentary elections in Denbighshire 1716–1741', *The National Library of Wales Journal*, xi (1959), pp. 105–23.

Twisden, Sir J. R., *The Family of Twysden and Twisden*, 1939.

Underdown, David, *Royalist Conspiracy in England 1649–1660*, New Haven 1960.

Vaucher, P., *Robert Walpole et la Politique de Fleury (1731–42)*, Paris 1924.

  ed., *Recueil des Instructions données aux ambassadeurs et ministres de France, Angleterre 1698–1791*, Paris 1965.

Vaughan, H. M., 'Welsh Jacobitism', *The Transactions of the Honourable Society of Cymmrodorion*, 1920–1, pp. 11–39.

Vernon, Edward, *The Vernon Papers*, ed. B. M. Ranft, Navy Records Society, 1958.

Victoria History of the Counties of England, *A History of Warwickshire*, 9 vols, 1904–69.

Voltaire, *Précis du Siècle de Louis XV*, 2 vols, Paris 1826.

  Oeuvres complètes, ed. Beuchot, 72 vols, Paris 1829–40.

Walpole, Horace, *Memoirs of the Reign of George II*, ed. Lord Holland, 3 vols, 1846.

  Correspondence (Yale edition), ed. W. S. Lewis, 39 vols, New Haven 1937–74.

Waugh, W. T., *James Wolfe, Man and Soldier*, Montreal 1928.

Westminster Elections [A collection of broadsides relating to parliamentary elections 1741–51].

Yorke, Philip C., *The Life and Correspondence of Philip Yorke, Earl of Hardwicke*, 3 vols, Cambridge 1913.

Index

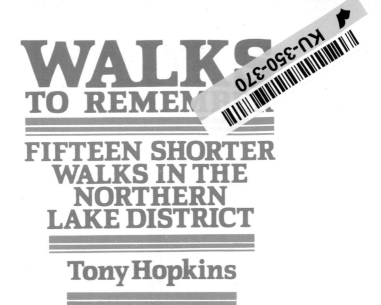

WALKS
TO REMEMBER

FIFTEEN SHORTER
WALKS IN THE
NORTHERN
LAKE DISTRICT

Tony Hopkins

The northern Lake District contains some of the finest upland walks in Britain, famous for their views and for the quality of the surrounding countryside. This book includes fifteen of the most interesting shorter routes with comprehensive interpretive notes, offering an insight into the wildlife, agriculture, history and landscape of the area. There are concise route descriptions, maps, photographs and drawings intended to be useful both on the day of the visit and as a momento to bring back pleasant memories. The walks are circular, starting from a convenient parking place and varying in length from three to eight kilometres. The majority are suitable for a wide range of age and fitness, some concentrating on lakesides and valleys, others on steep wooded slopes or fell tops.

Polecat Press

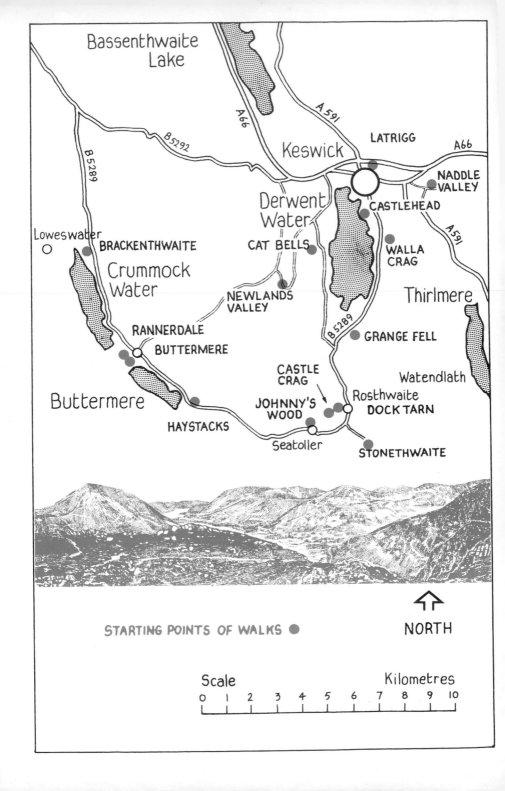

Bassenthwaite
Lake

A66

A591

B5292

Keswick

LATRIGG

A66

B5289

Derwent
Water

NADDLE
VALLEY

CASTLEHEAD

Loweswater

BRACKENTHWAITE

Crummock
Water

CAT BELLS

WALLA
CRAG

A591

NEWLANDS
VALLEY

Thirlmere

RANNERDALE

BUTTERMERE

B5289

GRANGE FELL

Buttermere

CASTLE
CRAG

Watendlath

HAYSTACKS

JOHNNY'S
WOOD

Rosthwaite
DOCK TARN

Seatoller

STONETHWAITE

STARTING POINTS OF WALKS ●

NORTH

Scale

Kilometres

0 1 2 3 4 5 6 7 8 9 10

Contents

Introduction

The unique scenery of the Lake District attracts millions of people every year, but on a brief visit there is little opportunity to discover where the best walks are, or to find answers to the host of questions that come to mind in the course of the day.

This book assembles fifteen of the most attractive and interesting routes in the northern Lake District, the majority requiring little previous walking experience or fitness, selected to illustrate the range c landscapes and habitats that characterise the area.

Selecting a walk

All the walks are circular, starting from places with ample room for parking, but they vary considerably in length, altitude and subject matter. An initial choice of wal may be made by consulting the table below:

| | FEATURES | | | | WEATHER | | | STANDARD | | |
	Scenery	Wildlife	Geology	Local History	Fog	Rain	Snow (lying)	Level of exertion	Length (in km)	Ascent involved (in m)
1 Latrigg	3	4	2	5	2	3	4	3	8	270
2 Castlehead	3	5	3	4	4	4	4	2	5·5	110
3 Walla Crag	4	4	2	2	1	2	2	3	6·5	300
4 Naddle Valley and Low Rigg	3	4	2	3	3	3	4	3	6	170
5 Cat Bells	4	3	2	3	1	2	1	4	6·5	370
6 Newlands Valley	3	3	3	4	4	3	3	1	6·5	70
7 Castle Crag	4	3	3	3	2	3	2	3	5	200
8 Johnny's Wood	3	4	2	2	3	4	3	2	3·5	150
9 Grange Fell	5	5	4	2	1	1	1	4	7·5	330
10 Dock Tarn and Watendlath	5	5	3	2	1	1	1	4	7·5	390
11 Stonethwaite	3	3	2	2	4	2	4	1	4	50
12 Buttermere	4	3	3	3	4	3	4	1	7	10
13 Hay Stacks	5	3	5	1	1	1	1	5	7·5	480
14 Rannerdale	3	2	3	2	1	2	1	3	6	200
15 Brackenthwaite	3	3	3	3	2	2	3	3	5	150

A wet, misty day on Hay Stacks

A scale of 1 to 5 is used to give some idea of the relative merits of each walk (1 = poor, 2 = fair, 3 = good, 4 = excellent, 5 = outstanding). The same scale is used to indicate the suitability of the routes in bad weather. A low score means that the route is hazardous in those conditions, whilst a high score means it is *comparatively* safe.

An assessment of the overall difficulty of each walk is given on the right (a high score indicating that the walk is strenuous), and on the extreme right is the total length of each walk and the amount of ascent involved.

Timing

No assessment of the duration of each walk is given because this will vary according to fitness, inclination and prevailing weather conditions.

As a general rule allow an hour for every 4 kilometres and add 15 minutes for every 100 metres of ascent; this should allow enough time for a few stops and distractions.

Preparation and safety

Boots or stout shoes are necessary on most of the routes, and a waterproof of some sort (preferably a kagoul) is indispensable. Take warm clothing — the fell tops can be cold even in the summer and conditions can deteriorate quickly. A small rucksack is useful to store items of clothing, bars of chocolate, identification guides . . . and walks books! Always err on the side of safety: consult the local weather forecast, give yourself plenty of time and don't be in too much of a hurry. Be prepared to turn back if conditions deteriorate, and avoid any tempting short cuts, especially on high ground.

Route descriptions

Please note that cairns are piles of stones used as route markers; GR stands for Grid Reference, given to help find the starting point of each walk on Ordnance Survey maps (all walks can be found on the 1 inch: 1 mile Lake District Tourist sheet or the 1 : 25000 North West Lakes Outdoor Leisure map); 'm' and 'km' refer to metres and kilometres. The metric system is used throughout: 1 metre = 1.09 yards, 1 kilometre = 0.62 miles.

The maps

A uniform scale of 1 : 25000 has been adopted for maps in the text. All features described in the body of the text are incorporated, and any walls and buildings of use in route-finding have been retained. Contours are in metres, north is always towards the top of the page, and the walking route is superimposed in a second colour with its starting point clearly indicated.

On the walk

Paths in the Lake District are heavily used and it is in everyone's interest to follow the Country Code. In particular, fasten all gates, keep to the recognised path, and take any litter home. Most of the routes follow recognised footpaths but there are several cases where no right of way exists and the path is by permission of the landowner. Please be particularly considerate when passing farmhouses or crossing agricultural land, leave machinery and livestock alone and, if you wish to take a dog, keep it under control on a lead.

The routes may change from time to time according to agreements between the National Park Authority, who administer the footpaths system, and the farmer. Stiles and gates may be changed too, so common sense should be employed when walking a footpath, no matter what a published guide may say.

Most of the Lake District lies within the boundary of the National Park; this accounts for an area of over 224,000 hectares, for which special conservation safeguards exist and provision for visitors is made. Wardens and Information Centres offer advice to walkers and officers liaise with landowners over land management and rights of way. The National Trust is strongly represented too, owning over 50,000 hectares and participating in management agreements to preserve both the landscape and the way of life. Thus the scenery described in this book is the product of many years of endeavour and is part of a national heritage, to be valued and enjoyed by everyone.

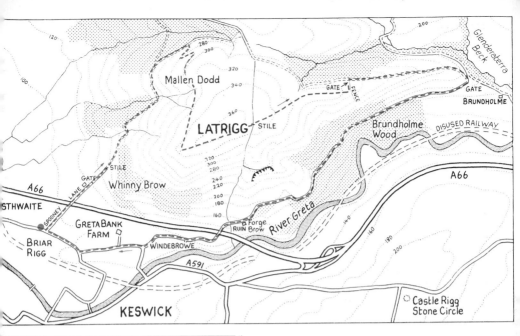

Walk One
LATRIGG

SPOONEY LANE — LATRIGG — BRUNDHOLME — WINDEBROWE; km

Latrigg has always been a favourite walk for the people of Keswick, offering a unique view over the town towards Derwent Water and Borrowdale, but it also provides one of the easiest routes to any worthwhile summit, with a gradual incline and a great deal of associated wildlife and history.

Start at GR 267242. Park on the Briar Rigg road opposite a sideroad to a small housing estate. Take the wide track leading north, signposted 'public bridleway to Skiddaw'. This is Spooney Lane.

The hedgerow alongside the main road is neatly maintained, reflecting a sense of harmony and order. Around the corner in Spooney Lane the situation is different, the hedge having at one time been allowed to grow rampant, too tall, too 'gappy' and too difficult to re-lay. The result has been the introduction of a wire fence with only fragments of the old hedge left to tell the tale. To appreciate the role that hedges once played in the area it is better to be on Latrigg with a view to Bassenthwaite, but a little further along Spooney Lane, just before the bridge, the section to the right at least offers a clue to its pedigree.

Within the space of a few metres there are bushes or trees of holly, ash, elder, hawthorn, sycamore, oak, dog rose, and beech. The diversity suggests that the hedge is very old, probably of medieval origin, and since it was planted on both sides of the track we can assume that Spooney Lane has been there for at least as long. The way back, past Windebrowe and Greta Bank Farm, will provide a few more clues . . . .

7

If it is spring there will be violets and Jack-by-the-hedge in flower, otherwise cow parsley, crosswort and woundwort will cover the verge.

Go over the bridge and up the track.

Before the A66 was built the field on the left stretched right back to Briar Rigg Road. According to the 1840 Tithe Map it was called Spoonah Close; the area ahead was Spoonah Green and the field to the right was called Groat Field. The groat (a silver coin worth 4d, i.e. 4 old pennies) went out of circulation in 1662, and the name perhaps refers to the relative size or quality of the field.

Continue past a building on the left, and through a wicket gate to the right of a five-bar gate. Continue up the track.

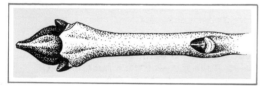

Ash twig

The track, which seems remarkably robust for such an underused route, was constructed around 1800 to allow farm machinery to get up onto the slopes of Latrigg.

The marshy ground to the right contains meadowsweet and yellow loosestrife, whilst the drier banks are inhabited by bramble and the inevitable foxglove. The wooded slope to the right is called Whinny Brow, and since 'whin' is Old Norse for gorse it would seem that gorse bushes have always been a feature of Latrigg.

The fenced area contains ash and larch trees, but close to the track there are several fine thickets of gorse, bursting with yellow flowers in early summer and producing a heavy coconut-scented fug which attracts bees. The foliage of gorse was once used as kindling wood and to fuel bakers' ovens; its capacity to burn fiercely makes it a notorious fire risk in an age of cigarette ends.

Go over the stile to the side of a gate and continue uphill, still keeping to the track which leads alongside a mature spruce plantation before reaching an 'S'-bend and a small stream or gill. At the fork just beyond the bend keep left with the plantation still to your left. Continue past the plantation and over another small bridge. The track bears left and begins to level out.

There is an excellent view to the left; Skiddaw dominates the north whilst to the north-west is Bassenthwaite Lake. The level ground between Bassenthwaite and Derwent Water attracted the first Neolithic farmers to settle in the Lake District and the rich alluvial soil has been intensively used ever since, either for pasture, corn or root crops. Turnip-growing was an especially important development in the area because it revolutionised the winter feeding of sheep, but like most innovations the turnip took a while to catch on; it was not until 1793 when a Mr Atkinson 'was the first in the fruitful and beautiful vale of Bassenthwaite that ventured to sow so much as four acres of turnips in a year; and it being in his younger days, he was sneeringly laughed at by his neighbours'. This observation was penned by William Dickinson in 1850, by which date turnips were an accepted winter fodder, though sheep were also given pine branches to nibble in the belief that the resin acted beneficially on the system of animals confined to such a watery diet . . . .

Just beyond the A66/A591 roundabout is Crosthwaite, its church visible beyond a school field. The church is dedicated to St Kentigern who arrived here about 553 whilst on his way from Glasgow to Wales. Apparently he was fleeing for his life, but when he heard about the people of the mountains who worshipped false gods he stopped off long enough to erect a cross in a clearing, hence the name Crosthwaite.

In more recent times the name Hardwicke Drummond Rawnsley figures prominently in local and national affairs. He was vicar of Crosthwaite at the turn of the century but is best remembered as co-founder of the National Trust. What is sometimes forgotten is that he was also a great activist and led several important campaigns to open the fells to walkers. Two thousand people took

art in a mass trespass along this path after
the route to Latrigg had been blocked. This
was in the late 1880s, long before access to
the countryside had become a national
issue.

**Continue along the track to the right of
another spruce plantation until a grassy
path leads three-quarters right up the
hillside.**

Opposite the path is a small group of
hawthorns, looking rather out of place
among the conifers. The flowers, produced
during the early summer, are prolific but
short-lived and the old name of May
blossom, referring to the appearance of the
flowers on May Day, was made nonsense
by the change from the Julian to the
Gregorian calendar in 1752.

**Walk up the steep grassy track, which zig-
zags several times before heading around
the slope of Mallen Dodd.**

Bracken clothes the ground but it is not
very dense, allowing other plants to survive
so long as they can also tolerate being
grazed heavily by Swaledale sheep. The
bushy grey lichen is called *Cladonia;* in
Scandinavia a closely-related species is the
staple food for reindeer.

The River Greta with Latrigg in the distance

**The path turns abruptly to the left on the
top of Latrigg. Before following this path
walk over to the right for an excellent view
southwards.**

Like many towns with a crowded history,
Keswick seems a disorganised jumble of
streets and houses, surrounded in this case
by a cordon of green fields which enhance
the beauty of the lakeside.

To the east of Derwent Water are Walla
Crag and Bleaberry Fell, on the south shore
is Borrowdale, guarded by King's How and
Castle Crag, and to the west is the fine
range of fells capped by Crag Hill and
Grizedale Pike.

**Now follow the path again which makes its
way north-east with the hilltop to your left
and a steep slope to your right. Continue
along the cairned path to an old drystone
wall (topped by a fence) with a stile in it.
Go through the stile keeping to the same
line on the other side.**

Walls can be old too and this one bears
several signs of antiquity, not least the
amount of moss and lichen growing on it.
The hilltop has no bracken at all, probably
because the soil is too thin and exposed

and spring frosts kill the young fronds. Heather and bilberry would grow here if it were not for the sheep. As it is the only place to find bilberry is in the crevices of the wall, and the ground cover is mostly fescue grass.

Moles are quite common here though their hills are not always obvious. Each mole excavates its own tunnel system and produces several hills in the process, but once it has finished the digging its whole life revolves around waiting for worms to drop in for a meal.

A mole has an active hunting period of about four hours followed by a similar period of rest, so that it gets through four 'days' to our one. For centuries farmers have been trying to eradicate moles ('mow-diwarps') from their land, and in this area they were once successful. According to a report submitted to the Board of Agriculture in 1797 their inspectors 'scarce ever saw a mole-hill upon the enclosed grounds of most parts of Cumberland', and they attributed this to the letting of the mole-catching, any fee being raised by local parishes. There are now a lot more of the creatures about, on in-bye and intake as well as on fells and commons, and the skilled job of catching them is a dying art. The latest form of pest control is to put worms laced with strychnine into the tunnels and trust to the moles' gluttony.

Keep to the path. After a little way there is a wood to your left. Walk parallel with this, still on the path, until you reach a fence (with old hawthorns). At this turn left, then right through a gate. Continue along the rutted track with the wood to your left. When the wood ends follow the crest of the ridge eastwards.

View from Latrigg summit — south clockwise to north

This is an ancient 'green way' known as Wigton Road. To the right the A66 spoils what would otherwise be an attractive view of the wooded banks of the River Greta ('Greta' is Old Norse for rocky stream), the Naddle Valley and St John's Vale beyond.

Ahead and to the left, the lower slopes of Skiddaw and Blencathra are separated by Glenderaterra Beck, with Lonscale Fell to the west and Blease Fell to the east.

The 'in-bye' farmland beyond Lonscale Farm comes to an abrupt end as the ground rises steeply. Beyond the last wall the vegetation is dominated by bracken and rushes and the quality of grazing is drastically reduced. This is the sort of country favoured by foxes, though these days they are of the red lowland type rather than the large grey-coloured variety hunted by John Peel in the early 19th century. Peel was born and raised at Caldbeck, over 15km to the north of here across the wilds of Skiddaw Forest, but it was nothing for him to cover that distance on foot with his 14 couple of hounds, and hunts of 110 - 130km were not unknown at about that time. Today there is still a Blencathra pack of hounds, kennelled at Threlkeld, and although the huntsmen still go on foot the foxes do not seem to be as energetic as they once were.

The path leads down to a gate. Turn right down the metalled road and follow it down to Brundholme Wood. There is an alternative path which bears off the road to the left; this offers a pleasant woodland/riverside walk but is not recommended if you are short of time or are tired. Instead, keep to the road.

At this point the woodland is mostly birch, and since its seeds need light to germinate

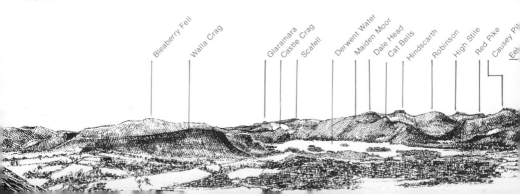

This is a sign that the original oaks were block-felled. Birch is often called 'the lady of the woods' because it is slim and graceful, but it is worthless as a timber crop and is considered a weed by foresters. There are other trees here however, including oak, sycamore and wych elm, with an understorey of hazel. A good mixed habitat which birds favour because it offers a variety of food and shelter.

Continue along the road for several hundred metres.

There are some very fine banks of foxgloves to the right, flowering profusely in most years. Once the flowers have died the seedheads make good table decorations, but make sure that all the seeds have gone if you are tempted to take any home. This is not just in the name of conservation but also to avoid a host of unwanted seedlings appearing in your garden. One of the nastiest of all alien plants, the giant hogweed, is thought to be dispersed not only by wind and water, but also by amateur flower-arrangers in search of something dramatic.

The road eventually leads out of the wood, with a small stone ruin to the left.

The area to the left is Forge Brow, a name dating back to the 16th century when this hillside overlooked the smelting furnaces at Brigham - 'the finest works of their kind in Europe', producing copper ingots for Elizabeth I.

Cross the A66 and bear right along the road.

The noise from the traffic can be irritating, but we have learned to live with progress in a way that would have appalled past generations. The first turnpike road reached Keswick in 1761, at first to unanimous celebration, but second thoughts soon gave way to deep misgivings by those affluent enough to have finer feelings about the environment. Residents like Wordsworth and Canon Rawnsley fought bitterly and with some success to keep railways out of the main valleys. But the ironworks of industrial Cumberland needed coke and a Penrith to Cockermouth Railway was duly constructed in 1865. The line passed through Keswick, just the other side of the river from here, and it brought the first real wave of tourism.

To walkers on the slopes of Latrigg the railway would only have been an occasional distraction. As Bradley wrote in 1901, 'At long intervals there is a rattle and brief commotion, a cloud of smoke, a stampede of wood pigeons, and a scuttle or rabbits, and the horrid thing is gone'.

Keep to the road, which continues straight ahead, past Windebrowe.

Windebrowe appears on the parish record of 1594. 'Old Windebrowe', the collection of buildings on the roadside, once housed a stables and is still used as such, by the Calvert Trust's adventure centre for the disabled which opened in 1978. Rainsley Calvert, who died in 1795 at the age of 21, was a close friend and supporter of Wordsworth, and it was his legacy of £900 which gave the poet freedom to become a full-time writer. Rainsley's older brother, William, lent the house to William and Dorothy Wordsworth who lived here for most of 1794 (during which the *Windy Brow Notebook,* including such poems as 'Salisbury Plain', was written).

A few metres along the road is the entrance

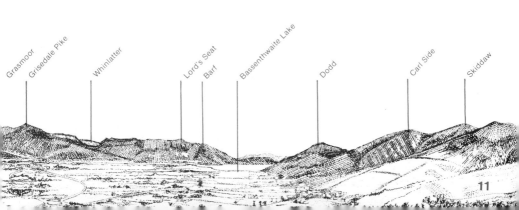

to Windebrowe, a 'mansion with shrubberies', listed as 'Greta Bank' on most old maps but renamed about 1920. A little further on are some fine old trees, the remnants of what must have been a majestic avenue. On the left as the road bears left is a superb oak, probably a pollard, its trunk slightly spiralled (perhaps it was twinned, two saplings together). Its top must have been lopped when still a young tree and the resulting set of shoots allowed to grow into sturdy ascending boughs.

Across the road at this point is a horse chestnut. Behind it is another oak, situated outside a small wood (actually an old orchard). Compare this oak with the one on the left of the road and it will be obvious that it was not interfered with in the same way. Now compare it with yet another mature oak standing out in the middle of the field. Obviously oaks can grow into different shapes; the one on the right close to the horse chestnut grew on the edge of, or just inside the wood, developing into a tall tree with few heavy side branches, whilst the one out in the field has always had light around it and has developed a semi-circular crown. Neither of these trees has moved but the wood edge has been pushed back, to confuse both the trees and local historians..

Continue about 50m along the track, where the road bears right.

Dog's mercury

Few trees are given individual names, but where they are it is usually with good reason; the oak to the left (where a track leads down to the river) is called the Hangman's Tree, its precise history obscure but probably tragic. The triple-stemmed oak in the field to the right bears a name too, the General's Tree, this time following a less sinister episode in the estate's history. In the 1930s Brigadier-General Spedding decided to improve the quality of his sheep stock by introducing a Border-Leicester ram. The ram (or 'tupp'), called John Wooley, was not of benign disposition and its owner was obliged on one memorable occasion to seek refuge in this tree. The experiment with Border-Leicesters was not continued.

Bear right, keeping to the road as it passes Greta Bank Farm and continues west to a junction.

Putting a few of the clues together it is now obvious that the hedge on the right, hiding a row of oak stumps, was part of the original estate and has outlived more imposing structures, buildings and trees, that may have stood close-by. Woodland plants like dog's mercury, growing along the verge, suggest that the hedge began its career even before Kentigern, not as an enclosure perhaps, but certainly as a fragment of woodland left after the first forest clearance.

Turn right, back to Spooney Lane.

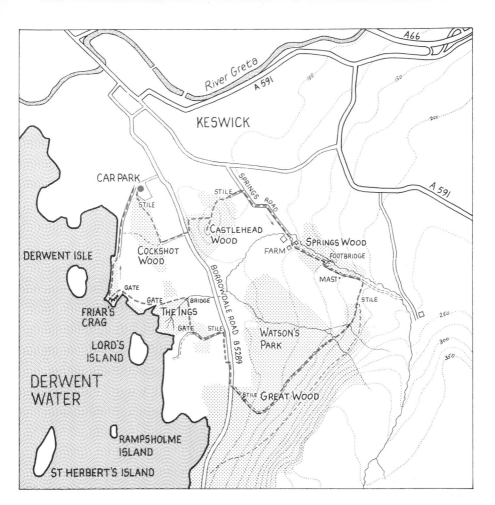

A gentle walk linking five ancient woods and incorporating meadow, pasture, lakeside and a splendid view of Borrowdale. In spite of the route's proximity to Keswick and the tourist honeypot of the north-east shore, most people find it disarmingly enjoyable. It is not wild or remote, simply beautiful.

Walk Two
CASTLEHEAD

COCKSHOT — GREAT WOOD — FRIAR'S CRAG; 5.5km

Start at GR 266229, on the lakeside car park just north of Cockshot Wood.

The grounds of the car park are worth a few minutes inspection because of the wide assortment of trees that have been planted, including whitebeam, cherry, field maple, beech, ash, oak and willow. During the early summer the grassy banks are interesting too, bugle, lady's mantle and pignut combining in an unusual association of woodland and meadow plants. Pignut, a delicate little 'umbellifer' rather like dwarf cow parsley, used to be sought after by country children who lived in blissful ignorance of the fact that a 17th century herbalist had recommended it for its aphrodisiac or 'venery' properties. The 'nut' is in fact difficult to locate without excavating an unsightly hole.

Make for the south corner of the car park, entering Cockshot Wood via a stile. Turn left and walk south along the wood edge.

This is not an especially imposing wood (wait until you see Castlehead); its oak and ash trees have been augmented by beech and sycamore, both introduced by man. Sycamore in particular is cordially hated by naturalists, which may seem odd considering it is a hardwood tree and hardwoods are what naturalists are trying to conserve. Sycamore's flaw is in its pedigree as a native tree; it has only been here for about 400 years and did not arrive by fair means. Oak, ash and most of the others got to Britain by spreading sedately westward over Europe as the ice retreated and the climate improved. About 5,500 years ago the English Channel severed the land-bridge and many plants and animals arrived at the French and Belgian coasts too late. Thus our native British flora is what got here before the deluge, and it took many centuries for man to provide some logical additions. Unfortunately all the associated insects and birds of the European forests could not be so easily transported, resulting in some very dull and lifeless woods.

Continue along the path for about 300m.

Cockshot got its name from Cock-shut i.e. twilight. It is a mixed wood and has a good proportion of oak with hazel growing as an understorey. Vernal flowers like wood anemone and dog's mercury make up the herb layer.

At the cross-roads of paths turn left, out of the wood and up a path with a hedge alongside it.

Some plants seem to like growing in the shade of hedges, the prime example being Jack-by-the-hedge or hedge garlic, which

grows here during early summer. The leaves are large and rounded and taste mildly of garlic (unlike ramsons, which despite what some books say is capable of fumigating every brain cell at the first bite). The flower spike is tall and when the little white flowers have fallen they leave thin green seed-pods. Look closely and you may find a tiny orange egg attached to one of the pods, laid by an orange-tip butterfly. The caterpillar feeds quite openly on the developing pods but is still well camouflaged, thin and green and probably smelling of garlic.

Over the hedge to the left is an attractive view of meadowland and pasture, with Skiddaw brooding in the distance.

The path leads onto the Borrowdale road. Cross the road and turn left towards the northern edge of the wood, then bear right uphill.

You are now among some of the finest trees in the Lake District, oaks of great character and distinction. It is heartening to see that there are also many young oaks too, presumably because Castlehead is not grazed by sheep which would nibble any seedlings to death. Regeneration of native woodland is a national problem largely caused by abuse and thoughtlessness.

Where the path levels out and the fence to the left meets the corner of a field, turn right, a detour which takes you to the top of Castlehead.

The view is remarkably good, especially to the south, of Derwent Water and its delta flanked by a dense skirt of trees and over-looked by open fells and peaks. A busy landscape, almost too full to bear analysis. Instead look at the rock on which you are standing, a fine-grained and very hard material called dolerite bearing tiny crystals of augite. In fact you are possibly standing on a volcano, for dolerite is an igneous rock forced in a molten state through the earth's crust several million years ago. That it does not resemble a volcano today is the result of weathering, in particular by the boulder-filled glaciers which have sandpapered away the surface.

Retrace your route back to the field corner on the wood edge and back onto the path. Continue north-east, downhill.

The footpath through Castlehead Wood, shaded by a mature oak

Bird song is a characteristic of these woods though it is often difficult to separate the sounds and identify the culprits. During May and June the trio of leaf warblers are particularly in evidence. The most memorable of these is the wood warbler which produces a jingle something like 'stip-stip-stititititititipswee'. If this sounds complicated then remember it as a single note that gains speed and ends as a trill. The willow warbler is responsible for another distinctive song, this time a descending ripple, which transcribes onto paper as 'se-se-se-se-see-see-su-su-suit-suit-sueet-sueetew'. Not surprisingly most people find it impossible to imagine this sort of jibberish as a lovely wistful bird song. The last of the trio presents no difficulty however, for the chiffchaff just goes 'chiff chaff'.

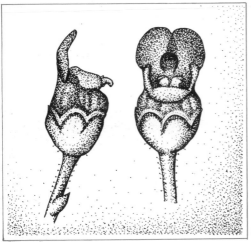

Figwort flowers

The path bears left and out of the wood via a stile. Continue along the tarmac track to a road, at which turn right, heading south-east.

This is Springs Road, a smart suburb of Keswick with some immaculate front gardens full of azalias and laburnums. There is a good view back to Castlehead which stands aloof but contained within the patchwork of meadows.

Continue along the road, which ends in a farmyard. Follow the footpath signs, over the bridge and between the farm buildings into Springs Wood.

This is a fine example of a coppice, the trees once managed for under-wood rather than timber, i.e. for poles which could then be used for basket making, fencing or for the local pencil-making industry in Keswick. Coppice woodland once covered much of England but over the past fifty years it has almost disappeared. Old people are often accused of looking back on their youth through rose-tinted glasses, but in the case of romantic walks along flower-covered woodland rides they are perfectly correct. There really were more flowers in the old days when the coppiced hazels allowed in plenty of spring sunshine, and primroses, bluebells and anemones produced dazzling mosaics of colour.

Walk uphill with the stream on your left, until just before a footbridge. Bear right along a broad track, which then bears left, along the edge of a wood.

This small wood is called 'North Willy Howe Planting' on the 1840 Tithe Map. The trees are mostly downy birch, with some rowan and sycamore. In the early summer the open canopy allows a carpet of bluebells and stitchwort to brighten the banks.

Continue past a radio mast until a path leads right, towards Great Wood. Follow this path, a wall to your left, and enter the wood via a stile. Walk downhill for a few metres until just after a small stream, when a large vehicle track can be seen through a clearing in the larch trees to the right. Bear right along a minor path to join this track and follow it downhill.

Today Great Wood and Watson's Park (to the right) are composed essentially of larch. They present a useful contrast with Castlehead, and bear witness to how native woodland can be sacrificed to profit or popular notions of beauty. Larch is one of the trees that never made it across the land bridge and had to be introduced (from the Alps) in the 18th century, not for its timber but as an ornamental tree to grace country estates.

Walk downhill along the track for several hundred metres (ignoring any side paths) until it meets a gate. Go over the stile next to this gate and bear right to the

Borrowdale road, at which turn right. Walk along the roadside for about 100m then go through a stile on the left and bear right through a small wood to a gravel drive. Turn left and after about 75m go through a wicket gate to the right and into another wood.

This is The Ings, an example of alder and willow 'carr' (marshy woodland) with a profusion of meadowsweet, yellow flag and marsh marigold. There is also figwort, a tall plant with a square stem and tiny round purple/red flowers, much frequented by wasps. The leaves are often eaten-away until they resemble green lace; the creature responsible for this is the grub of a little weevil called *Cionus*. Most weevils are boring little things (literally — they bore through leaves and seeds) but the adult *Cionus* is very attractive and can be found sitting on the seed-heads, but *very* well camouflaged!

Go over a footbridge and bear left until another wicket gate leads you onto parkland on the lake shore.

The east shore of Derwent Water, looking south

Derwent Water now becomes the abiding influence, and Lord's Island, to the south, attracts immediate attention. It is steeped in history, most notably because of its association with the unfortunate Radcliffe family.

Sir Francis Radcliffe fled to the island after being driven out of Northumberland by Parliamentary forces, but his manor house on Lord's Island turned out to be an insecure retreat and was destroyed in 1640.

In 1715 his descendant James Radcliffe, third and last Earl of Derwent water, exhibited the same fatal family trait of being on the losing side, this time taking up the Jacobite cause. He was imprisoned in the Tower of London and would have been spared had he acknowledged George I and the Protestant religion, but he remained loyal to his cousin James Stuart and he was beheaded on February 24th, 1716 at the age of 27. Bright red lights were seen in the sky, the first recorded appearance of the aurora borealis or northern lights, which were referred to thereafter as Lord Derwentwater's Lights.

An obvious path bears right over two small footbridges, leading to a wooded knoll just after a small bay.

This view of Friar's Crag and Derwent Water may give you an uneasy sensation of déjà vu. In fact, it has appeared on so many chocolate boxes and calendars that its image is probably imprinted on half the subconscious minds in Britain. Even the great Victorian traveller John Ruskin considered it 'one of the three or four most beautiful views in Europe'. His opinion was tempered by nostalgia, however, for as a child his first memory was of being taken by his nurse to the brow of the crag where 'the intense joy, mingled with awe, that I had in looking through the mossy roots, over the crag, into the dark lake, has associated itself more or less with all twining roots of trees ever since'.

Like Castlehead, Friar's Crag is made of dolerite, similar in composition to the basalt of Fingals Cave or the Giant's Causeway.

Go through the wicket gate, left and up around the point of Friar's Crag. From there walk north along the lakeside to join a metalled road.

The island close-by to the west is Derwent Isle (sometimes called Vicar's Isle) which is the largest of the Derwent Water group and was once a little enclave for the families of German miners, working the nearby lead and copper mines in the 16th and 17th centuries. It is recorded in the Crosthwaite parish register that in the twenty years after 1565 a total of 176 christenings took place involving German fathers, and one of the descendants of those families, Sir John Rawlinson, became Mayor of London.

Continue north along the road.

To the left are jetties and landing stages offering steam-boat trips over the lake.

The car park is a little further on, to the right.

The Ings in spring; an alder wood carpeted by marsh plants

18

Walk Three
WALLA CRAG

GREAT WOOD — ASHNESS BRIDGE — WALLA CRAG — RAKEFOOT; 6.5km

Walla Crag is one of the best-loved of the lower Lakeland Fells, its panorama quite breathtaking and well worth the modest climb involved. The walk also offers woodland, bracken-covered slopes beneath precipitous crags, high moorland and a fine view over Derwent Water.

Start at GR 272213. Park in Great Wood car park, 2.5km south-west of Keswick, just above the Borrowdale road. Leave the car park by a stile next to a gate, on the south-east side of the parking area. The path curves quickly up and right, to a signed junction. Follow the southern route, way-marked 'Ashness Bridge'.

This part of Great Wood makes you wonder how the place got its name (on the Tithe Map it is called Waterage Bank Wood), but it was once a tract of majestic oaks, a wilderness held in awe and rarely entered.

Fragments of the original wood still survive, but as islands amid more recent conifer planting. Above the path to the left are larches, not without their own beauty especially when, as in this case, there are also rowans and ash trees to break the uniformity.

To the right is an area of coppiced hazel and small saplings, too young as yet to obscure the view of Cat Bells and Causey Pike on the other side of Derwent Water.

Continue to a small footbridge.

The little stream is called Cat Gill, described in 1759 as still being a likely stronghold of wild cats, 'the most fierce and daring animals we have'. The report, by Clarke, goes on to observe that they 'seem to be of the tyger kind', and that twelve were killed during Whitsun week not far away. Not surprisingly the wild cat became extinct in England by the early 19th century.

A reduction in the level of keepering in the Scottish Highlands this century has resulted in a rapid extension towards the Border, so perhaps wild cats will recolonise Cumbria before too long and return to former haunts. If they did it would probably be some time before anybody realised it; wild cats are very shy, not daring or fierce, and certainly not inclined to brush around people's ankles.

The damp face of the rock to the left of the stream is overhung with honeysuckle, the flowers of which have an indescribably beautiful scent. In shadowy conditions the plant produces no flowers however, and its old name of woodbine is more appropriate. The folk ballad 'Spencer the Rover' is just one of many traditional stories referring to the plant:

'With the night fast approaching, to the woods he resorted, with woodbine and ivy his bed for to make.'

Holly and ivy grow here also, linked by their choice of soil and a thread of pre-Christian history. They are endowed with magical power, the holly male and the ivy female, proof against evil and an important part of the mid-winter festival.

Ivy

19

Go over the footbridge; the path descends with a wall to your right.

On the other side of the wall is one of the better remnants of Great Wood, some sturdy oaks clothed in lichens and looking good for another century.

leader climbs up trailing the rope behind him, which he clips into small metal 'nuts' that he places in crevices in the rock, whilst the second holds the end of the rope firmly. Should the leader slip, the second holds the rope and the metal nuts act as pulleys, stopping the leader falling all the way

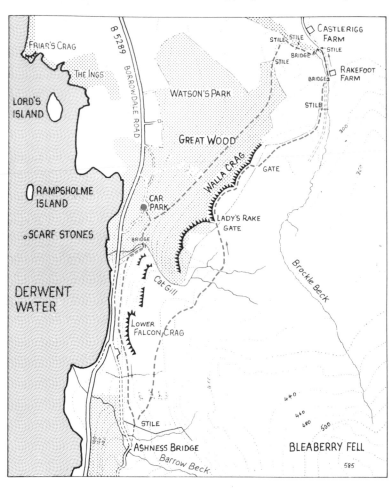

After a few metres the path bears left leading onto a more open hillside with high crags to the left.

This is Falcon Crag - named after the peregrine falcons which still haunt the general area. Look at Lower Falcon Crag and you are likely to see climbers spreadeagled on the 53 metre-high rock-face, for this is a popular climbing route. In each climbing party there is a leader and a second; the

down. The second climber follows with the comparative safety of a rope from above.

Natural history and climbing are often thought to be incompatible (especially when climbers indulge in 'gardening' to clear vegetation from clefts and ledges), but birds of prey like the peregrine have had to learn to co-exist, to cope with a certain level of disturbance.

After passing the second buttress (Lower Falcon Crag) the path rises gently and splits; go straight on, along the path way-marked 'Ashness Bridge'.

There is a good viewpoint to the right of the sign. The 'Jaws of Borrowdale' to the south-west are impressively toothed, but the most remarkable feature is how heavily wooded they seem. This is partly an illusion, the major woods stacked in a line to mask fellsides and fields, but there is no doubt that there really is a high density of tree cover, most of it hardwood timber. The exaggerated slopes and compressed perspective lend the view a flavour of J.R.R. Tolkein, the road to Rivendell.

The path rises gradually via a short series of steps, then crosses a narrow stream.

Usually a quiet tinkling little gill, but storms turn it into a torrent of flying boulders. To the left, uphill, is a low evergreen shrub, a juniper, bearing small dark berries which take two or three years to ripen. Crush a few spiky leaves and they will give off a strong refreshing smell just like gin, the product of volatile oils called monoterpenes. Juniper has a reputation as an aphrodisiac, or as a 'resister of Pestilence', but it can be poisonous and should be treated with respect. It is, incidentally, the favourite foodplant of the elk.

Continue to a ladder stile over a wall.

If you have the time and inclination, go over the stile and walk to Ashness Bridge, about 250m away. Just upstream from the bridge the stones are worn smooth by countless photographers cuffing their boots or elbows trying to frame the perfect picture. It is one of the most photographed scenes in Britain, Derwent Water and Skiddaw in the background and the little packhorse bridge in the foreground. Walk back to the ladder stile and cross it.

A few metres from the wall turn obliquely uphill; the path is sometimes rocky but usually clear on the ground.

There are one or two more juniper bushes, neatly clipped by sheep but still looking healthy. Juniper has one of the best pedigrees of any Lakeland tree, having arrived shortly after the Ice Age when the climate and soil would not support other species.

The view north of Derwent Water is dominated by the islands, particularly St Herbert's Island to the left and Rampsholme to the right. Between them lies a tiny scattering of rocks called Scarf Stones, actually lying due south of Rampsholme. This is a favourite loafing place for waterbirds, especially cormorants, who are shy of people and are often subject to unofficial 'control' because of their efficiency at catching fish.

Eventually the path levels out and becomes grassy.

There are several marshy places, worth inspecting because they contain interesting plants such as cross-leaved heath and butterwort. The latter species was known as rot-grass because it was supposed to cause foot-rot in sheep, but it got its more usual name because it was thought to protect the dairy from fairies. The leaves are pale green with curled edges, bluntly pointed, with a slightly slippery surface designed to catch flies and thereby provide the plant with essential nutrients.

Continue along the wide path, heading north-east.

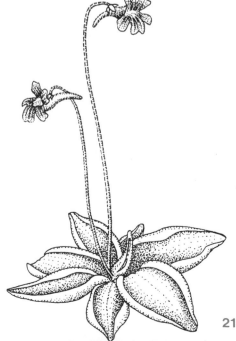

Butterwort

21

To the right there is a fascinating patchwork of vegetation: heather, bracken and mat-grass. Surprisingly sheep find mat-grass, *Nardus stricta*, virtually inedible and it usually grows in the most impoverished conditions, often on the sites of ancient clearings. In the winter it turns white, contrasting with the brown bracken and black heather.

The view to the south-east unfolds gradually, a fine sweep of heather moorland rising to Bleaberry Fell. Heather is the food-plant of some of the most dramatic upland insects such as the northern eggar and emperor moths, both of which have day-flying males who career erratically over the moor at break-neck speed trying to find females. They can detect a potential mate at a range of several hundred metres, a feat made possible by incredibly sensitive feathered antennae capable of registering a few molecules of scent. The emperor is on the wing in April and May, the northern eggar in May and June.

The path bears right, contouring around a headstream of Cat Gill.

There is a good view to the left, over Derwent Water; directly opposite is a green corridor to the Newlands valley, framed between Cat Bells to the left and the forested knoll of Swinside to the right. Behind Newlands can be seen Barrow and Causey Pike, with Hopegill Head and Crag Hill in the distance.

To the north-west is Bassenthwaite Lake, owned by the National Park Authority and one of the least accessible of waters. The more people encouraged to enjoy the countryside the less attractive it can become, and this is particularly true for the wildlife associated with lakes. It seems only right that there should be a few quiet places where access is partly restricted.

Continue north-east then north, to a wicket gate.

Heather moorland is still the major feature to the right, most attractive in late August when the flowers cast a mauve or purple wash over the whole landscape. At other times these are 'black lands', and Bleaberry Fell, rising to 585m (1,932ft) can be rather dour and foreboding. Bilberries (bleaberries) are rather a scarce crop because the bushes are heavily grazed by sheep, but a search of the less accessible banks and crags may produce enough of the blue-black berries in July to make a pie, a gastro-nomic marvel with a transatlantic reputation.

Go through the wicket gate.

The gap to the left, the deep scar on Walla Crag visible from miles around, is Lady's Rake. This was supposed to be the escape route taken by Lady Radcliffe in the 17th century, fleeing with the family treasure from Parliamentary forces who were attack-

View from Walla Crag summit — south-west clockwise to north

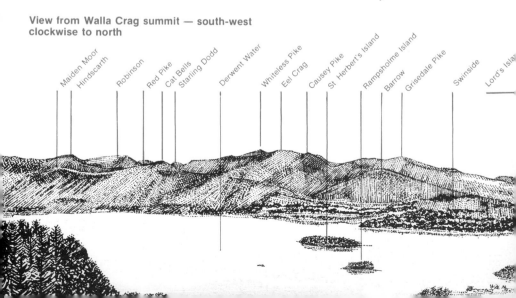

Maiden Moor Hindscarth Robinson Red Pike Cat Bells Starling Dodd Derwent Water Whiteless Pike Eel Crag Causey Pike St Herbert's Island Rampsholme Island Barrow Grisedale Pike Swinside Lord's Isla

Mat-grass, bracken and heather; Bleaberry Fell in the distance

ing Lord's Island. Why she chose such a tortuous route is a mystery; gold coins found among the boulders in subsequent years offer convenient corroboration.

Continue to the summit.

A mighty view, worthy of a much more exhausting climb! The distant peaks are impressive, but so too are the woods and fields in the foreground: Watson's Park, mostly larch trees, then a gap to a narrow ribbon of woodland screening a white house, then another gap to the domed oakwood of Castlehead. To the left, on the lakeshore, lies The Ings, with Friar's Crag to the left and Cockshot Wood (with its large car park) a little way beyond.

To the left of Keswick look for Crosthwaite Church, in line with the lower slope of Thornthwaite Forest on the eastern shore of Bassenthwaite Lake. This was the pivot about which civilisation flourished during the Dark Ages, and is of more recent literary interest as the resting place of Robert Southey, a Poet Laureate little remembered by posterity.

From the summit cairn walk along the path parallel with the crag face.

The trees on the summit of Walla Crag are mostly birch with a few rowan, having grown up after a disastrous fire in 1925 which removed most of the existing cover.

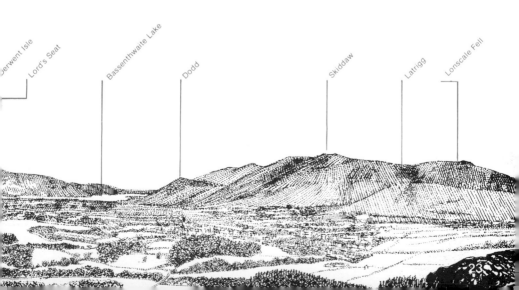

Derwent Isle   Lord's Seat   Bassenthwaite Lake   Dodd   Skiddaw   Latrigg   Lonscale Fell

23

The parallel path leads to a wicket gate through a wall. Walk along the wide grassy path to rejoin the wall, then continue alongside this and downhill, bearing left to cross a stile alongside a gate.

The gateposts are slate slabs, traditional in the Lake District and much more hard-wearing than they look. To the right is the Brockle Beck (Brock = badger of course!), an attractive stream drawing its water from peat-capped fells, and therefore nutrient-poor and acidic in nature. The banks of the beck are wooded with ash, rowan and birch, but there is a scrubby area dominated by bramble which produces some fruit in the autumn. There are several hundred different species of brambles, so it is hardly surprising that some bushes seem to produce better blackberries than others. Compare the leaves and you may find two or three different types in one small patch.

Continue downhill, cross a footbridge and turn left down the road and past Rakefoot Farm. About 100m past the farm entrance is a signpost to Spring Farm. Turn left down to a stile and go over this, then across the field and over a footbridge. Turn right and follow the beck downstream.

There is a bank of woodland still to the right, mostly of ash and beech. These two trees rarely grow together except where they have been deliberately planted. Ash produces a light and dappled shade, beneath which plants like the celandine and anemone can flourish, whilst beech forms a dense dark canopy offering few opportunities for 'vernal' (spring) flowers.

Go over a stile and along the narrow path with the stream still to your right. After crossing a second stile turn left, waymarked 'Great Wood', and continue to another stile leading into the wood. Follow the path down between the trees, ignoring any right turns; continue to a junction with a vehicle track and follow this, still obliquely downhill.

Mostly larch trees now, but there are mossy oak stumps here and there, for much of the year acting as headstones in a quiet woodland graveyard. A few flowers have survived the transition, including the wood sorrel, its small shamrock-shaped leaves often carpeting the banks. Wood sorrel was once used as the basis for a sauce or as part of a salad; try a single leaf, sharp and refreshing, but not recommended in large doses.

Carry on south-west, bearing right when the car park comes into view.

The north-east shore of Derwent Water, Keswick to the top right

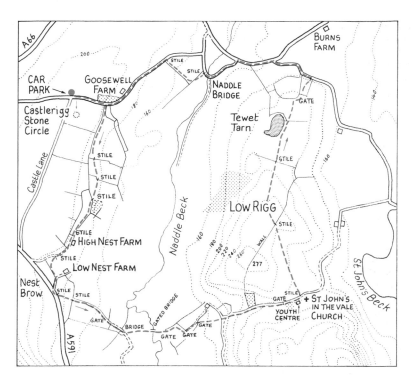

Walk Four
NADDLE VALLEY & LOW RIGG

CASTLERIGG — ST JOHN'S IN THE VALE CHURCH — TEWET TARN; 6km

A walk of great charm rather than grandeur, a combination of low fell and green pasture in which pastoral elements are strong, though the 'Out with Romany' impression of pre-war simplicity is misleading.

Park at GR 292237, on the roadside opposite the entrance to Castlerigg stone circle.

Start with a detour; the route goes along the road and straight past the entrance to the stone circle, but it is impossible to pass by without walking up the field to stand among the stones. Father West, writing in the 18th century, described it as a 'wide circle of rude stones; the awful monument of the barbarous superstition which enslaved the minds of ancient times'. This assessment may have been far from objective, but in truth nobody really knows what stone circles were for.

The Castlerigg or Keswick Stones were put into place in the Bronze Age, probably about 3,000 years ago; there are 48 of them and they are not quite in a circle. Fact then gives way to fantasy, and a host of theories have been put forward to account for such megaliths, the most bizarre being that they were galactic computers, constructed of macro rather than micro chips. The area around the stone circle was once cultivated, a fact revealed by the surrounding ridge and furrow marks. This suggests that our

25

Castlerigg Stone Circle

more recent ancestors were less impressed by the monument than by the comparatively level ground which could be used for crops.

From the gate go east along the roadside, i.e. right when facing the road from the gate.

The hedgerow is remarkably rich in herbs. Some of these, such as woundwort and herb robert, are typical of uncut road verges everywhere, but there are others like wood sorrel and herb bennet which are woodland species and rarely colonise open ground. So this hedge may be the skeleton of an ancient coppice: the variety of trees and bushes (ash, hazel, wych elm etc.) would make it a likely explanation, and it is a pity it has been so badly neglected.

Continue along the roadside until a footpath marked 'The Nest' leads right. Go down the field and make for a stone stile in the wall.

The plantation to the left provides a shelterbelt, a narrow ribbon of trees just wide enough to offer protection to stock in severe weather and to accommodate pheasants for winter shooting. The upper part has been replanted and will be allowed

to mature before another section is cut down. This provides continuous cover whilst allowing a crop of trees to be harvested.

Go through the stile, bearing slightly left and to the left of a bend or kink in the wall ahead. Go through another stile into a third field, this time making for a ladder stile in the right-hand corner, alongside a small plantation.

The trees are mostly pine and larch, again maintained as shelter for stock.

Follow the path to the right of a hedge. This is replaced by a wall as you approach High Nest Farm.

To the right of the path are several sturdy hazel trees, though 'trees' is perhaps the wrong word; bushes might be more accurate. This is as big as they ever seem to get and their natural habitat is as a shrub growing beneath taller trees. Hazel gets its name from the Anglo-Saxon 'haesel', meaning 'command', and wands or sticks of hazel were used long before teachers discovered canes.

Go through the gate and onto a metalled track.

26

This is High Nest, full of fascinating details; past the byre try to find the unusual 'date mark', the vine, the toadflax on the wall. An engaging and apparently ageless world, yet vulnerable to every breath of change.

Continue down the tarmac drive to a stile on the left just before a cattle grid. Cross the stile and walk down the field. Bear a little to the right, to make for a cattle grid on another metalled track below. At the track bear right, with Low Nest Farm to the left, towards a main road.

The hedge to the right, bearing honeysuckle and wild raspberry, is yet another ancient one; the clue this time is wood horsetail, growing on both sides of the track and resembling a finely-structured garden horsetail.

Horsetails have come through the last few hundred million years with little change to their structure. They are closely related to ferns and bear 'cones' rather than flowers, and produce spores rather than seeds. Years ago, before brillo pads were invented, horsetails were used to clean pots and pans. Feel the stem and you can understand why, though the type sold for scouring pads was of a different species and much coarser than the wood horsetail.

The roughness of the stem is caused by tiny deposits of silica (as in sandpaper), a useful adaptation to put-off hungry insects and sheep.

At the main road (on Nest Brow) turn left, and, after 50m, go left at a stile. Cross the field to another stile through a tall drystone wall.

An excellent place to look over the Naddle valley towards High Rigg. The sides of the green and fertile valley end abruptly, meeting the bracken-covered lower fells at a stone wall without any intermediate enclosures or 'intake'. This gives the impression that the fell is neatly contained, like a film-set for the well-known fairy story about a magic cooking pot which buries a village in a great dome of lumpy porridge. Fossilised porridge is perhaps an apt description for the present appearance of the glaciated volcanic rock which forms the fell, but it hardly does justice to its scenic qualities. It is probably a gigantic 'roche

moutonnée', shaped by ice moving over its surface.

From the stile go left and then right around the field edge, following the boundary down to a gate. Go through this and along the farm track.

To the left is a marshy area, the ideal habitat for snipe. During the spring they can be heard 'drumming' overhead, a sound created by air vibrating through the outer tail feathers as the bird descends in a display flight. The sound carries a surprising distance and, like the song of the skylark, seems to fill the sky without any point of origin.

Reed grass

27

The small group of birch trees beyond the fence provides a feeding ground for that most beautiful of game birds, the woodcock. Both snipe and woodcock are shot at but they are extremely difficult to hit. A much more efficient method of catching woodcock for the pot was employed by local poachers; this was a trap known as a 'sprint', an ingenious device involving a line of stones with a gap in the middle across which was set a snare. Woodcock dislike stepping over stones and prefer to look for a convenient gap or gateway.

Walk along the track to a small footbridge over the drainage channel. Bear left just after the bridge, off the track and onto a grassy path. Head towards a white-gated footbridge over the Naddle Beck.

The water is fast and clear with submerged clumps of crowfoot (a sort of aquatic buttercup with white petals) and a border of reed grass.

There are few clues here to the schizophrenic nature of upland streams, usually friendly but capable of ferocious violence. Even the benign becks flanking High Rigg are capable of occasional outbursts. In 1749 there was a memorable storm when 'the inhabitants of the vale [of St John's] heard a strange buzzing noise . . . for two hours together, before the breaking of the clouds . . Catchety Gill swept away a mill and a kiln in five minutes, leaving the place where they stood covered by huge rocks and rubbish, three or four yards deep'. This must have been unusual even by Lake District standards because the inhabitants 'who were scarce less astonished . . than they would have been at the sound of the last trumpet . . climbed the neighbouring tree, and others got on top of hay stacks'. The fields on the valley floor are mostly down to hay or pasture, an indication that flooding still prevents arable crops from being grown with any confidence.

Continue across the bridge and along the path for about 50m to a wicket gate by the side of a five-bar gate. Go through this and across the next field by keeping close to the fence on your left. A wicket gate then leads to the left up a farm track.

The fields are rather more varied here,

perhaps kale or a root crop grown as fodder for Friesian cattle. The pasture is rich too, a mixture of grass and clover providing much better food value and ultimately a good milk yield.

After about 100m leave the track for a wicket gate on the right and continue straight on over rocky outcrops (cairned) to a metalled road.

Looking to the right it is now worth remembering the view across from Nest Brow; this is the meeting point between fell and pasture and it is marked by a very definite boundary wall. The terrain changes completely too, back onto familiar rocks and pebbles.

Follow the track as it climbs steeply, then levels out before approaching the grounds of Carlisle Diocesan Youth Centre and a small plantation of trees.

Before reaching the gates, look right to the open fells. Two small trees attract attention apparently growing out of shallow rock faces on the exposed hillside. They are rowans, a species noted for its resilience and magical power. According to Icelandic legend, Thor was saved from the swollen waters of the River Vimur by catching hold of a rowan, and in Britain stories abound in the north and west about the protection afforded by a rowan branch. But not in the south of England, where it is a tree of suburban gardens and is known as the mountain ash. Presumably its lonely appearance on high hills in the uplands singled it out as a force against evil, protecting the byre and buttery from witchcraft.

The greatest threat to any vegetation on the fells is sheep, and the reason these rowans have escaped their attention is because sheep cannot climb cliffs. Heather and bilberry survive in much the same fugitive way.

Go through the gates and past the Youth Centre. Just beyond it, and almost completely hidden from view, is a church.

This is the church of St John's in the Vale; go through the gate for a walk around the churchyard, which has several interesting

features. The present building dates back only as far as 1845 but there has been a structure of some kind here for much longer.

There is a mysterious well towards the south-west corner, overshadowed by a canopy of yew, holly and rhododendron. Interesting to speculate on how many weary travellers drank from the cup and what unpleasant germs they picked up as a result.

The gravestones bear familiar local names, folk born and raised in the parish. The only wanderers commemorated are the Edmondsons who found their way to South Africa, America and Argentina, at a time when most of their neighbours probably thought Carlisle was a frontier post.

There is also a stone dedicated to John Richardson, a dialect poet of the 19th century who taught at the adjacent school, of which there is now no trace.

When you have finished looking at the fronts of the headstones try looking at the backs, where the clean air has enabled a riot of lichens to transform them into an abstract picture gallery.

From the church cross the road and go over a stile, onto the open fell. Bear slightly to the right, keeping the higher ground to the left and making for a distant wall. The path becomes more distinct as you continue north.

Skiddaw is ahead, with Blencathra much more obvious to the right. Quarries scar the lower slopes of Threlkeld Knotts to the east, culminating to the north-east in the famous Threlkeld Quarries which extract micro-granite from what is probably a laccolith — an intrusion pushed up into a dome beneath the older rock. Unlike good quality slate, granite is only worth quarrying if there is immediate access to a road system for cheap transport.

At the wall, go through the stile. Again the way is not clear on the ground; bear ahead and slightly right, through the shallow gap

29

with Low Rigg to your right. **Bear right, making for the right of Tewet Tarn which should now be visible to the north. Cross a fence in the dip via a stile to the left, then continue over the ridge, still making for the right of the tarn.**

Tewet Tarn, known locally as Tewfit Tarn, is very shallow and has a reputation for freezing early and providing skating practice. 'Tewet' is a colloquial name for lapwing and describes the call of the bird just as well as the more widespread 'peewit'. Try to think of other birds named after their call and you may find it surprisingly difficult. In fact there are four or five, including obscure ones like 'oriole' and obvious ones like 'cuckoo'.

A wall lies ahead. Go over the stile, about 80m up from the tarn, then continue straight ahead (north) for about 100m to a rocky knoll with a wooden signpost.

There are hawthorn bushes just before the knoll, nibbled by generations of sheep into some very strange shapes. The only reason the bushes survive is the protection afforded by their thorns, which deter sheep from trying to reach the new leaf growth.

Bear right alongside a wall; follow this as it turns left, then go through a gate and diagonally right, down a field to the road. Go through the gate and left along the road.

To the right is Blencathra, its elegant saddleback rising to 868m (2,848ft). The high plateau of Mungrisdale Common and Skiddaw Forest stretch beyond, hidden from view but the nearest thing to wilderness that the Lake District has to offer.

In the foreground is Burns Farm. Around the old core are several new buildings added over recent years to house machinery or stock. To the left is a silage clamp, a feature appearing more and more in upland farms. To winter stock requires a great deal of fodder: hay is too unreliable (requiring dry weather for successful harvesting), so silage-making was introduced. Instead of needing a dry haystack, grass for silage is chopped up and rolled in a great pit or clamp with black plastic draped over the top to keep air out. Old tyres are usually used to weight the plastic down; not

very attractive, but efficient. Apart from the obvious visual change, the disadvantage with silage in lowland England is that it is cut earlier than hay, so meadow flowers do not get a chance to produce seed and soon disappear; hence no cowslips. In the Lake District silage is often cut at about the same time as hay, and the chief conservation problem is not the loss of flowers but the increased pollution caused by the massive increase in the use of nitrogenous fertilisers for silage crops.

At the junction turn left onto the main road then first left again.

The bank to the left is covered with bracken and male fern; bracken used to be called lady or female fern and it is interesting to compare them and see what 19th century naturalists considered feminine.

Freud would have an explanation of course particularly for Victorian entomologists who discovered dowdy little moths and gave them names like true lovers knot and maiden's blush.

The road bears right, over a bridge.

This is Naddle Bridge; look to the right where there is an alder grove and a sloe thicket. The thorny cover attracts birds like buntings and warblers which are able to nest in comparative safety. Their chief predator here is the stoat which is a very efficient hunter and is capable of reaching any nest built close to the ground.

There is a gate and a stile on the left side of the road about 30m after the bridge. Go through the stile bearing right across the corner of the field, then through a gateway and across the corner of the next field to a gate. Turn right before the gate and follow the edge of the field uphill to a stile. Go over the stile and turn left along the road.

The road passes Goosewell Farm, another fascinating group of buildings with an old whitewashed byre set amid modern storage and stock sheds. Don't be too surprised to see a peacock around the place — farmers often keep unusual pets.

Continue along the road, up the hill and back to the car park.

Walk Five
CAT BELLS

**GUTHERSCALE — CAT BELLS —
MANESTY PARK — BRANDELHOW
— HAWES END; 6.5km**

*Visitors to Keswick and Derwent
Water are quickly seduced by the
distinctive features of Cat Bells, and
this is one of the most popular of all
the minor fells. The route suggested
here includes the ridge and peak of
Cat Bells, involving two sharp
gradients but sublime views, returning via beautiful parkland on the
lake's shore.*

Cat Bells with Derwent Water to the left

**Start at GR 246212. Park at Gutherscale car
park, reached by following the Grange road
for 3km south of Portinscale. From the car
park follow the side road back towards
Keswick.**

After a few metres the trees to the left give
way to a surprisingly good view both north
and west. Skiddaw dominates the skyline
above Portinscale and Keswick. It is formed
of soft grey shale and siltstone which
weather easily in frost and rain, so that
there is no craggy peak but many cascades
of fine scree. Most of the final shaping of
this landscape came not from glaciers
during the Ice Age but from 'periglacial'
activity, the period of freezing and thawing
that followed in its wake.

Closer at hand is the dome of Swinside,
clothed in a coniferous plantation of pine,
larch and spruce and, across the Newlands
Beck, the treeless whaleback of Barrow.
Just left of the scree area beneath the
flanks of Barrow is Farm Uzzicar, named
after Husaker Tarn. The tarn was drained in
the 13th century but the 'new lands'
reclaimed in the process still provide a
name for the whole valley.

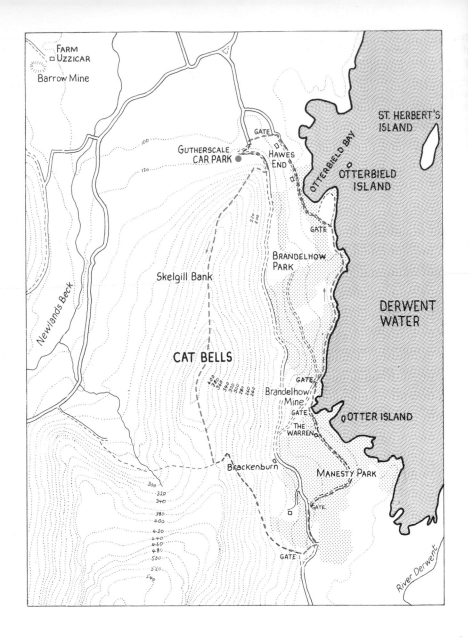

At the junction with the main road bear right, along the Grange road. After about 100m, opposite a sign marked 'Cat Bells ridge', bear right, up a trackway.

The wide track and erosion show how popular the route is. The most common plant here is bracken, but foxglove is also characteristic. Trampling prevents it from flowering, and the broad leaves are not so obvious as the tall flowering spikes. Foxglove, known by all sorts of nicknames such as 'thimbles' and 'deadmen's bellows' contains a toxin called digitalin. In very minute doses it is used medicinally to treat certain heart complaints, but like so many traditional cures it can be lethal in large doses.

fter about 50m a smaller path turns sharp
ght, off the main track. Follow this as it
g-zags up onto the ridge.

is tempting to stop on one of the 'false
eaks' along Skelgill Bank. Take the
pportunity to look out over Derwent
'ater. The islands in particular demand
tention; the nearest is Otterbield. 'Bield'
eans 'place of shelter', but otters are
ncommon in Cumbria now and are
nlikely to return to such an exposed
treat. Behind Otterbield is St Herbert's
land. Herbert was a 7th century hermit
no believed in the contemplative life. He
as a close friend of St Cuthbert, the
opular Bishop of Lindisfarne who also
ent a remarkable amount of his time on
nall islands, such as Hobthrush (off Holy
land) and Farne. The saints met once a
ear, presumably to exchange prayers
ther than gossip, and died on the same
ay in 678. Beyond St Herbert's is
ampsholme Island, and further left
wards the far shore are Lord's Island and
erwent Isle — of which more on walk 2.

ontinue along the crest of the ridge,
eeping to the worn path and avoiding the
ippery grassed slopes.

arrow will still be an obvious feature to
e north-west. Find Farm Uzzicar again
nd you will see, a little to its left, the spoil
eaps of Barrow Mine. Its most prosperous
eriod was in the 1880s when there was a
-foot wheel and a 20 horse-power steam
ngine. Prior to that in the middle of the
th century it had been worked by a
ommunity of self-employed miners each
aying a small tribute to the Keswick
ompany. Many of these singular
aracters hoarded the ore (mostly galena,
errusite and blende) and stored it in
nderground chambers, presumably so that
ey could retire early and live off the
oils. A miner's life was hard and
angerous however, and over the years
cret hoards have occasionally been
scovered, suggesting that the rightful
vners died before they could cash-in their
vings.

llow the path up to the top of Cat Bells
ast the grass-covered remains of some
ry old mine workings on the ridge crest).

om Cat Bells the head of the Newlands
lley looks incredibly verdant, hayfields

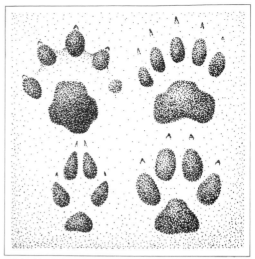

*Animal footprints; otter (top left) badger (top right) fox
(bottom left) and dog (bottom right)*

and pasture sheltered in a lattice of tree-
lined walls and hedges, the improved 'in-
bye' land contrasting sharply with the
bracken-covered fells. Most of the fields are
the result of the great enclosure awards of
the 18th and 19th centuries: before then
there would have been a more open system
of pasture and woodland, less obviously
contained in the basin of the valley.

**From the summit the path descends, still on
the ridge, to a wide flat area before
ascending again. Do not follow the path
uphill again, but from the lowest point of
the flat area turn left towards Derwent
Water, downhill on the path guarded by
rails. The path zig-zags steeply at first and
then slants south-east until level with a
wood on the left.**

Badgers inhabit the nearby woods, and
their tracks can sometimes be seen in
muddy places on the fells where they have
been out at night foraging for food. The
footprint (emblem of the Cumbria Naturalists'
Trust) is distinctive, broad and with five
toes rather than the four associated with
dog or fox prints. Badgers, known locally
as 'pates' or 'grays', were virtually extinct in
the Lake District by the end of the 18th
century following a couple of centuries of
persecution. A bounty of a shilling a head
(literally) nearly finished them off but they
have increased considerably this century,
especially in the southern fells.

Continue alongside the wood (ignore paths joining from the left) to a gate, at which turn left onto a road. Walk left along the roadside for about 300m, then turn right along a metalled track which leads through a gate into Manesty Park.

Manesty, bought by the National Trust in 1905, is very Victorian. Their idea was that woodland should contain a variety of form, shape and colour, and since British trees often weren't up to the required standard, foreign ones brought back by adventurers were introduced. Fortunately, Borrowdale still has many pieces of unspoiled native woodland so it is possible to forgive former excesses and enjoy what is, in fact, a very attractive combination of oak and larch. Wordsworth hated larch trees, but they have the advantage of being deciduous (losing their needles in autumn), allowing some shrubs and flowers to grow in the dappled shade.

In theory most woods should have a shrub zone beneath the canopy, but often this is restricted by grazing animals like deer or sheep which eat anything within reach. The old holly bushes in Manesty Park have a browse line about a metre from the ground, suggesting there are plenty of sheep about with a taste for holly-prickles.

The metalled track leads through the wood to a slate-built house ('The Warren') on the left.

Otter Island — minus any otters — is just offshore in Abbot's Bay, screened by the trees to the right, and is well worth a detour

View from Cat Bells summit — south clockwise to north

for a better view. Back on the main route the track goes through an interesting marshy area with birch and willow trees (native and natural) and rhododendron (Himalayan and introduced).

Continue for about 200m, go through a five-bar gate and along the path between a house and garages, with old boathouses to the right.

There is an extensive area of mine waste just after the house; this is what remains of the Brandley or Brandelhow Mine, dating back many hundreds of years and one of the oldest in the Lake District. It was a lead mine, yielding galena and cerussite, but also some blende (zinc sulphide) and even a little silver and gold. The problem was water, which eventually defeated every effort to keep the shafts open, including the introduction of a steam engine in the middle of the 19th century.

After crossing the mine waste bear left and follow the fence for a few metres before going through the gate to the right and into Brandelhow Park.

This was the first property bought by the National Trust in the Lake District. The Trust was founded in 1895 and its first secretary, Canon Rawnsley, was vicar of Crosthwaite, just west of Keswick. He knew Brandelhow very well and its acquisition for the nation in 1900 must have given him a great deal of satisfaction.

This path must also have been walked regularly by Hugh Walpole, who lived at

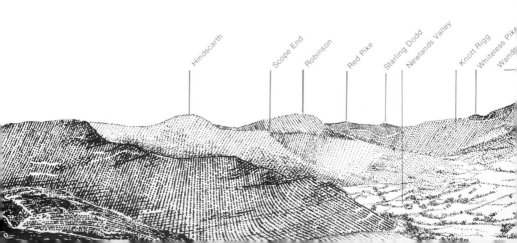

Hindscarth Scope End Robinson Red Pike Starling Dodd Newlands Valley Knott Rigg Whiteless Pike Wand

rackenburn a little way to the south-west, or it is the most direct route from there to ne shore of Derwent Water. Walpole was a rolific novelist and wrote several long tories *(The Herries Chronicle)* set in Sorrowdale and Keswick, but most literary ritics are now dismissive about his work. His name, nearly household in the 1920s nd 30s, is now virtually forgotten.

Srandelhow is rather different to Manesty; nere are some majestic Douglas firs and nese seem particularly attractive to quirrels; not grey squirrels but the native nd much more endearing red. They are oisy animals, chasing each other from tree o tree or dropping cones from overhead ranches and chattering with agitation. They are not always easy to see however, nd patience is not always rewarded. During the autumn and winter red squirrels ave a blackish or dark brown tail, but by ne following summer this has been leached almost white. The coat is moulted wice a year but the ear tufts and the tail nce only — hence a sudden change from vhite to black.

Follow the well-worn track and, when a maller path bears right, go down to the vaterside; a path leads parallel with the hore.

Derwent Water is very shallow compared with most other Cumbrian lakes. When the reat ice sheets melted at the end of the Ice Age (the 'retreat' of the Ice Age) they umped an equally great amount of silt and ebris, which filled up the wide valley of the Derwent. Bassenthwaite Lake and Derwent

Water were joined for a long time, and the land separating them is still very low and marshy. Because it is so shallow (about 22m maximum) Derwent Water does not have any char, a fish characteristic of the deeper lakes. On the other hand both Derwent Water and Bassenthwaite have the vendace, an obscure little whitefish found nowhere else in England. After severe weather vendace are sometimes washed up on the shore, but that is about the only time that they are seen, for unlike the trout they do not rise to any bait.

The curious plant growing in the shallows is quillwort, a primitive non-flowering species most closely related to horsetail.

After several hundred metres of lakeside the path leads through a gate and into a field. The direct path goes left here, following the line of the wall, but a detour along the shore and around the small raised headland offers splendid views and adds little in distance.

Otterbield Bay lies just to the north of the headland, its indented shore collecting silt which in turn has allowed *Phragmites* reed to colonise the shallows. Reed beds are uncommon on most of the larger lakes, the main exception being Esthwaite (to the west of Windermere) which is much richer in nutrients.

Otterbield Island is again visible from the headland, with St Herbert's Island beyond. Beatrix Potter used St Herbert's Island as the setting for her story about Squirrel Nutkin, in which the squirrels boated out to Owl Island to collect hazel nuts.

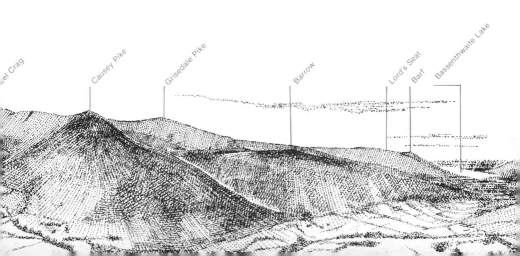

Leave the field via a track and raised walkway which bears right into another field. Continue along this path, bearing left when this divides and taking the higher level to pass close beneath a house and up to a metalled track. Turn right down the track, which passes to the right of Hawes End Centre. Continue for about 50m to a wicket gate on the wooded bank to the left.

The commonest bird along the civilised borders of Derwent Water is the chaffinch, which has become accustomed to the easy living provided by tourists. Chaffinches sit in the trees overhead waiting for people to drop crumbs or uncover seeds on the ground, and in many respects they behave like diminutive vultures. They can be recognised by the white bars on their wings and shoulders, and by their call which has earned them their local name 'spink'.

Go through the gate and bear right, around a grassy knoll to meet a drystone wall. Turn left to meet the road, at which turn left again and walk over a cattle grid to a road junction, then along the road and back to the car park.

The south-west shore of Derwent Water, Otter Island in the foreground

Walk Six
NEWLANDS VALLEY

CHAPEL BRIDGE — LOW SNAB — KELGILL — LITTLE TOWN; 6.5km

It is possible to split this walk into two halves and take these independently (see map, page 38). The upper section of Newlands Valley is very beautiful but difficult of access, and the route suggested is one of the few that keeps to the level valley without suddenly launching itself onto a ridge or steep stream-side. Instead, it concentrates on hay meadows and pasture below the mine-scarred hills of Scope End, Maiden Moor and Cat Bells.

Park on the road verge on the east side of Chapel Bridge, GR 233194, just south of Little Town. Walk over the bridge and go through the gate to the left after about 50m.

There are drystone walls on either side, covered with the coloured spots and dabs of lichens, especially *Lecanora* (white), *Candelariella* and *Xanthoria* (yellow). Lichens are very singular plants; they live for a very long time, can withstand considerable periods of drought, are very sensitive to pollution, and are used in the preparation of dyes and antibiotics. The most curious thing about them, however, is that they function by a form of symbiosis (team work) in which fungi create the outer shell and framework and algae make the food. This complicated arrangement was discovered in the last century by Beatrix Potter.

Walk along the track towards a small church.

Just before the church on the right is a gateway with a 'slope stone', a slate slab with holes in it to take the wooden rails or beams that preceded gates.

Newlands Church is very pretty, mid-European in appearance, painted white and surrounded by sycamore trees enclosed by a neat stone wall. The tiny schoolroom to the left was added just over a century ago but was closed (as a school) in 1967.

Take the left turn, opposite the church, marked as a private road to Low Snab.

The view to the right includes Causey Pike, its unusual cone-tipped summit rising to 617m (2,035ft). To its left are Scar Crags, weathered dramatically into a series of acute ridges and grooves like the heading of a curtain.

Ahead, the valley of the Newlands Beck forks, Scope Beck going off to the right and the main beck continuing due south. Between them lies Scope End, leading upwards to the considerable summit of Hindscarth.

The road goes over a small bridge; go straight on, through the gate, alongside a field and through another gate towards Low Snab Farm.

This is one of the most attractive views of a Lakeland farm in its timeless setting. The slopes of Scope End are grazed by Herdwick sheep from the farm; the nearest neighbour to the south-west is Gatesgarth (by Buttermere), and the distance between the two farms is about 6km.

Apart from the sheep the farm also has a small herd of Ayrshire cattle, kept for their milk. They are preferred to the more usual Friesians because they are less bulky and easier to manage in the small byre.

Go through the gate (close it carefully) and through the farm, taking care not to disturb any work in progress.

Most old farms in the area date back to the period between 1650 and 1750 and have been shaped by function and climate since then. The farmhouse is to the right, the byre and hay barn to the left. High up in

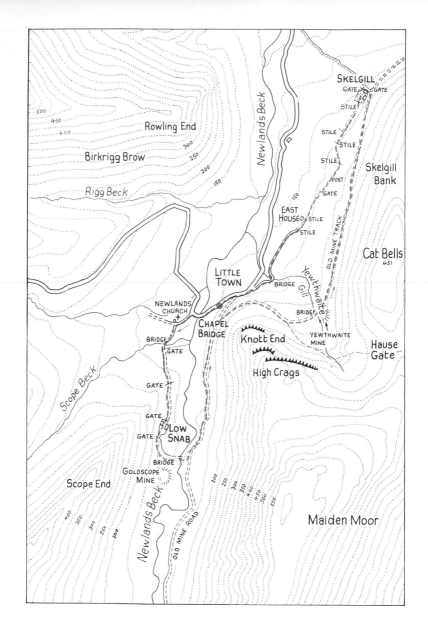

the wall above the byre door is an old pigeon loft, a rare feature in Lakeland and a legacy from the days when there was little fresh meat in the winter and a pigeon pie or two came in handy. This was in the 17th and 18th centuries when farmers could not provide enough hay for their sheep and some of the flock had to be slaughtered in the autumn. The carcasses were cut into 'collops' and hung in open chimneys to smoke dry, a process commemorated in 'Collop Monday' when children were allowed a special feast on the Monday preceding Lent.

Go through the gate at the far end of the farm and continue with the wall to your left.

he great mound of spoil to the right is
om the Goldscope Mine, first mentioned
the 13th century and subsequently one
f the most productive of all the Lakeland
ines. Two parallel veins of lead were
orked, running north-east to south-west,
f which the east lode was up to 4.2m thick.
iagonal to this was a rich 2.7m vein of
opper, and there was some silver and
ome gold also. Little wonder that the
iermans who developed the mine called it
iottes Gaab' (i.e. God's gift), a name the
cals soon corrupted to Goldscope.

he mine finally closed operations in the
iiddle of the 19th century. Apart from the
uge heaps of spoil the only visible features
emaining are the adits or entrances, called
ie Pan Holes, on the slope of Scope End.

**he wall bears left; follow the path which
ads parallel with the wall and down to a
ridge over the beck.**

here is still quite a lot of surface debris to
he right, but it is sobering to see that the
nly monument to hundreds of years of
uman endeavour is an unsightly scatter of
ubble. Some information about the mine
an be deduced from old records, but the
tory of the social and working conditions
ias probably been lost for ever.

ihead are the steep slopes of Maiden
Moor, whilst to the right the beck leads
outh to the 749m (2,473ft) peak of Dale
Head, flanked by High Spy to the east and
Hindscarth to the west. The rocky buttress
utting out on the left side of the valley is
alled Castle Nook.

**Continue over the bridge to join a main
rack after about 100m.**

his is the old mine road leading to Castle -
iook Mine and Dale Head; the copper mine
it Dale Head was opened at the turn of the
7th century by Daniel Hechstetter, a name
hat crops up time and time again in the
Elizabethan exploitation of the Lake District
nines. Most were subsequently closed
either by force or by indirect pressure in
he English Civil War, but many had a
econd lease of life during the Industrial
Revolution.

Turn left and walk along the track.

)rystone walls like the one on the left are
ised as shelter by many small mammals

such as voles and weasels. These rarely
show themselves, however, and the only
creature likely to be seen coming out of a
wall crevice is a wren. This tiny bird not
only nests among the stones but also finds
enough insect food there to keep it alive
throughout the winter. Most insectivorous
birds migrate, but the wren always stays in
its own territory and risks starvation if
weather is severe. After two or three mild
winters the wren becomes the commonest
bird in Britain with up to ten million
breeding pairs, but numbers can crash
dramatically, especially in high fell country
where alternative habitats are limited.

Wren

The view to the left is of the beautiful upper
section of the Newlands valley: hay
meadows, farms, and tree-lined hedges. On
the steep south-facing slopes of the
adjacent fells can be seen two carpets of
trees, the famous Keskadale and Birkrigg
oaks. These small woods climb to an
altitude of about 500m and are thought to
be at the limit of the tree's climatic range in
this country. They have much in common
with Wistman's Wood on Dartmoor but are
composed of sessile rather than
pedunculate oak. Whilst many of the Borrowdale woods were planted, there is little
doubt that these curious stunted and
deformed trees are the descendants of the
original canopy that existed more than
7,000 years ago.

**Just before the track bears right, and with
Chapel Bridge across the field to the left,
there is a green path which angles up
through bracken to the right, below a small
crag. If you wish to complete the whole
walk (a distance of another 4km) take this
path.**

39

If, however, you wish to finish the walk at this point keep to the main track for a few more metres, then turn left down the bank and to the wall end, over a stile at the fence, and left to the car park.

Assuming that you have decided to continue . . . . follow the green path which angles right to join another old mine track, at which continue right.

Ahead on the east side of the Newlands valley is Cat Bells (see walk 5) with the wooded dome of Swinside to the north: to the immediate right is Knott End, the lowest of a triple tier of crags rising via High Crags to Maiden Moor. The west side of Newlands has not yet resolved itself and is dominated by Birkrigg Brow and Rowling End, on the shoulder of Causey Pike.

Continue along the track, bearing right, with the settlement of Little Town to the left. There is now a wall to the left and the track straightens.

The coll or cleft in the ridge between Cat Bells and Maiden Moor is called Hause Gate, 'Hause' meaning a pass.

The untidy mounds on the left bank of Yewthwaite Gill are what remains of Yewthwaite Mine, worked first in the mid-18th century. It was very profitable compared with most other local mines, partly because the shafts were shallow and the ore was easy to extract, requiring a minimum of equipment. Like many mines it suffered closure, only to be reopened and reworked in the mid-19th century. At its peak it was producing 426 tonnes per year: cerrusite, galena and pyrites, worth nearly £6,000 — a fortune for the owner considering the small overheads.

The track follows the wall to the left, then leads over a bridge.

This is Yewthwaite Gill, though at this point the stream itself is usually subterranean. There is spoil above and below the track; a little way beyond the bridge (turning left then bearing right) is an interesting cobbled yard, the most visual evidence of what must once have been a bustling, noisy place.

From the deserted working continue north-north-east for several hundred metres along the track, with the steep slope of Cat Bells to the right.

Beatrix Potter knew this area very well in the late 19th and early 20th centuries; she visited Little Town several times on holiday and staged the story of Mrs Tiggywinkle or the meadows and the lower slopes of Cat Bells. The door of Mrs Tiggywinkle's house is somewhere amongst the bracken to the right of the path, a magical spot the exact location of which was known only to Beatrix Potter, and perhaps to Lucy of Little Town who followed the hedgehog looking for her 'pocket-hankins and her pinny'. Beatrix Potter did much more for the Lake District than write children's stories however; she was a well-respected naturalist who did a great deal of work on fungi (she illustrated a definitive book about toadstools), and with the royalties from her books she bought hundreds of acres of land which she donated to the National Trust.

Eventually the track descends, with the buildings of Skelgill to the left. Turn left onto the road and go through the gate, then bear right in front of the white house. Turn left off the road, along a path and through the gate to the right of this house. This leads through a small plantation of trees to a gate; go over the stile next to this gate and along the green path heading south-west.

Down the hill to the right is an old farm, probably dating back to the late 17th century when the 'long-house' was popular. This allowed the farmer to be under the same roof as his cattle, though why he found this so desirable is a mystery. The smell of cattle was once thought to ward off disease, so perhaps the legendary longevity of farmers was due to ammonia rather than to regular exercise.

Follow the grassy path across the rough pasture and meadowland, crossing two stiles over fences and a ladder stile over a wall. The path then bears slightly right, away from the hedge, making for a post marking the gap through an old field boundary. From here the path continues to the left of a derelict hedge, goes through a wicket gate and follows a ridge (another old field boundary), still heading south-west.

The traditional field system has long fallen into disuse and the hawthorn hedges are almost moribund, though the old banks harbour many wild flowers.

Newlands Church, with Little Town and Cat Bells in the distance

The grassland is predominantly of the 'bent/fescue' type, i.e. *Agrostis* and *Festuca* grasses with occasional crested dogstail, cocksfoot etc. On good ground most fields are planted with better quality grasses like timothy, but gradually even these give way to 'weed' species offering a poorer yield.

Ahead is Little Town at the foot of Maiden Moor, with Scope End in the distance, backed by Dale Head to the left and Robinson to the right. The latter, a peak of 732m (2,417ft) commemorates Richard Robinson who once owned it; immortality in place-names is fickle and one would have expected someone to come up with a more descriptive name in subsequent centuries.

Continue for several hundred metres, crossing old hedge-lines and small streams, **and passing a cottage ('East House') to the right. Go over the stile to the right of a gate, then cross the corner of the field to another stile, leading to a trackway. Walk along the trackway which bears left, over a bridge.**

This is Yewthwaite Gill again, which meets Newlands Beck a little way to the north-west. Newlands Beck eventually feeds into Bassenthwaite Lake. The fields in this area are more functional: for much of the year they hold Swaledale ('Swaddle') sheep or store cattle. The latter are very demanding on winter feed but they are not selective grazers and improve the quality of the pastures by eating-off the less palatable rushes and coarse grasses.

The track bears right to meet the road, at which turn left, through Little Town, and down to the car park.

Walk Seven
CASTLE CRAG

ROSTHWAITE — LOW HOWS WOOD — CASTLE CRAG; 5km

The superb view from Castle Crag is the main object of the exercise, but there is a lot to be seen on the way, especially on the attractive river Derwent and its associated woods and pastures. Much of the route is over gentle terrain, but the final approach is steep and stony and requires some care.

Park at Rosthwaite, either on the roadside on the Keswick (north) side of the village GR 258149, or at a walled car park up the metalled track opposite the Post Office (the end house). The walk begins on this track, heading west away from the road. The track leads to Yew Tree Farm then bears slightly right.

The walls of the farm buildings are of grey slate interwoven with rounded boulders picked from the riverside. Look at the corner of the hay barn on the right; the slates are 'watershot', meaning they are angled downwards so that any rain blown into the gaps runs out again. Minor features like this have been evolved over centuries of hard-earned experience. Hay needs to be kept well ventilated but dry, so a constant through-flow of air is provided by a slatted 'window' on the western face of the building. The roof is of local slate, hard-wearing but difficult to cleave, large heavy pieces at the base decreasing in size to the apex, totally unlike the uniform materials encouraged by modern builders.

Carry on down the gravel track, with stone walls on either side.

Just over the wall on the right is a curious low wooden roof hiding an equally curious concrete structure, a sheep dip, though the dip itself is lost among the various accessories such as the forcing pen, designed to sort out the sheep and to regulate proceedings.

At one time sheep were 'salved' with a mixture of tar and butter, believed to 'promote the growth of wool, and enable the fleece to better resist the wet'. These days a dip suffices; there are many unpleasant parasites on the fells trying to get under the fleece of sheep, so dipping is an essential seasonal exercise involving the use of a strong organophosphorus pesticide. Dieldrin used to be used, but it was banned in 1965 because it was having a drastic effect on wildlife. Predators like the peregrine falcon fed on other birds that had picked up the poison, and the cumulative concentration resulted either in death or sterility. Following the ban imposed on the really nasty pesticides (called organochlorides), the peregrine population has undergone a spectacular recovery and there are now pairs on most suitable Lakeland crags.

At the river bear right, keeping to the riverside track towards a bridge.

A straight, swift-running reach of the Derwent with a deep central channel, its volume of water depending on rainfall over Seathwaite Fell to the south-west.

A pair of dippers usually holds a territory here and can often be seen flying to and fro, low over the water. Dippers look like giant wrens but their characteristic white 'bib' is only visible when viewed head-on, and the chestnut-brown back and short whirring wings are often the best clues. Dippers are noisy birds; they have a loud call ('clink') and a curious song. This is best heard during the winter, because the dipper is one of the earliest nesting birds and is feeding young when most other species are just getting down to selecting sites.

Cross the packhorse bridge and bear right, following the river north on its west side.

Just after the bridge on the right is a small enclosure of oak, ash and rowan, planted with an eye to the future. No naturally-set

eedlings can survive the constant grazing, so
the 'generation gap' of trees has to be bridged
by artificial means.

**Go through the gate and bear right;
continue parallel to the river. The track
makes for the left of a tree-covered knoll
before heading north-east to High Hows
Wood.**

The river is still close by. High Hows Wood is
of very varied structure: oak, birch and hazel,
ash, rowan and holly. Close to the river there

The river is to the right, screened by a small
knoll and a healthy covering of shrubs and
small trees. This type of vegetation is ideal for
birds like the willow warbler which are hidden
from view amongst the foliage, but can find an
ample supply of insect food. Bird-watchers
find these conditions particularly frustrating
because the birds fly about continually and
rarely offer a good view for identification;
Wordsworth must have had this in mind when
he wrote

'Alas! the fowls of heaven have wings.'

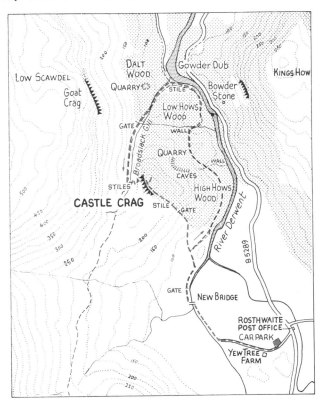

are also alders, not easy to describe except
that the leaves are dark green with a blunt or
indented end rather than a point. Alders are
always associated with water and their orange
seeds, dispersed from small round cones, are
often carried downstream to be eaten by
ducks, finches, mice or, a chance in a million,
to grow into another tree.

**A well-defined path leads through the wood,
with an attractive rocky bank of oaks to the
left, before descending to a flat area of
marshland and scrub.**

Most insectivorous birds arrive from Africa in
April however, so there are a few weeks at the
start of each breeding season when oakwoods
have not grown sufficient leaf cover to
obscure everything and birdwatchers have an
opportunity to tick-off specialities like the
wood warbler and the pied flycatcher.

**Continue along the path, past a wooden sign
to Grange, then up to the left, through a
tumbled-down wall to an old quarry.**

43

There is a cave to the left, damp but shallow, and some old quarry spoil colonised by larch trees.

The path makes its way to the right past the heaps of slate debris and leads uphill back into the wood.

The high wooded crags and quarries often ring with the sound of jackdaws. In the late summer and autumn the birch a little further along the path on the left is colonised by fly agaric toadstools, bright red with white spots and the kind that appear in many fairy stories. Fly agaric belongs to the *Amanitas,* a group that includes death cap and destroying angel, our most deadly fungi. Most people in this country have a policy of not eating toadstools unless they are proved to be harmless, but in France this idea is reversed and everything is eaten unless it is known to be poisonous. Because the death cap looks so unremarkable it has been the cause of many fatalities, whilst fly agaric is distinctive and easy to avoid. In some European countries fly agaric is sprinkled with sugar and placed on windowsills to attract and poison flies, but it has also been used down the centuries as an hallucinating drug or stimulant, often with unfortunate consequences.

At a path junction turn right, descending to a gap in a drystone wall. Go through this and over a flat grassy clearing towards the river, then bear left to keep by the riverside.

In heavy rain this flat area on the river bend is turned into an island, a shallow ox-bow to the left linking with the main river and

sending a stream of water over the raised pathway. The river is lined with alders, their seeds attracting redpolls and siskins.

The path gains height to a gap through the rocks, then leads to a stile and descends again towards a small footbridge.

A good place to stop for a few minutes, though the river bend is too accessible from Grange to make it secluded, and there is a by-road just across the river. This beautiful reach of the river Derwent is called Gowder Dub, 'dub' being a deep pool.

The neck of Borrowdale, opening out to north and south, is where local people are supposed by tradition to have built a great wall to try to stop the last cuckoo from leaving, taking with it the last of the summer. The cuckoo (or 'gowk') sailed just clear of the cam stones, and one of the Borrowdale farmers is supposed to have exclaimed that had they built the wall a little higher they would have caught it. Like so many good folk-tales this one is linked with several other places around Britain, but it has special relevance to this area where the inhabitants of the dale were once innocent victims of the sort of joke now associated with the Irish.

Turn left before the footbridge, going up a track signposted as a bridleway to Seatoller.

Low Hows Wood is to the left, Dalt Wood to the right across Broadslack Gill.

The track crosses by a footbridge to the other side of the gill, then heads to a gate and out of the wood.

View from Castle Crag summit — east clockwise to west

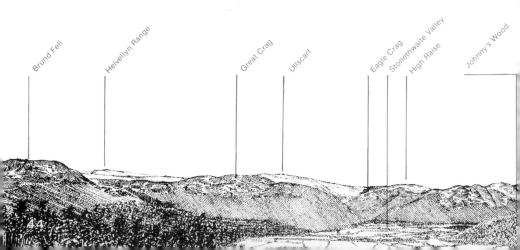

Brund Fell   Helvellyn Range   Great Crag   Ullscarf   Eagle Crag   Stonethwaite Valley   High Raise   Johnny's Wood

44

Derwent Water and Skiddaw, from Castle Crag. In the foreground are the densely wooded slopes of Borrowdale, obscuring the River Derwent

The old track was obviously well used by pack-ponies and was the main route to Rigghead Quarry, but has long been neglected. According to P.B.M. Allen such ancient by-ways have reverted 'to the use of the ghosts of those who made and used them'. Once out of the shadows and through the gate any unpleasant sensation should be dispelled by the view to the right, the rugged slope of Low Scawdel sprinkled with bonsai trees and bushes trying to make the most of thin pockets of soil.

Continue up the track, which is crossed by several small runners or streams, often culverted.

There is a sheep fold to the left, an essential enclosure used for centuries to assemble stock or provide shelter for ewes. The shape of the pen varies according to function, topography or tradition.

Carry on to a flat grassy area with a large cairn, to the left of a stream crossing. Leave the track here and bear left, steeply uphill for about 50m to a wall stile, then to a ladder stile. Go over these and the fence immediately beyond, and take the zig-zagging path uphill.

A tiring last section towards the summit, and because of the slate (quarry waste again) the ascent should be taken carefully. Pine trees have managed to colonise the steep slope, showing that there is not a great deal of rock-slippage away from the path. Pine survives quite happily on thin dry soils, and it is possible that some of these trees are the descendants of post Ice-Age arrivals dating back more than 9,000 years, long before the oak trees took up residence.

The path leads to a flat grassy shelf with a cairn.

Alder leaves and Catkins

It is tempting to continue straight to the top, but stop awhile for the view south, unbeatable on a clear day when the river, green flat fields, walls and hedges, and the buildings of Rosthwaite crowd the foreground in fussy detail compared with the uncompromising peaks all around.

Take the path north, to the top of Castle Crag, just past the trees.

The summit cairn bears a dedication to the

memory of John Harmer and ten other soldiers from Borrowdale, mostly of the Border Regiment, who fell in the Great War.

Derwent Water, with the iron-grey bulk of Skiddaw behind, is the focal point of the view north. Much closer is the village of Grange, which has an honourable history dating back at least to the monks of Furness who developed it as their abbey farm. Borrowdale was purchased by Furness from Alice de Rumelli in 1209, a holding extending from Sty Head and Great Gable to the south-west to Ashness and Dock Tarn to the north-east.

Just across the river Derwent to the right (east) is the Bowder Stone, a giant rock mostly obscured by trees but a favourite tourist attraction. Wordsworth, and Hutchinson before him, described it as resembling a stranded ship; their imagination was obviously keen and more ethereal than our own.

From the summit there is only one way down — the way that you came up. Cairns help to locate the top of the slate zig-zags. At the bottom cairn walk forward about 50m to a ladder stile over a wall close to some trees.

Obviously, ladder stiles have the advantage of not necessitating a gap in the wall, but they also avoid any contact with the stones and this means that the vital cap or camstones are not dislodged — the prelude by which walls begin to disintegrate. The making of drystone walls was a valued skill, now largely irrelevant in an age of barbed wire but still practised because landowners receive financial support to keep the characteristic landscape intact.

A proper drystone wall is broad at its base, has several 'through stones' (often slate) for support, and has its two faces infilled with rubble or 'hearting'. If it is not damaged by careless walkers a wall will last for at least a century, virtually free of maintenance.

Descend steeply left, parallel with the wall, to a wicket gate. The path then skirts left to begin a sinuous descent through open woodland to emerge by a fence gate to join the approach route. Retrace your steps alongside the Derwent to Rosthwaite.

Slate on Castle Crag ▷

Walk Eight
JOHNNY'S WOOD

SEATOLLER — JOHNNY'S WOOD — SCALECLOSE; 3.5km

A walk of two contrasting parts. The first is dominated by a marvellous Borrowdale oakwood flanked by the upper reaches of the river Derwent, the second by Scaleclose and Little Gatesgarthdale beneath High Scawdel and the shoulders of Dale Head and High Spy.

Start at Seatoller car park, GR 245138. Take the path to the left of the toilet block, between the farm buildings and, after 20m, bear right to a five-bar gate. Go through this into an open field.

To the right, beyond the stone wall and across the narrow valley are the Borrowdale Fells, a craggy and inhospitable block rising to Glaramara a little way to the south. The drystone walls in this district are all made from boulders collected from the riverside. Why bring slate from local quarries when an unending supply of ready-graded stone was available close at hand? Borrowdale folk were regarded as slow and backward by the sophisticated inhabitants of Keswick, but they were not stupid.

After about 50m a narrow path bears right, away from the main track. Take the smaller path with a drystone wall to the right. Continue to a wicket gate, through a wall on the right, and along the edge of the wood.

A group of holly trees lies just to the right of the path. Holly is dioecious, a term apparently invented by sadistic biology teachers who would have it pronounced dy-ee-shus, meaning that the male and female flowers are carried on different trees. In this group there is one male tree, producing enough pollen to ensure a fine show of winter berries on the neighbouring female trees.

Look closely at the holly leaves and you will notice that they are more prickly at the base than at the top, a defence against browsing animals. Also, many of the leaves have pale brown blotches on them, caused by the tiny grubs of leaf-mining flies called *Agromyzids* which tunnel into the leaves and feed on the soft inner tissue.

At the gap in the old wall bear left, to keep parallel with the river rather than going down to Folly Bridge. Continue alongside the wall to a five-bar gate leading back into Johnny's Wood. Go through the gate and down the track as it descends to the river, with a stone wall on the right and woodland to the left.

This is a hanging sessile oakwood, and a real charmer. Between great moss-strewn boulders and deep clefts the oaks usually manage to push up straight solid trunks, but their growth is clearly affected by the awkward conditions. There are two species of oak in Britain, and there is a general misconception that the sessile is suited to the rough slopes in the north and west whilst the pedunculate is the tree of the flat lowland plains. In fact although the sessile does show some preference for well-drained acid soils it would grow very well over most of England given the opportunity. Unfortunately it has suffered from a very bad reputation among nurserymen, and although sessile oak is a slower grower in its early years its mature timber is at least as good as that of the pedunculate. The lovely Borrowdale woods may not provide ideal conditions for timber but they are an ideal habitat for rare plants and animals, so much so that they are classified by the Nature Conservancy Council as 'clearly in the first echelon of Grade I sites'.

The track leads to a wicket gate. Go through this and bear left, over a rocky promontory by the river. The path levels out again once it is past the river bend.

impressive, certainly, but sometimes the Derwent can be downright violent. Look at the far bank, in the process of being sliced away bit by bit to reveal great boulders amongst the glacial drift. The water has also sculpted hollows in the river bed and rarely allows rolling stones to stay around long enough to gather any aquatic moss.

wall corner. Continue to the left of the farm building and along another wooded section of the route.

This spot is particularly good for ferns, presumably because it is damp and heavily shaded. If you spend five minutes here you are bound to notice that there are many

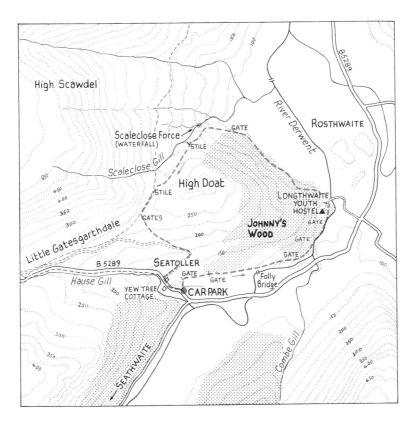

Upland reaches of rivers are uncomfortable places for plants and animals, but look for grey wagtails hawking for flies on the water's edge; they are finely-featured birds coloured grey, yellow, black and white, and are sufficiently common to be anticipated on most riverside walks.

Continue as the path heads north-east through another gate and into the grounds of Longthwaite Youth Hostel. Walk in front of the building and along the metalled track for a few metres. Where the track bears to the right however, you bear left, over the grass to make for a path to the left of the

different kinds. They include great filigree bunches of lady fern and, growing on tree stumps and in damp clefts, polypod and the exquisite beech fern, considered by many to be the most beautiful of them all. None transfer well to gardens, but the Victorians (who else?) went through a craze which saw several of the rarer species all but obliterated.

Continue along the stony track, with the wood to your left.

The fence is there to keep out sheep rather than humans. Grazing animals have prevented any regeneration of oak trees for

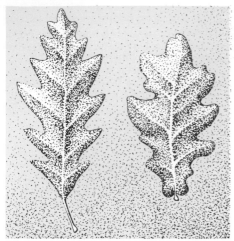

Leaves of sessile (left) and pedunculate oak

many years, but steps have been taken by the National Trust to plant young trees and protect them until they are past the palatable stage.

Until this century the Borrowdale woods, like those of Furness to the south, were worked as an economic concern and their coppices were managed with great care. When woodland products were no longer needed the coppices fell derelict and have been in a geriatric state ever since. Apart from the oak, hazel is the dominant tree. It rarely grows more than five or six metres tall and often goes unnoticed, but during the early spring, when the oak is still in tight bud, it opens out a flurry of catkins or 'lambs' tails' which respond to every breath of wind by delivering clouds of yellow pollen. Unlike holly, hazel is monoecious, carrying both male and female flowers on the same tree; look at the twigs that have the catkins and you should find one or two tiny red tufts on the end of the thick green buds. These are the female flowers which will develop into cobnuts.

Borrowdale was once renowned for its nuts, but hazel bushes need a lot of light and the long period of neglect has resulted in a much reduced crop.

Keep to the wood edge until the track bears uphill to the left, to pick up the line of an old drystone wall. This leads past a National Trust sign to your left and through an old gateway. The track continues to bear left, leading out onto a grassy hillside.

To the north is a fine view of Castle Crag, a cone-shaped hill crying out for a castle. The nearest thing to a ruin today is actually the remains of a slate quarry, which did away with the original earthworks of a Romano-British or Iron Age settlement. The name Borrowdale comes from the Norse 'borgas dalr', the valley of the fortress, so it must once have been an impressive or memorable feature.

Take the grassy track slanting up to the left, following a ruined stone wall on the right. Where the wall ends a path leads downhill into a little wooded valley hiding Scaleclose Force. *Do not take this* but bear left and follow the wide grassy path as it meanders uphill to a wall. Continue with the wall on your left, to take a ladder stile to the left.

The wall has parsley fern growing in it, a plant which prefers high rocky places although it looks as if it ought to be in a herb garden. It does not smell like parsley at all and behaves like any other fern, producing spores rather than seeds.

The noise at this point is produced by Scaleclose Gill, a fast-flowing little torrent with its attractive waterfall hidden by the trees.

Go left uphill, contouring along a rather indistinct grassy path around the hillside for several hundred metres until a ladder stile can be seen to the right, in a stone wall.

To the left is a craggy knoll called High Doat. Jackdaws are usually in evidence, looking like small crows but delivering a noisy 'jack' instead of a 'caw'.

Jackdaws are a nuisance in some villages because of their habit of dropping sticks down chimneys. On crags like this it is easy to understand why they do it. There are no good nest sites in the vertical crevices, but if a stick can be lodged across a narrow gully a platform can be built-up by simply dropping more sticks on top of the first one. Deserted houses sometimes have their chimneys bunged up by thousands of sticks dropped by hundreds of persistent jackdaws; this does not seem to happen so much on open crags, presumably because even the most optimistic birds can see when it is not going to work.

To the north-west is High Scawdel, a shoulder of Dale Head which manages to obscure the main peak with impressive ease.

Bear right, towards the stile.

The dip in the ground should be crossed with care; it is a bog quite capable of wetting your ankles but containing some quite interesting plants, so if you have reasonable boots on it should be worth the inconvenience. The plant to look for is sundew, out in summer and autumn but very easy to overlook as it is usually quite tiny. It has round red-green leaves with sticky hairs which catch gnats and thereby provide the plant with essential nutrients. Sundew gained its name from the globules on the tips of the leaf-hairs, which look like dew but do not evaporate in the hot sunshine.

Gerard (of *Herbal* fame) wrote that 'cattle of the female kinde are stirred up to lust by eating even a small quantitie'. Check that there are no debauched cows about before

you continue.

Cross the stile and turn left along the well-used track. Continue for several hundred metres.

Ahead and to the right is the road to Honister, snaking its way up a nasty incline which once had the R.S.P.C.A. campaigning against cruelty to pack horses. The route has changed somewhat and the original road is now no more than a green track, but the incline is as severe and modern cars complain a lot more than lowly horses ever did. Ahead and to the left is the Seathwaite fork of Borrowdale, famous for being the wettest inhabited place in England.

Under such circumstances one wonders why it continues to be inhabited; the annual rainfall is about 322cm.

The path ends with two adjacent gates. Go through the left one and take the wide grassy path downhill. At the stony track turn left and continue downhill to Seatoller.

Bridge at Longthwaite

Seatoller once had a manor, now reduced in status to a house but still a cut above the local cottages. There used to be a toll house too which is how some people think that the village got its name, but the Old Norse 'saetr' (summer pasture with the alder tree), is a more likely origin.

Yew Tree Cottage, on the right, is dated 1628, and has a yew tree outside it. Was there always a yew tree there, and, more particularly was it *that* yew tree? The answer is that it probably was not — the popular idea that yews grow to be hundreds or thousands of years old is a myth, propagated by people interpreting the Domesday Book too literally.

Continue to the car park.

You will probably find a cordon of chaffinches around your car; they seem to know when lunch is imminent.

Grange Fell

Walk Nine
GRANGE FELL

TROUTDALE — GRANGE FELL — WATENDLATH — HIGH LODORE; 7.5km

This route incorporates some of the best-known spots in northern Lakeland, yet it manages to do so within the context of a varied and exciting walk, using the woods, fells, falls and settlements as integral parts of a landscape rather than as snap-shot images.

Start at GR 262183. Park on the roadside close to the Borrowdale Hotel, 5km south of Keswick on the main road. Walk south on the right side of the main road for several hundred metres until the roadside path ends on a bend. Cross the road (carefully!) and turn up the gravelled track, signed 'Troutdale Cottages'.

The track is shadowed to the left and right by trees and bushes: copper beech, yew and laurel to the left, ash, hawthorn and elder to the right. Perhaps it is its sickly appearance and unpleasant smell that have given elder its dubious reputation. Evil is said to befall anyone who burns or cuts it down and tradition identifies it as the tree used by Judas for his suicide.

By contrast, enchanters' nightshade, which grows in the shade beneath the ash trees on the right, is a rather insignificant plant for such a portentous name, and has no particular magical associations.

A little further along the track is a very beautiful oak wood, growing on the steep north slope of Grange Crags.

At the end of the track is a five-bar gate.

Go through this and on for another 100m until a path bears left to meet a small stream.

The stream is called Comb Gill. About 50m from the main stream is a smaller tributary which runs through a series of narrow walled troughs, the remains of fish ponds built at a time when fresh trout was a welcome addition to the local diet.

The cropped grass on the banks of the stream is colonised by thyme and pignut as well as the usual trio of acid-grassland flowers — foxglove, tormentil and heath bedstraw. 'Bedstraw' was a name applied to any plant used to stuff a mattress in the days when it was prudent to replace the material regularly and get rid of the associated fleas.

After about 100m on the streamside bear right, away from the stream, uphill past a large boulder and through a birchwood.

The rock face to the south-east is Black Crag, containing one of the most famous of the Lake District climbing routes, Troutdale Pinnacles. It was first scaled by two local Borrowdale climbers, Mayson and Mallison, in 1914, at the end of a twenty-year golden age that had produced a generation of adventure-seekers. Those were the days when you shot your chums with a Thornton-Pickard folding ruby camera and crammed into the Wastwater Hotel to watch your heroes play billiard table fives. On the climb itself you were recommended to wear a Norfolk jacket fastened by bulldog buttons, and your footwear would have consisted of wet-day socks, shepherd's walking boots and clinkers.

Follow the path uphill, across a small side-stream and up towards a wall with, at its end by the main stream, a stile.

The craggy woodland was once the home of badgers, hence the name 'Brock Bield' on the map. The ground probably slopes too severely for oak to take a firm hold, so birch has remained the dominant tree. Birch is very short-lived, rarely surviving for more than a hundred years — by which time it has usually been superceded by other species. It is a pioneer of open ground and its seeds are unable to germinate in the shade of existing woodland, so in most situations its presence is a sign of previous clearance or the relief of grazing pressures.

Most mature birches are attacked by the polypore fungus, which sends out large hoof-shaped brackets from the trunk of any affected tree; these tough outgrowths were once used as razor strops, and the fine wood-dust caused by the decay was used by Swiss watch-makers as a polish. Apart from these obscure and obsolete uses foresters have afforded birch only one major virtue — that its sap makes a highly potent wine.

Go over the stile and up the steep path which bears away from the stream for a while.

The more enclosed canopy keeps the atmosphere damp and allows ferns to flourish. The humidity is also responsible for the surprising number of large black slugs (of a species called *Arion ater*), which seem to enjoy a crawl over the path.

Continue uphill to join a very stony path leading even more steeply up a wooded gully onto level open ground. About 100m further on is a fence and stile. Go over this and follow the narrow path up a heather-lined defile.

At the top, a detour of two or three metres on the left will bring you to a rocky knoll with a superb view of Keswick and Derwent Water. To the right (east) is Brown Dodd, to the left Cat Bells and Maiden Moor.

The path now descends towards a wall, at which bear right, keeping the wall to your left. Continue for several hundred metres; the path eventually leaves the wall and bears right, through heather.

Small heath butterfly

Down to the left is a rushy hollow called Long Moss. During the summer small heath butterflies will be on the wing here. They are tawny-brown in colour, and, like all the other members of the 'brown' (Satyrid) family of butterflies, have false eye-spots near the tip of the wings designed to frighten or distract birds. Years ago the large heath, a species characteristic of upland mires, probably occurred here as well, but it is now very rare in the Lake District. Most of the other classic mountain insects like the mountain ringlet butterfly and the orange-tailed bumblebee *Bombus monticola* are still found in this area, but there are few extensive 'mosses' left in Cumbria and the large heath has been unable to adapt to drier habitats.

Continue over the hill brow and join a substantial drystone wall. The path keeps to the right of this wall; after about 100m there is a ladder stile. Cross this and follow the grassy path which leads downhill, over a small stream, and towards a sheep pen.

The view to the right is of the narrow neck of Borrowdale, with Castle Crag (topped by a memorial cairn) the most eye-catching feature. Further south is the River Derwent and Johnny's Wood, with Base Brown and Great Gable in the distance.

The most notable insect of drier heath areas is the tiger beetle, a handsome bright-green creature which runs and flies at incredible speed and spends its life terrorising grubs and caterpillars. Like most predators it is unreliable in its habits, and is at its most active on sunny days. Each tiger beetle probably disposes of hundreds of 'pests' like the heather beetle and the anchor moth, but real heroes remain anonymous and there are no dialect poems dedicated to insects.

Walk past the sheep pen and up the short steep rise. At the top of the path is a junction. Turn sharp left and continue uphill through heather towards Brund Fell. The main path bears right between summit pinnacles.

A scramble of a few metres to the right will bring you to the top of Brund Fell, with an outstandingly craggy panorama typical of the volcanic rocks at the heart of the Lake District. The slabs and boulders bear scars from the Ice Age, lines etched by stones embedded in sheets of ice.

54

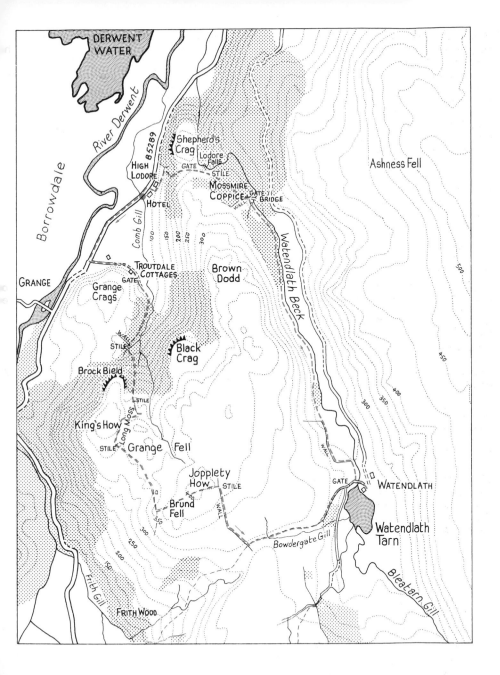

Back on the path, continue east-north-east over the craggy fell. Keep Jopplety How (a distinctive steep-sided hill) to the left and head downhill to a ladder stile over a wall. Cross the stile and turn right, following the wall downhill for several hundred metres.

To the left is some very marshy ground, so keep as close as possible to the wall. Swaledale sheep, identified by their black faces with white muzzles, inhabit the drier ground and are the commonest breed in the area. The world population of the other characteristic breed, the Herdwick, probably stands at no more than 50,000, centred on Borrowdale where most tenancy agreements stipulate that the more traditional breed should be continued, but the Swaledale is considered more cost-effective and numbers have increased considerably in recent years.

Eventually a wide gravel track is reached, at which turn left. At first there is a fence to the right, but towards Watendlath this is replaced by a wall.

The view ahead and to the right is transformed by the appearance of Watendlath Tarn, either deep indigo or lead-grey depending on the state of the wind and weather. On the far side of the valley is a steep hillside incised here and there by tree-lined gullies, rising eastwards above Watendlath to the cairned summit of High Tove. Less than 2km the other side of this 515m hill top is Thirlmere, but because of the intervening spine of hills the distance by the road from here to the north shore of the reservoir is about 17km.

Follow the track down to Watendlath. Just before the packhorse bridge is a gate to the left.

This is the route to follow, but a short detour into the hamlet is hard to resist. The name 'Watendlath' has caused a great deal of speculation among would-be etymologists, culminating in the translation 'the barn at the end of the lake', with 'vatn' translated from Old Norse as the lake and 'endi' as the end. What 'lath' was is not so easily deduced, but the temptation to turn it into

View from Brund Fell summit — north-west clockwise to south

something appropriate has proved almost overwhelming.

Across from the bridge is a barn and a stable; to the right of this is Caffle House, a large whitewashed building offering refreshment to weary walkers. On the far right, flanking the southern side of the settlement, is a series of farm buildings lending the place an authentic flavour, vital to its credibility as the setting for much of Hugh Walpole's *Herries Chronicle*.

Go through the gate on the west bank of the stream. Follow the path for several hundred metres, first alongside the stream, then left at a wall and bearing right beneath the crags. Continue alongside the wall until the path bears right to bring you back to the stream, then keep close to its bank and continue north-north-west.

The water of Watendlath Beck provides a reliable source of insects for pied and grey wagtails, and for the common sandpiper and dipper. Wagtails have a special liking for gnats and other small winged creatures, and when the insect season is over they move downstream or, in the case of the pied wagtail, drift away to farmyards and fields to try a more varied diet. The sandpiper deserts the country entirely, spending the winter in southern Africa, leaving the dipper as the only regular inhabitant of the waterside during winter.

Keep to the path which eventually crosses a footbridge over a small sidestream, then enters a lightly-wooded area and leads to a stone wall with woodland behind and a footbridge to the right across Watendlath

Griesdale Pike Causey Pike Maiden Moor Cat Bells Skiddaw Bleaberry Fell High Seat Watendlath V

Watendlath in December

Beck. Do not cross the bridge but turn left.
Continue for about 50m with the wall on
your right until you reach a wicket gate.
Go through this and walk down the
woodland track.

This is Mossmire Coppice, a block of
sessile oak trees bedecked by mosses and
lichens. Look closely at the trunks and you
will probably find them alive with ants, not
the little black creatures that suddenly
appear in suburban kitchens but big red

wood ants on patrol from their impressive
nests on the forest floor. The ants coming
down the trunks will have scoured the
foliage in search of other insects and will
be dragging their victims (often other ants)
back to the nest to satisfy a million pairs of
hungry mandibles.

If you find an anthill don't get too inquisit-
ive. When ants get angry they squirt formic
acid at any intruder, producing a shimmer-
ing blanket of gas which quickly brings

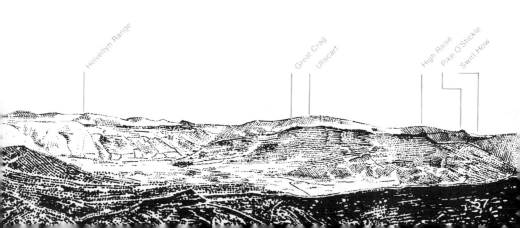

tears to the eyes. Green woodpeckers, which inhabit this wood and feed almost exclusively on ants when they are in season, deliberately wade-in among their prey allowing the formic acid to fumigate their plumage.

Continue along the track for about 200m, to a rocky gap with wooded slopes to left and right. Just as the track starts to descend towards a stream, take a path which bears left. Go over a stile and bear left again. A little further on is a wicket gate.

To the right are the famous Lodore Falls, partly obscured in the summer because of the undergrowth, but this seems only to enhance the mystery of the place. In 1829 Parson and White's Directory observed that on the nearby crag 'oak ash birch holly and wild rose, hang in wanton luxuriance'. So they still do, but the accompanying description of Lodore as the 'Niagara of

England' was taking enthusiasm a little too far.

The damp atmosphere of the gorge encourages ferns and mosses to grow in particular abundance, earning it a mention in many botanic text books. It is also of interest to geologists, forming a shelf between the Borrowdale Volcanic Series of rocks and the Skiddaw Series. But most of all Lodore attracts attention because it is noisy, bustling and beautiful.

About 50m further on, close to a small side-stream by a clump of young birch trees, the path forks; bear left, continue on through a gap in an old wall, then follow the obvious path which zig-zags downhill into Borrowdale, through open woodland to emerge by a stone wall. Go left, through High Lodore Farm to the main road and the Borrowdale Hotel.

Stonethwaite Valley, with Eagle Crag in the distance

Walk Ten
DOCK TARN &
WATENDLATH

ROSTHWAITE — WILLYGRASS GILL — DOCK TARN — WATENDLATH; 7.5km

A very varied walk, starting along the Stonethwaite Beck but ascending suddenly and steeply through woodland to exposed fell, with notable tarns and a few mires along the way. As with most routes that include open fell landscapes, keep this for a reasonably clear day.

Park at the Keswick (north) end of Rosthwaite, on the east side of the road at GR 258149, or at the car park just up the track opposite the Post Office (the end house). Take the metalled track going east on the Keswick side of the Post Office, signposted 'Hazel Bank Hotel'. This leads to a bridge.

It is remarkable how level the bed of the beck is, and how vividly the blue-green stones shine through the water. The structure of a watercourse is a product of several factors, of which the velocity of the current is the most important. At anything more than a metre per second the flow is described as 'torrential' and there is no chance of any silt or sand settling to provide an anchorage for aquatic plants. Occasional 'spates' or flash-floods dislodge or shuffle even the largest stones, settling them again to form a regular, level bed. Apart from the fish, most aquatic animal life is found under the stones; creatures like mayfly nymphs and freshwater shrimps emerge from their shelter at night when they are not so likely to be eaten by wagtails and water shrews.

Cross the bridge and take the right turn before Hazel Bank Hotel.

Hugh Walpole had this house in mind when he wrote *Rogue Herries* — the first book in the long Herries saga. The house is reminiscent of the novels: solid and reliable.

Walk along the walled track with the river on your right.

The bushes on the right are hazel and bird cherry; neither achieves great stature but they are attractive in their season and thoroughly British.

Across the beck is the back of Rosthwaite, and with one notable exception the rear view is just as interesting as the front. The houses are very square, the windows small and functional. Compare the walls and roofs of neighbouring dwellings; thick irregular slates are the genuine article, but even they do not last forever and have had to be replaced in some cases.

Continue along the track.

After the village the most obvious features are the high walls. To the left are some narrow fields, old enclosures used as pasture but without any shelter for stock, so the walls serve a dual function. Most of the drystone walls in the Lake District are the result of 18th or 19th century enclosure awards, but some go back much further — perhaps a thousand years — when flat valley land was cleared around key communities. These settlements bear the suffix 'thwaite', an indication that they date back to the times of Norse settlers arriving from Ireland in the 10th century. Rosthwaite was 'the clearing marked by, or surrounding, a cairn'.

Across the river valley to the right (south-west) is the other fork of Borrowdale, leading away to Seathwaite. Johnny's Wood (see page 48) lies in the foreground.

Follow the track, alternately closely walled or across open fields, for several hundred metres until another track (from Stonethwaite) joins it from the right.

Stonethwaite is another ancient settlement, this time requiring no translation — the name probably records the sheer frustration of trying to clear a few acres of ground in what still seems to be the pebbliest place in

Buzzard

There are several features of interest if an excuse is needed to rest, such as Willygrass Gill, noisy but pretty, with its attractive little gorge to the right of the stile.

The trees are sessile or Durmast oaks, and although they are the natural tree cover for acidic soils on western hillsides they were probably planted as an economic crop, either to replace existing tree cover or poor quality sheep walk. The only good reason for not extending rough grazing over all the common land during the 18th and 19th centuries was if a better return could be secured from woodland industries. The major occupations involved were bark-stripping to produce tannin for leather manufacture, and charcoal-burning to produce fuel for smelting.

The only clues left today are the trees themselves — they often have two or three stems instead of a single trunk, a sign that they were once coppiced (i.e. cut off just above the ground) to force the growth of additional shoots.

At the top of the wood follow the cairned path, easier now, past a small stone structure used as a sheep fold.

This is a good place to stop and look over the valley; the quick ascent through the wood makes it possible to appreciate the contrast in both landscape and land use. These upper fells have always been remote from the farms below, especially in winter.

Prior to the Agrarian Revolution, a percent-age of each man's flock of sheep had to be killed every year because of insufficient grazing. Life among the farmers and shepherds was very frugal in such isolated valleys, and there are several contemporary accounts of unmitigated squalor. It says much for romantic duplicity that Gilpin, writing in 1772, saw things rather differ-ently:

Their herds afford them milk; and their flocks, cloaths . . . the sheep and shep-herds are clothed alike; both in the simple livary of nature.

Cumbria. Across the valley is Bull Crag, topped by Hanging Haystack, a good place to look out for buzzards which like to soar above the wooded crags in search of rabbits or carrion. They are the most likely birds of prey to be seen in the area, though there are also sparrowhawks, peregrines and kestrels.

Continue south-east, through a gate and as before, with the wall to your right.

An alternative to the stony track is to walk along a parallel grassy path a few metres up the hillside. The wood to the left is of oak but the more open lower slopes also contain a few ash and holly trees, both en-couraged by farmers who once used them as fodder.

Go through the next gate (where all the

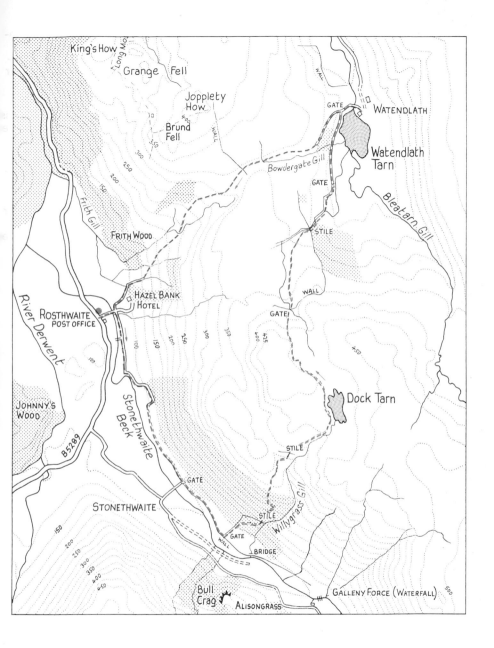

enant and yeoman farmer alike rejoiced at ie arrival of the turnip at the end of the 3th century. Henceforth there was no need ir any return to autumn slaughter and noked carcasses ceased to clutter cottage resides.

The view south is dominated by Eagle Crag with Greenup Edge on the opposite (eastern) side of Greenup Gill. Three kilometres beyond Eagle Crag is High Raise with, two kilometres further in the distance, the Langdale Pikes.

**ontinue around the head of a little valley
nd over a stile.**

here is an impressive view to the right, a
ne sweep to Greenup Gill and its head-
ater towards High Raise.

he path makes its way through some
turdy heather, a plant which needs to be
urnt or cut down every few years to
ncourage fresh growth, and which often
uffers from overgrazing.

**ollow a path alongside a stream to Dock
arn.**

he tarn probably got its name from the
Old English 'docce', meaning a water lily or
ther aquatic plant. High altitude tarns like
his are often very acidic and few water
lants do well, except those specifically
dapted to them such as the curious little
wlwort. The same is true for most birds,
hough the common sandpiper, known
ocally as the 'willylilt', is a regular visitor
uring the spring.

**ake the path along the nearside (i.e. west
ank) of the tarn, past a knoll to the left.
he path continues north-west with a
oggy area to the right.**

umbrians have almost as many names for
ogs as Eskimos do for snow. This one
robably qualifies as a 'flother', a rather wet
ype with sphagnum moss and bog cotton.
he little islands, protected from sheep,
ave clusters of bog asphodel — one of the
oveliest of upland plants, producing bright
ellow flowers in August.

**ollow the path north, descending to a gate
n a wall.**

n the distance Watendlath Tarn and its ad-
acent green fields catch the eye like an
asis in a wilderness. The wide sweep of
narshy ground ahead is colonised by a
lassic plant community composed of bog
nyrtle and purple moor grass. Bog myrtle
s an unattractive name for a low straggly
hrub with few outstanding features, but
he crushed leaves give off a gloriously
ppetising smell. Before the introduction of
ops it was used to flavour beer, providing
he brew with enough body 'to make a man
uickly drunke', according to Gerard's
Herbal.

Watendlath Beck and Tarn

Purple moor grass is also rather inconspic-
uous for most of the year, producing a tall,
rather sparse head of purple-brown seeds.
But during the late summer and autumn the
old stems turn a warm orange, bringing an
unexpected change of colour to the wet-
lands and fells. The leaves curl back and
break off in the autumn winds, earning the
plant its country name of 'flying bent'.

**For about 200m the path is quite clear, but
then it fades and is difficult to make out.
Keep on the same line, however, heading
slightly to the right with Skiddaw on the
skyline. After a few hundred metres of
gentle descent the various small paths join
together, then bear right to follow a wall to
a ladder stile where four enclosure walls
meet. Go over the stile and follow the clear
path by a stream and stone wall down to an
enclosed lane. Go through the gate.**

To the right (east) is the lightly wooded
scarp slope above Bleatarn Gill, which
feeds into Watendlath Tarn. The gnarled
trees by the track are ash pollards, their
branches cut back so that they often seem
half-dead. The twigs of the ash are thick
and brittle, tipped for most of the year by
sooty black buds. An Anglo-Saxon cure for
deafness ran as follows: 'take a green stick
of ash, lay it over a fire, take the juice that
comes out, put it in wool, and stick it in the
ear'. A desperate remedy!

**Continue along the track towards Watend-
lath. Just before the wicket gate on the
edge of the hamlet is a path leading
obliquely to the left, signposted to Rosthwaite. This is the route to follow, but a
short detour into Watendlath will add little
to the total length of the walk.**

There is also a little tea room, not to be
dismissed lightly. Watendlath Tarn is
charming, circled by a ring of water lilies
and stocked with trout — less like an
upland tarn than a large village pond.

Before the Dissolution of the Monasteries
this area was owned by the Cistercians of
Fountains Abbey in Yorkshire, who fished
the waters and tended their flocks in
splendid isolation, for this is a curiously
lonely place even on a sunny day when
tourists are everywhere.

From the Rosthwaite turn walk uphill, heading south-west.

After several hundred metres the ground levels over a wide hill brow, with Jopplety How and Grange Fell high to the right. Alongside the track runs a line of telegraph poles, not pretty but important to the local community. Many features of modern civilisation are obtrusive in the countryside and none more so than power cables and telegraph wires. The Friends of the Lake District waged a successful battle in 1937 to prevent electricity pylons invading the area and most power lines now run underground, but the cost prohibits a total cover up.

Follow the track, stony in places, as it winds downhill through light woodland. Just before a small stream (Frith Gill) turn right through a gap in the wall, descending again to rejoin the stream a little further down. Cross it via a raised walkway, continue past Hazel Bank Hotel and turn right, back to Rosthwaite.

A wall stile

Walk Eleven
STONETHWAITE

**STONETHWAITE — GALLENY
FORCE — JOHNNY HOUSE —
ALISONGRASS; 4km**

*A short walk over level ground, often
stony and difficult during very wet
weather when the fells can brood
ominously on all sides, yet remarkable for the ease with which quiet
rurality gives way to apparent
wilderness, and for the constantly
changing character of Stonethwaite
Beck.*

**Start from GR 263137. Park in Stonethwaite
village, close to the telephone kiosk if this
is possible. From this kiosk take the track
leading towards the beck.**

Close to the cottages the track is overhung
with wild cherry.

A notice on the bridge states that it was
erected in 1899 but had to be rebuilt in
1979. Being swept away or damaged by torrential spates of water is the normal fate for
most bridges in Cumbria, and accounts for
the relative scarcity of picturesque stone
structures.

From the bridge the whole valley seems to
be heavily wooded, especially downstream
where the Borrowdale oakwoods cover
most of the lower slopes. 'Thwaite' means a
clearing however, and there is little doubt
that early settlers found a terrace here from
where they could begin to push back the
wildwood and create pasture for their stock.

**Go over the bridge and through a gate to
the junction with another track. Turn right.**

The deformed trees are ash. Cutting off the
branches at head-height is a process
known as pollarding, a traditional form of
management designed to provide a self-
renewing crop every few years. It used to
provide farmers with a dual harvest, the
wood being sent away to make tool handles
whilst the foliage and bark were fed to
stock. Unfortunately cheap imports of
hickory from the New World killed off the
market for ash wood, and it was discovered
that dairy cattle produced poorer milk
yields when fed on ash leaves.

Pollarding may produce deformed trees but
for some reason it increases their life ex-
pectancy, and most of Britain's oldest trees
were pollarded at some time in their youth.

**Follow the trackway up the valley, keeping
the wall to your right.**

A very stony track; the larger boulders to
the left have been colonised by interesting
plants such as foxglove and parsley fern,
contrasting with the wall itself which is in
heavy shade and has little growing on it
except a few lichens.

The open ground between the track and the
oakwood is grazed by sheep, and there is a
small circular fold or pen used by
shepherds to hold flocks temporarily or to
provide shelter for ewes with lambs.

**After a few hundred metres the wood on
the left begins to recede and, after passing
a small larch plantation, the path leads over
a small bridge across Willygrass Gill.**

Pollarded tree

65

The view to the right is of Bull Crag, a steep wooded slope with an attractive jumble of rocks. Large black birds will probably be crows, but *very* large black birds might be ravens. They keep to the upper crags above the tree line and are usually seen either singly or in pairs. Considering their size and bulk, ravens are masters of flight and will often perform acrobatic tumbles and twists for the sheer pleasure of it. They are still common in the Lake District, despite persecution and a bad reputation. The Ancient Greeks thought that rubbing a raven's egg into your hair prevented it from going grey, but apparently there was a risk that the magic might be too powerful and turn your teeth black.

Continue along the track for another few hundred metres to pass a group of yew trees and a small stone ruin.

Yews are often associated with habitation, and particularly with churchyards. In pagan times the tree held great spiritual significance and was planted in sacred places, so when Christianity took over the sacred places it also took over the yew. When a venerable old tree died it was replaced with a new one, and so on down the years.

This group of yews has examples of both sexes, the male developing little green or yellow flowers in the summer and the female producing bright red arils in autumn. The aril contains a clear sticky go enclosing the seed, and for some reason thrushes find this irresistible.

Keep to the same track. After a slight rise level it descends again to lead through a gate.

The track is very stony and is in the process of being eroded away by the beck. The channel fills very rapidly after rain; this is because it is fed by many small streams or gills taking run-off from the immediate

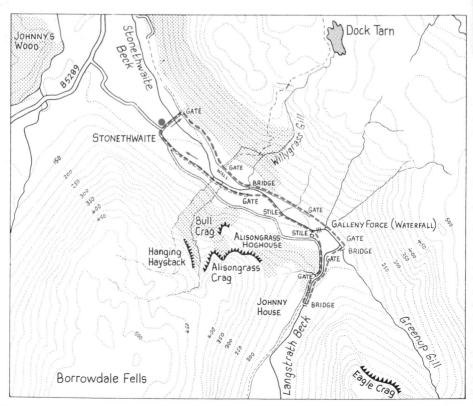

w trees and sheep fold, Stonethwaite Beck in the distance

lls rather than from distant headstreams.
he small waterfall, called Galleny Force, is
est viewed from the other bank on the
eturn leg, but is still worth a look.

little way ahead is a sheep-fold. Take the
icket gate to the right just before this is
eached, leading to a footbridge over
reenup Gill.

ooking at the bare stones and the fierce
urrent it is difficult to believe that anything
an live in the water, but several insects
ave adapted themselves to the conditions
nd are to be found clinging to the
ndersides of submerged stones. The most
ramatic are the larvae of mayflies and
oneflies, which have incredibly flattened
odies and long tails. They are full-grown
the spring, just before they change into
dults, but are very nimble and difficult to
tch. Along with caddisfly larvae they are
e chief food-source for the trout and for
erside birds like the dipper.

**Go over the bridge and through a wicket
gate.**

To the left is one of the most desolate
valleys in the whole area, guarded by Eagle
Crag, which lost its eyrie many years ago.
Eagles were never popular with farmers:
'The devastation made on the fold, in the
breeding season, by one eyrie is computed
as a lamb a day' wrote Father West in the
18th century. He also described how this
site was destroyed by a shepherd 'let down
the summit of this dreadful rock by a rope
of twenty fathoms'. The rope referred to
was paid for by general subscription, and
was kept in Borrowdale for this express
purpose. No doubt the eagles tried to
rebuild again and again for they are
remarkably faithful to traditional sites, but
in the end they went the way of all
predators.

**Walk alongside the Langstrath Beck for a
little way before bearing left to pick up the
path.**

This gives you the opportunity to explore a beautifully sculpted little chasm through which the beck runs. There are cascades of white water and deep pools refracting the green or turquoise of submerged boulders. The colour comes from chlorite contained in the volcanic rocks.

Walk south-west along the grassy path, marshy in places, through a gap in a ruined drystone wall, to a footbridge over Langstrath Beck.

A substantial bridge which seems out of proportion to the amount of traffic it carries. Presumably anything less robust would be washed away when Langstrath Beck asserted itself. The banks are overhung by some fine downy birches, their trunks less white than silver birch and their young twigs slightly pubescent. There are also some rowans, which produce lovely orange berries popular with wine-makers.

To the left the dale of Langstrath leads away to Esk Hause, the wettest place in England. Langstrath is one of the least spoiled and least visited of the main valleys,

just as desolate as the route alongside Greenup Gill and reaching much further into the core of the Lake District.

The surrounding fells are reputed to 'attract the vapours', and there is often a soggy blanket of cloud hanging over the dale head.

Go over the footbridge and turn right. Follow the track to a gate.

There is an old oak tree to the right. Oak produces its foliage quite late into the spring, usually just after the ash. The rhyme 'ash before oak and we're in for a soak' is therefore a safe enough prediction in most years. Another weather-inspired verse, 'If the thrush sings 'fore Candlemas Day it does nowt after but repent and pray' is a saying based on a much better appreciation of Lake District weather. Candlemas is February 2nd, and thrushes have a nasty habit of starting too early after a mild winter.

By the middle of the summer oak leaves are usually peppered with holes, having been the food for a vast array of caterpillars,

Stonethwaite village

arrow

ugs and beetles. More species of insects
eed on oak than on any other tree, and
rom the end of June the foliage begins to
ear the scars. It is not an unequal contest,
owever, for the oak produces tannins
which gradually make the leaves inedible.
nsects therefore have to time their
reeding season to coincide with the period
f early leaf growth.

**Keep to the track, which veers left away
rom the beck only to rejoin it after 200m. A
rack then bears left, towards a small build-
ng, but avoid this and instead go over a
tile to keep close to the beck.**

Upstream the beck is at its most beautiful,
ot to be passed without stopping for at
ast a moment's contemplation.

he little hut to the left is a 'hogg house',
uilt not to accommodate pigs (which were
nown as 'gris'), but young sheep or
oggs'. The normal practice in the 18th
nd 19th centuries was to keep the replace-
ent stock in these buildings during the
orst of the winter and feed them on hay.
When the young sheep were into their third
ear they were introduced into the flock, by
which time they were robust and healthy
nough to survive and bear lambs.

**Continue along the path; the ground rises
lightly to a ladder stile, after which it levels
ut to a wide grassy shelf.**

his is an area popular with campers. As
ell as the usual yarrow and foxglove there
 a healthy population of plantain, a low-
rowing plant appearing wherever man
upsets the normal vegetation. Red Indians
called it 'white man's footprint' and Nature
Reserve wardens find it in all sorts of
unwanted places, and probably call it
something worse.

Carry on north-west towards Stonethwaite.

Quite suddenly you are entering an
agricultural landscape of level pastures and
ash pollards. This area can have changed
little since the 13th century, when it formed
part of the thriving vaccary (dairy farm) of
Stonethwaite. It was so desirable a property
that the abbeys of Furness and Fountains
squabbled for years over ownership, until
Edward I was obliged to confiscate it. This
was in 1304; the Abbot at Fountains must
have been a shrewd businessman for he immediately offered the King 40 shillings and
got the place back without any redress
from Furness.

**Go through a gate and along the road back
to the car park.**

Look at the gardens as you go by, phlox
and magnolia, Victorian to the core. The
walls of the cottages are whitewashed, layer
upon layer of the stuff, until after a few
centuries the surface has grown to
resemble thick icing. Byres and outbuildings were not painted — air whistling
through gaps in the walls kept cattle free
from T.B., and hay cool enough to prevent
fermentation or spontaneous combustion.

Continue along the road to the car park.

Walk Twelve
BUTTERMERE

A CIRCUIT OF THE LAKE; 7km

A walk of reflected glory, the fells mirrored in a sheet of glass. Buttermere is one of the few lakes with a footpath right around it. The steep fells on either side, wooded on the lower slopes but dramatically unnamed, contrast with the level pastures to the north-east and southwest and the smooth surface of the water. The 'Buttermere Round' was one of the most popular Victorian walks; they eulogised it in a way that would seem excessive even by modern holiday brochure standards, yet much of the praise was wellmerited. It is varied, easy underfoot, and suitable for all ages.

Start at GR 174169. Park in the village car park close to the Fish Hotel. Facing the hotel bear left, following a wide track signposted as 'public bridleway to Buttermere'.

The Fish Hotel figures in a famous story. Mary Robertson, who lived at what was then the Fish Inn, fell in love with a dashing gentleman calling himself the Honourable Alexander Augustus Hope. He had arrived in Keswick in July 1802 and the country girl of 18 was so infatuated that by October they were married. Doubts among the local gentry resulted in a series of sensational revelations; the man turned out to be John Hatfield who had left two wives and a pile of debts behind him. He was hanged for forgery in September 1803 leaving Mary alone and with child. The story of the Keswick Imposter and the Buttermere Beauty became the subject of many a

Fleetwith Pike, from the north-west shore of Buttermere

soulful ballad, displaying little respect for poor Mary Robertson who had to live on in the village, older but wiser.

The track soon turns left. At the gate go over the stile on the left and continue along the main track as it bears right.

The hedges may not look very ancient but they have probably been here for several hundred years. Their age can be estimated by counting the different species of trees or bushes along a 30m section, each species adding a hundred years to the total. Within a few metres of this gate there are hawthorn, ash, hazel, elder, dog rose and sloe, suggesting that these hedges might have been here as field boundaries when Buttermere first got its name (translated as 'mere surrounded by good grazing land').

Walk along the track to a footbridge; go over this and bear left.

Just across the bridge is a birch tree bearing curious bunches of twigs looking rather like displaced crows' nests. They are called witches' brooms for obvious reasons, but the magic involved has more to do with chemicals than sorcery; fungi and/or bacteria attack the branches which respond by throwing out a chaotic tangle of buds and twigs.

Cross Sourmilk Gill, and make for the gate across the rough boulders.

Sourmilk Gill, which cascades down from Bleaberry Tarn, divides Scales Wood from Burtness. The latter is dominated by larch. Nobody really knows when larch was introduced into Britain, but it was certainly here in the early 17th century. By 1800 it had become a plantation tree and the subject of a long-standing argument about the wisdom of sacrificing tradition to rapid profit. Today even larch is considered to be too slow-growing to be of great economic value, and the current craze is for spruce.

Continue along the lakeside track, with the woods to your right.

The open canopy of larch and birch lets in a good deal of light, so there is plenty of vegetation on the woodland floor. Compare this with the dour spruce plantation a kilometre further along the track.

This section of Burtness Wood is good for fungi in the late autumn. The most common toadstools are *Russula* and *Boletus*. *Russulas* usually have watery-purple or red caps with white stem and gills, whilst *Boletus* species are easy to recognise because they have tiny pores rather than gills, giving the underside a sponge-like appearance. *Boletus* are very chunky solid-looking toadstools, and have incredibly thick stems designed to hold the cap rigid and let the spores drop straight out.

The track goes through a gateway in an old drystone wall and into a much less varied section of woodland. Continue south-east until the wood ends at a gate and you are out on the open fell.

There is a good view across Buttermere to the left. The water is very clear, often with a slight turquoise cast produced by slate dust washed down from Honister Quarry by Gatesgarthdale Beck. It is a very infertile lake, second only to Wastwater in its lack of nutrients and therefore its shortage of aquatic plants, but it contains the char — a rare salmon-like fish once prized as being 'more luscious and delicious than the trout'. Char are only found in deep lakes, and Buttermere at 29m probably only just qualifies.

Behind the lake are the craggy fells astride Hassnesshow Beck. This area was once known as the last breeding site for golden eagles in the Lake District. Eagles eat young lambs and their presence in sheep country has always caused hostility among farmers. Add to this a good helping of persecution by gamekeepers and it is hardly surprising that they disappeared over a century ago. The long-awaited return to Cumbria came in 1969; since then they have nested successfully a few miles away and a pair may yet come back to these crags.

Walk along the path to cross Comb Beck to the right of a small larch wood.

The steep fell to the right is very impressive, the peaks of High Stile and High Crag linked by Comb Crags and the ice-sculpted bowl of Burtness Comb. This area holds another interesting animal story, because forty years ago a strange creature was discovered high up on Burtness Comb. It was brought down to Gatesgarth Farm and became a family pet, looked after by the farmer's daughter who had a way with animals and already had several foxes about the place. The mysterious animal turned out to be a pine marten, and it is strange that none of the local people recognised it: martens were once widespread in the district.

Pine martens were called 'sweet marts' to distinguish them from evil smelling 'foul marts' or polecats, which were known to have a liking for chickens and were quickly exterminated. But the pine martens did little harm and were far more elusive.

Pine marten

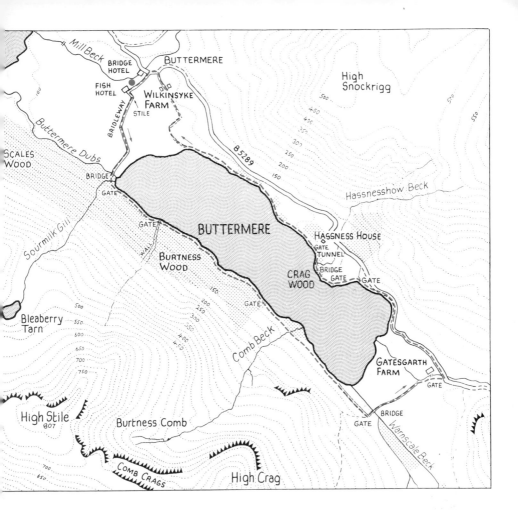

Perhaps they still inhabit the high woods and fells of Ennerdale; certainly they still survive in Grizedale Forest and are known to be great wanderers.

Eventually the path runs alongside a wall.

Ahead are Gatesgarthdale and Warnscale, two deep valleys gouged out a million years ago by glaciers converging from Honister and Great Gable. They met at Fleetwith Pike, and when the ice melted all that remained of the underlying rock was the sharp ridge of Fleetwith Edge. Little pieces of the Lake District were carried all over northern England, to be dumped as far south as the Cheshire Plain.

Turn left just after a sheep-fold, towards a gate. Go through the gate and along the straight track, over Warnscale Beck and on to Gatesgarth Farm.

Originally there were three farms, each with its own flock of Herdwick sheep. Gatesgarth is the only one still functioning; it maintains a genuine tradition in a place otherwise dedicated to tourism, and there are often interesting activities in progress. Observe from a distance and try not to get in the way. The busiest time is probably September and October when the autumn sales are in progress and the holding pens are full.

Sheep carry two identification features to establish ownership. The most obvious is the smit-mark on the fleece, usually red and

73

derived originally from local haematite. The second is the lug-mark, a hole clipped in the ear to provide permanent proof of origin.

At the main road turn left, go over the bridge and continue for several hundred metres until the open shore is reached. At the small parking area take the path along the lakeside, signposted 'Buttermere via lakeshore path'.

This is the best part of the lake for fly fishing. Buttermere has an unusually wide assortment of fish species, but they are rarely found in the same section of water; trout prefer the shallows whilst pike and perch are most common close to the north-east shore where the edge shelves steeply.

Follow the path around the rocky eastern lake shore, through a wicket gate across a field, through another wicket gate and towards the pine trees of Crag Wood.

Interesting to compare the Scots pine growing in a gap close to the shore with those on the edge of the field a little to the north-east. Those growing in the group are tall and straight with few lower branches and a characteristic platform of foliage at the top. This is what we expect pine trees to look like, but they only grow like this because they have to compete for light. Look at the ones at the wood edge, more rounded with hefty boughs and a lot more greenery. Beautiful trees, native north of the Border but introduced here many hundreds of years ago.

Go on a few more metres towards a foot-bridge.

Pines were not the only trees to be re-distributed around Britain in the dim and distant past. There are some attractive beech trees here, this time brought up from the south of England.

The tunnel on the shoreline path around Buttermere

Buttermere, from the north-west

The ground beneath the trees is usually littered with the opened husks of beech nuts, known as mast. Mice and squirrels seem to prefer acorns if they have the choice, and in any case the mast crop is unreliable and bonanza years are infrequent.

Cross the footbridge; the path now follows a much rockier course around the lake shore, and through a short tunnel.

The tunnel was built in the last century at the instigation of George Benson who owned Hassness House. He wanted to keep his men busy during the winter and must have been pleased with the result. An idle fancy to while away the idle moments; whether his men followed the same reasoning is another matter.

Go through a wicket gate and through some attractive parkland of lime, beech and sycamore. At the end of the lake continue straight ahead and then bear right, over a rocky piece of ground.

The gain in height offers a good view of the flat alluvial land that links Buttermere to Crummock Water. The lakes were once joined, and the flat deposits of silt and pebbles hardly seem enough to keep them apart.

Follow the waymarked track, through Wilkinsyke Farm and on to the village.

Wilkinsyke, one of the 17th century farms at the core of the Buttermere community, is a gem, especially for those who believe in the dog and stick image of agriculture. The path goes right through the yard, so take care not to put your foot in anything.

If you have time, look round the village and try to sort out which are the really old buildings; most of them have an interesting story to tell, though few inhabitants apart from Mary Robertson have gained fame or notoriety. A minor exception is John Norman, who lived in the terrace of white cottages at the northern end of the village and had the misfortune to be on HMS *Bounty* with Captain Bligh.

Walk Thirteen
HAY STACKS

GATESGARTH — SCARTH GAP — HAY STACKS — GREEN CRAG — WARNSCALE BECK; 7.5km

The most difficult walk in this book, involving a long climb up Scarth Gap and some rock-hopping in high country. The beauty and variety of scenery make it irresistible however, and many fell connoisseurs such as Wainwright hold it very close to their hearts, only lamenting that it is not a little higher. Save it for a clear day; any mist will not only obscure views but may also make parts of the route dangerous.

Park at the National Park car park at the southern end of Buttermere, on the Honister road opposite Gatesgarth Farm, GR 196150. Cross the road and go through the wicket gate just before the bridge, sign-posted 'public footpath to Scarth Gap'.

To the right is Gatesgarthdale Beck which draws its water from Honister. A local legend tells of a time in the 14th century when the beck ran red following a skirmish between Freebooters and English Border-ers. The Freebooters, rustlers of the Graeme clan who had crossed the border to steal cattle, laid a trap between Honister and Yew Crags; the English Borderers, marching from Borrowdale, walked straight into it. The result was bloody and brief and both chiefs were killed.

Across the sycamore-lined beck is Gates-garth Farm — though its byres and buildings are on this side, to the left of the path. There were once two other farms in the vicinity and a chapel on the roadside opposite Gatesgarth Cottage, but the community dwindled and has lost any individual identity.

After the farmyard bear left to go through a wicket gate and along a track with a wall and fence to the right.

To the left across the pasture is Low Raven Crag, rising sharply on a knife-edged ridge or 'arête' to Fleetwith Pike. On the lower slopes to the left is a small white cross, placed as a monument to Fanny Mercer, a girl killed in an accident in 1887.

Continue along the track towards a bridge.

The green pasture has been used as in-bye for sheep grazing for hundreds of years, always stocked with Herdwick sheep. Nobody knows how the breed originated; there is a story that a ship from the Spanish Armada was wrecked on the coast and forty sheep were rescued. Recent genetic investigation has shown some affinities with Scandinavian breeds so it seems more likely that the Herdwick's ancestors were introduced by Norse settlers, probably in the 10th century.

The name Herdwick or 'Herdwyck' is derived not from the actual name of the breed but from the traditional habit of leasing a farm to a tenant with a 'herd' of sheep. In hill country it is not practicable to take a flock from one farm to another because sheep take a long time to get to know the best grazing and shelter, so the flock is 'heafted', considered part and parcel of the farm.

Cross the bridge and continue along the track to a gate.

The view all around is of a glaciated land-scape, especially the basin of Warnscale to the left which was hollowed-out by hund-reds of metres of ice. Warnscale Beck is little more than a silver thread lost in an amphitheatre, though it is the focal point of the dale head. Ahead and to the right are the buttressed peaks of High Crag and High Stile with, between them, a classic 'cirque' (or cwm or corrie) called Burtness Comb, which held its core of ice high above the main valley now occupied by Buttermere. The reason the fells on the south-west side of the valley are so craggy is that the rocks of their upper slopes, being of the Borrow-

Autumn at Gatesgarth Farm; a pen full of Herdwick sheep

dale Volcanic Series, have not weathered as easily as the older Skiddaw Slates, on which Buttermere actually sits.

Go through the gate and up the rather stony path which zig-zags steeply before finally bearing sharp left on a long but gradual ascent heading for Scarth Gap.

A little way after the turn is a wicket gate, a convenient place to look out over Warnscale Bottom to the left. The dominant feature is the marshy lower reach of the beck and its outfall with the grey stony shore of Buttermere. The green pasture-land ends abruptly to the south-east and it is possible to make out several drainage channels cut through the tussocky, rush-covered marshland to divert flood water away from the fields. During very wet weather this whole piece of land can disappear under a sheet of water, and the high water-table has obviously killed many of the pine trees on this side of the beck.

On the far side of the valley is Fleetwith Edge rising to the 648m (2,126ft) peak of Fleetwith Pike. The track arcing around its foot is the return route.

The path takes the easiest line obliquely up the hillside, making for the gap between two rocky crags.

The upper one of these is High Wax Knott, the clefts of its face lightly covered with heather and some small bushes of holly and rowan. This is a good place to look

Alpine lady's mantle

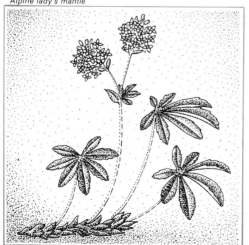

ahead to the Hay Stacks massif which can look remarkably doomy if the weather has turned bad. If a heavy mist has crept over Big Stack (the outer tooth) then it is time to think seriously of retreating the way you have come. Thick mist is the bane of any walker, though William Gilpin once wrote a piece entitled *The Beauty of Fog* in which he noted that 'among the beautiful appear-ances of fogs and mists, their gradual going off may be observed'. This is an aesthetic exercise you may wish to be spared.

The path contours to a gap in an old en-closure wall, then ascends Scarth Gap Pass, following the cairns.

Around the rocks and boulders are several flowers, among them a true mountain species called alpine lady's mantle. It has obscure yellow flowers but the leaves are distinctive, multi-fingered and resembling a miniature laburnam. Sheep graze most of the exposed patches but there are some better clumps hidden in the higher clefts.

Continue for about 200m over the flat brow of Scarth Gap. This leads towards a line of posts.

The posts are an old boundary, separating Ennerdale from the wilds beyond. To the right is the tip of Ennerdale Forest, a dark and sad place full of regimented conifers.

Just before the posts, bear left to follow a path which gains height very gradually for about 150m then, at a small cairn, turn sharp left up a steep and stony scramble marked by cairns to a grassy shelf or promontory, at which bear left.

A really excellent view soon opens up to the north-west, over Buttermere and Crummock Water and, if the day is very clear, to the Solway Firth and the Scottish hills.

Bear right, spiralling up to an iron post.

The view is now of the south face of Fleet-with Pike. It is remarkable how in very good visibility distance is foreshortened and deceptive, but the sheep-fold at the foot of the bracken-covered slope gives some idea of scale.

The path bears left of the next iron post, then left and uphill to yet another.

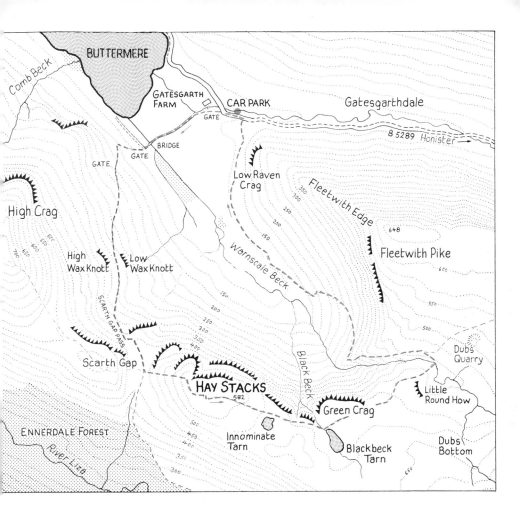

From here there is a good view west to Ennerdale. Even before the Forestry Commission planted the valley it was rather dour, though in medieval times this country was well-wooded and was called Ennerdale Chase, between the great deer preserves of Derwentfells and Copeland. On the southern shore of Ennerdale Water is a small deciduous wood once famous for its red deer, and it is recorded that as late as 1675 it contained 'Hartts and Staggs as great as in any part of England'. So this was a favoured area, perhaps following a tradition dating back thousands of years, for the dale is littered with enigmatic fragments of pre-history, culminating in the

mysterious cairn on Boat How above the wood already mentioned.

The fells towards Ennerdale Water are less rugged than those close to Buttermere because the rock is igneous, an intrusion of pink granophyre which weathers quicker than the blue-green Borrowdale Volcanic Series. Further away to the west of Ennerdale Water the geology changes again, to the heavily weathered Skiddaw Slate.

Go to the left of a small shallow tarn, then left of another iron post and up to the summit of Hay Stacks.

In fact the summit takes the form of a ridge, 50m long, with posts at its north and south pinnacles. This is very convenient in that it is possible to concentrate first on the north view without being too distracted with what is over your shoulder. The northern panorama also has the advantage of catching the best of the light, offering a magnificent sweep from High Crag in the foreground, across Crummock Water to Whiteless Pike, then Crag Hill, Robinson, Causey Pike (in the distance), Hindsgarth and Fleetwith Pike.

Having spent a few minutes on the northern pinnacle of the ridge (in fact this is probably the higher of the two at about 582m (1,909ft)), pick your way over the rocks to the south post. The north side of Great Gable and its neighbours is usually in deep shadow and this flattens the perspective. They menace and threaten rather than invite the walker; Scafell Pike, to the right of Gable, has an undeniable attraction however, being the highest peak in England. Of the other goliaths Pillar, to the south-west, rivals Great Gable in its presence and power. The north face of Pillar Rock is visible, which earned the rounded mountain its name and makes it a favourite with climbers.

From the summit scramble down to the cairned path which makes its way south-east close to the northern edge of the mountain block. Take care not to stray from the path. Make for the left of the tarn.

This is Innominate Tarn, which seems a silly name considering it was once known as Loaf Tarn. Presumably when the little loaf-shaped islands eroded and sank that name was considered inappropriate, since when it has remained innominate, i.e. unnamed.

Most of the tarns in the area are very poor in aquatic plants because their water is drawn from thin peat overlying hard volcanic rocks, which will not weather to release any minerals or nutrients. The Borrowdale Volcanics originated about 450 million years ago as a series of volcanic islands, their lavas, dust and debris of a similar type to those found in the Andes today. The precise date for any igneous rock is difficult to judge because there are no fossils to provide comparative clues.

Descend through a gap, passing to the right of a rocky outcrop, and down the cairned path.

A fine vista of Buttermere and Crummock Water suddenly opens on the left, framed by a cleft in the rock wall through which Black Beck runs. Blackbeck Tarn, which appears after a few more metres of walking, is a much prettier piece of water than the others encountered, edged by a moss carpet and with an obvious catchment and outfall.

Cross the stream just to the left of the tarn, then head north-east with Green Crag to the left and a wide marshy basin to the right.

View from Hay Stacks summit — north-west clockwise to south-east

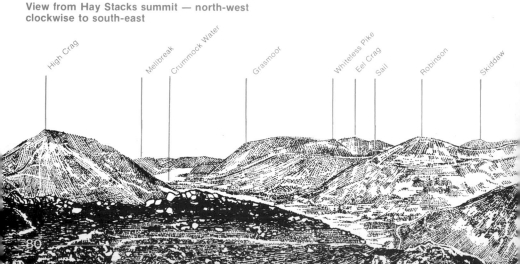

Innominate Tarn, Great Gable dominating the distant view

The bogs and puddles to the right resemble a tundra landscape, dominated by heather and *Sphagnum* moss. Squeeze the moss and you will see why it is so popular with gardeners making hanging baskets; it retains water. A similar property for centuries earned it a role in war-time as a combat-dressing, absorbing blood. One of the most interesting characteristics of *Sphagnum*, however, is that it is the prime constituent of peat, and its raw undecayed remains often go down more than a metre, the waterlogged conditions preserving both the moss and other plant remains like pollen grains. These tell scientists what the vegetation was like thousands of years ago.

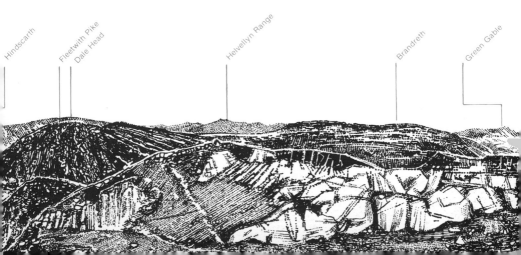

Hindscarth   Fleetwith Pike   Dale Head   Helvellyn Range   Brandreth   Green Gable

The path bears left of the rock outcrop of Little Round How, then descends a little to cross Warnscale Beck.

To the right is Dubs Bottom, the wide basin collecting run-off water from Grey Knotts and Brandreth which finds its way to Buttermere via Warnscale Beck. Ahead is the relic of Dubs Quarry, an eyesore of blue slate spoil.

Bear left along a narrow path through heather, joining a track after about 200m. Continue left.

The track is an old quarry road which winds tortuously down to Gatesgarth. Warnscale Beck to the left has attractive cascades and waterfalls, flanked by rocky promontories which provide pleasant vantage points. Ahead on the left is the sinister north face of Hay Stacks.

Warnscale Bottom, with Buttermere and Crummock Water in the distance

The track turns sharp right, then bears left.

An impressive view, like looking from a balcony high up in the Albert Hall.

The scree slopes of Hay Stacks support few trees other than rowan, but the west face of Fleetwith Pike also has yew, holly and hawthorn. Further down the valley is a clump of mature Scots pine, planted for shelter.

After another sharp left turn the track bears right and descends more gradually.

The lower slopes to the right are covered with a dense canopy of bracken for much of the year, which eliminates most other plants. To the left is a good view of Buttermere Fell and the ascent route to Scarth Gap.

Continue along the track which bears left to meet the road. Turn left to the car park.

Walk Fourteen
RANNERDALE

BUTTERMERE VILLAGE — HAUSE POINT — RANNERDALE — GYLL WOOD; 6km

A very varied walk with excellent views of Crummock Water and Buttermere, a look at several interesting little woods, and a good stride up grassy paths and a hidden valley.

Park in Buttermere village. Start at GR 174169 facing the Fish Hotel, and walk right to a car park. Leave the car park at its far right corner (beware of chickens!) and follow the way-marked path towards Crummock Water, keeping to the left of the stream.

The old village of Buttermere once had a Scandinavian-style 'click mill' to grind oats and rye. This was situated several hundred metres upstream and predated the Victorian enlargement of the village for the tourist trade.

To the left across the flat pasture is Scales Wood, a fine oakwood very different in character to the larchwood of Burtness on the east side of Sourmilk Gill. Above Scales Wood runs an old enclosure wall, then there is a steep slope before a wide corrie created and fashioned by ice, called Ling Comb. 'Ling' is another name for heather, and even from this distance it is possible to make out a thick collar of the plant clothing the hillside beneath Lingcomb Edge.

Continue along the path for several hundred metres until a bridge crosses the stream.

The symmetrical mound of woodland on the shore of Crummock Water is called Nether How, whilst across the beck to the right is Long How. How (or 'Howe') means a burial mound, and these two small hills are said in the novel *The Secret Valley* to be the resting place for English soldiers following a battle against the Normans. The details are all fictitious of course, but perhaps both these hills were burial sites at one time.

Today they are heavily wooded and are rich in wildlife. There seems to be a constant two-way traffic of birds between the two sites; wood pigeons are the most numerous, but great-spotted woodpeckers and jays are also regular commuters. Jays, noisy birds, are most noticeable in the autumn when they are much less shy and are busy collecting acorns. It has been calculated that each jay picks up an average of 3,000 acorns a year, burying them in nooks and crannies for winter food. Not all the acorns are found again of course, and it is possible that these birds are prime agents in the spread of oakwoods, far more important than the more obvious squirrels.

The relationship between acorns and jays has been known for many years. Writing in the 18th century William Cowper observed (of an acorn)

Thou wast a bauble once: a cup and ball,
Which babes might play with, and the
thievish jay
Seeking her food, with ease might have
purloin'd
The auburn nut that held thee . . . . .

Turn right and cross the bridge, then turn right again and follow the beck back upstream for about 75m.

The strange wooden structure across the beck is a watergate, a device to prevent sheep from creeping around the sides of the stone walls into greener pasture via the stony bed of the stream. Whatever the volume of water the hinged gate will act as a barrier without interrupting the flow.

The path divides; follow a rather steep path which bears left, away from the beck, and north-east through Long How.

The ground soon levels-off and the wide woodland path is very attractive. The oaks are at their most lovely in June when the leaves are still fresh and cock redstarts are searching among the mossy stumps for insects.

The path leads to a wicket gate and onto a main road. Turn left for about 100m then right (the line of the former road) and continue until it rejoins the metalled road again. Keep on the road around a double bend, then take a gently rising green path right, up the hillside.

bedding, so it is of little value to farmers. Neither is it a foodplant of many insects, only a sawfly, a few bugs and beetles, and a nondescript moth called the brown silver-lines, so it is of little interest to the naturalist.

Continue along the path for about 200m, at which point stop for a view over Crummock Water.

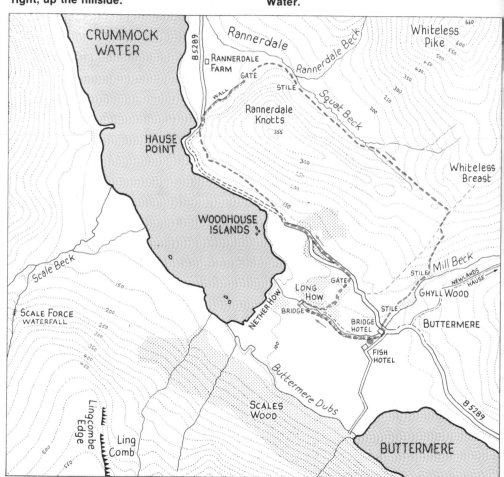

Bracken and gorse are usually taken as indicators that the soil is deep and of sufficient quality at least to grow a good grass crop. Fortunately for the visitor the Lakeland farmers are encouraged by grants and subsidies not to damage the visual beauty of the lower fells by 'improving' them. Bracken is poisonous to stock for most of the year and is no longer used for

The name is probably derived from 'Crombok-watre' i.e. crooked water, which is appropriate as the south quarter is distinctly kinked. There are several islands, all close to the shore and covered by birch and heather which provide shelter for visiting grey-lag and Canada geese. The cormorants are not so fussy and often sit exposed on the rocks of the Woodhouse

A Herdwick sheep on the slopes of Rannerdale Knotts

slands to dry their wings.

Across the lake is an arc of flattish land marking the outfall of Scale Beck. This wide grassy area was once inhabited by an Iron Age or Romano-British tribe and several stone huts have been discovered, suggesting it was a favoured settlement. Scale Beck soon gains height, bearing to the left (south) where a furrow of trees screens the famous Scale Force, a 47m (156ft) cascade of water marking the geological boundary between the old, soft Skiddaw Slate and a harder intrusion of granophyre.

Ignore any paths to the right and continue up the main path to a rocky outcrop.

Herdwick sheep are usually to be seen around this spot, possibly enjoying the view. Their fleece was once used undyed to make a tweed called 'Hodden grey', but today the wool of most upland breeds is used for carpets. The view ahead from the brow of the hill is of the road flanked by Crummock Water to the left and the imposing bulk of Grasmoor to the right.

Descend steeply to join the road again. Turn right almost immediately and go up the track with the wall to your left.

The steep, lightly-wooded slopes of Rannerdale Knotts cast a heavy shadow over this section of the walk. The drystone wall encloses in-bye pasture towards Rannerdale Farm and was built from that side with the cam of capstones protruding this side. It takes two men a day to build about six metres of wall, and each half-metre of stones weighs about a tonne. Anything less than its present height and the wall would not be stockproof, for sheep are capable of amazingly silly vertical scrambles.

Wheatear

Despite its name this is a very attractive stream, ash-lined, with some unassuming little falls and a conversational babble. The lower slopes of Rannerdale Knotts, to the right, are littered with boulders which provide breeding sites for wheatears, one of the most attractive of the upland birds with a distinctive white rump. This identification feature earned the bird its name, but propriety corrupted the vernacular 'arse' to 'ear'.

The rock boulders from Rannerdale Knotts are paler than those from a kilometre to the south or north; recent geological investigation has suggested there was probably an intrusion or injection of molton rock beneath the surface which baked the local stone and gave it its distinctive khaki colour.

Continue to a wicket gate, after which the path bears right.

Grasmoor to the north is still the major element in the landscape but closer at hand to the east is Whiteless Pike, a 654m (2,159ft) beauty which, from this angle at least, looks as though it has escaped from an alpine calendar. Separating the two mountains is Rannerdale Beck.

Follow the path right, past a tree, to join Squat Beck.

Walk along parallel with the stream to a ladder stile over a wall to the right. After crossing this continue south-east, still parallel with Squat Beck.

After a while the valley seems to open out, the stream falters, and Rannerdale takes on a silent aspect, as if waiting. Rannerdale was the site of a great 11th century battle between the English, under Earl Boethar, and the invading Normans, under Ranulf le Meschin, in which there was much bloodshed and the English for once were victorious. Historians will say that no such battle actually happened and that Nicholas Size invented it for his novel *The Secret*

View from col at head of Rannerdale Valley — south-east clockwise to north-west

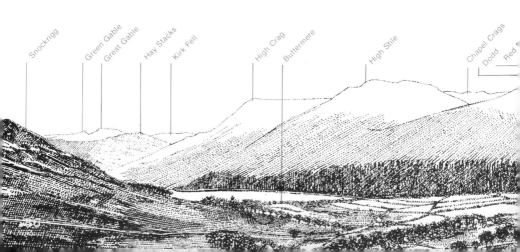

Snockrigg   Green Gable   Great Gable   Hay Stacks   Kirk Fell   High Crag   Buttermere   High Stile   Chapel Crags   Dodd   Red

Squat Beck in November

valley, but there is no doubt that for some reason the Normans failed to penetrate into the northern Lake District, and the Domesday Book is strangely silent about the area. So perhaps Norman ghosts linger on the hillsides to right and left, lamenting their defeat.

Continue up the dale, keeping to the path.

Minor detours may be necessary around marshy dips and hollows; the worst ones are covered with bog moss which is usually bright green and therefore easy to avoid. There are dozens of different kinds of bog moss, all very beautiful if you have boots and can peer closely at them. Botanists like David Bellamy may slosh around with reckless zeal but such commitment is unnecessary; look for the beautiful red-flushed species called *Sphagnum rubellum*, growing on the drier hummocks, among the more usual *Sphagnum plumulosum*. To the left several small streams run diagonally to meet Squat Beck, their deeply furrowed courses cutting through Skiddaw Slate.

Crummock Water

Mellbreak

Look back down the valley for a distant view of Loweswater.

The crest is reached quite suddenly between rocky outcrops to either side.

The block of hillside immediately ahead is High Snockrigg, with Robinson (736m) a little to the left. Further to the right, beyond Buttermere and Warnscale Bottom, are the craggy peaks of Hay Stacks with Great Gable behind and to the left. The route up Hay Stacks via Scarth Gap, described in walk 13, can be seen towards High Crag.

Turn right, down a broad grassy track for about 100m, then take a left turn where the paths divide and descend the steep path in the direction of Buttermere village.

To the left is the Mill Beck and the road to Newlands Hause. Whiteless Breast is on the north side of this, with Knott Rigg in the distance.

Turning back to the south-west, across the Buttermere—Crummock Water valley is

Crummock Water from the south-east, above Buttermere village

Lingcomb Edge again. This time look to the left, to the peaks of Red Pike and High Stile.

High Stile and its associates to the south-east are composed of hard volcanic rocks called the Borrowdale Volcanic Series or Greenstone, whilst most of Red Pike consists of an intrusion called Ennerdale Granophyre capped by a baked layer of Skiddaw Slate which has given the peak a smoother silhouette.

Continue the descent diagonally left until a path leads off left again, down to the edge of a valley wood. Make for a gated stile, go over this and turn right. Continue parallel with the Mill Beck.

This is Gyll Wood, a very steep 'hanging' sessile oakwood once used as a coppice and now owned by the National Trust. To the left is Mill Beck, making its way through an attractive little gully down to the Bridge Hotel.

Go through the stile, left at the road then right to get back to the Fish Hotel.

Walk Fifteen
BRACKENTHWAITE

LANTHWAITE — BRACKENTHWAITE HOWS — CRUMMOCK WATER; 5km

Brackenthwaite Hows stands at the strategic meeting place between the north-west fells and the green corridor of Lorton Vale. The river Cocker meets the Derwent just outside the National Park boundary at Cockermouth, 11km to the north, but long before then the hills have lost their grandeur and the lattice of fields has become the controlling influence on the landscape. This walk embraces a view of the vale from the foot of Grasmoor and Whiteside, then crosses farmland and common to Lanthwaite Wood and the shores of Crummock Water; there are several moderate inclines but nothing too severe – an appropriate finale with some abiding impressions of northern Lakeland.

Start at the Lanthwaite car park, GR 158207. Walk north past the farm then bear right along a track through open fell.

The view is totally dominated by Grasmoor to the right, an awesome 846m (2,791ft) peak which from this angle looks impossibly steep. In fact there is a straightforward walking route from the other side which can be reached by following Liza Beck to the head of Gasgale Gill and up onto a grassy plateau, but this still involves more than 600m of ascent. To the left is Whiteside, 702m (2,317ft), but of less dramatic aspect. Whin Ben on its southern flank is,

by contrast, small and neat, topped by heather and a muff of bracken but with a few relict frills of gorse at its foot.

'Whin' means gorse, so it can be assumed that when the first Norse-Irish settlers arrived they found the slopes heavily clad with the plant and used it for kindling and grazing.

After a few hundred metres a track junction is reached. Bear right, to reach Liza Beck.

The fan-shaped weir is edged by rushes, identified by their round, spiky leaves. Soft round rushes were once harvested and used as a crude form of domestic lighting. The tough husks were stripped away to reveal wads of white spongy pith which were dipped in sheep fat and used as primitive candles, called rush lights.

Bear right, heading upstream for about 100m, cross the footbridge and follow the path uphill. After a few metres the path divides; take the left fork and head north, keeping close to the wall.

In the distance to the left (west) is Holme Wood, a large block of mixed conifers with some curiously-shaped plantings of larch. Loweswater lies at its foot but is totally obscured by a wide dome of farmland and Brackenthwaite Hows. The hamlet of Loweswater (just visible) was once an important little settlement, and by the 12th century it had its own chapel. It did not have a burying ground however, and corpses had to be transported to St Bees, more than 20km to the south-west. They were 'buried in woollens' first (one of many legal stipulations brought in to protect the woollen industry), then strapped to a horse and carried up the hillside to a first stopping point at the boulders beyond Holme Force ('Grey Mare's Tail'), from thence across Burnbank Fell and to the Cumbrian coast.

Continue for several hundred metres, with the wall to your left.

To the right are the frost-shattered screes of Whiteside End. The rock is Skiddaw Slate, a 500 million-year-old bed of shale laced with hard sandstone slabs and more recent bands of quartz. To avoid the current confusion implied by its title geologists have recently taken to calling the rock the 'Skiddaw Series', a much better name for such a varied assortment.

The pasture to the left is grazed by a herd of Highland cattle, kept for beef, though the need for hardy stock has been superseded with the introduction of wintering sheds. The longhorn ancestors of the Highland breed were brought into Britain from southwest Europe by Neolithic settlers, and probably graced Lorton Vale several thousand years ago.

The extensive walling of lower fells for fields or 'intak' was a phenomenon of the 18th and 19th centuries, particularly following enclosure awards by the government, but the history of walling goes back longer than this and there were many periods of enclosure, usually dictated by necessity, as, for example, when groups of medieval farmers tried to grow corn in the valleys and needed to exclude stock.

Look for a wicket gate through the wall to the left. Go through this and follow the wall, ahead then right, then straight down to a stile by the Liza Beck. Cross this at a footbridge, then turn left down the road.

Skylark nest

Take care on the road; cars are moving quickly on this section of the B 5289. The wall on the right is set into the bank, enabling plants like polypod and parsley fern to thrive, whilst the verge in summer contains wood sage and red campion.

Just after Beck House is a gate on the right waymarked 'path to Scale Hill'. Go through this and west, past Pickett Howe.

The rocky knoll to the left (south) marks the edge of a mixed plantation, dominated here by oak. To the north is an interesting farmstead, the farmhouse to the right and a fine 'bank barn' in the centre, its imposing rear doorway built to accommodate loaded carts. To the left are some low outbuildings possibly built as a kennel or pig sty, then on the far left a new shed and silage clamp.

Proceed along the wall for about 300m then, when the wall veers right, continue uphill straight ahead over tussocky grassland and heath, making for a solitary rowan tree with a mixed fir plantation on the hillcrest beyond.

The route is very indistinct but keep heading south, uphill towards the fir trees.

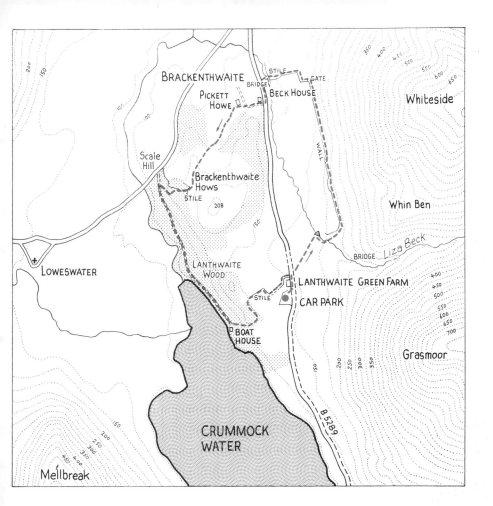

he ground is marshy at first but the
ussocky grassland soon dries out and the
nd is in fact very old pasture, excellent for
ild flowers and nesting birds like the
kylark. For several centuries lark's tongue
aspic was a popular delicacy, as was lark
e. 'If the number of individuals sacrificed
the exigencies of the kitchen can be
usted to supply a criterion, the skylark has
ong been a very abundant bird in Lakeland'
as the observation of H. A. Macpherson in
892, a wry if guarded criticism of the
aditional slaughter. Today skylarks are the
ost widespread of all our breeding birds,
estricted in some areas by changes in
griculture but still abundant.

ast the rowan tree continue in the same
**line. There is an indistinct path which
improves further up the hill. Make for the
wood, with a stone wall ahead and to the
right.**

Just before the wall is a very hummocky
area; look closely and most of the
hummocks will be found to bear clusters of
rabbit droppings. Far from wishing to
conceal their daily functions many animals
actually use them to mark their territories
on the most exposed vantage points they
can find. Because rabbits are herbivores
they produce vast quantities of fibrous
pellets which build and fertilise the hummocks. Carnivorous animals do the same
sort of thing but not in such profusion.

91

Naturalists learn a great deal about the habits and food of wild animals by looking for their droppings, though to an untrained eye one stool can look much like another. The scent is the vital factor however, and even to unsophisticated nostrils an otter 'spraint' smells not unpleasantly of fish-oil and musk whilst the rather similar-looking mink dropping produces an unutterably evil stench. So if you see someone on his hands and knees sniffing a rather questionable substance, there is a chance he might be involved in a scientific investigation.

Rabbit

Rabbits are not as common as they used to be. They were introduced into this country as a source of food, probably by the Normans, and have a long history of exploitation in carefully controlled warrens; but the population suddenly escalated to about 100 million in the early part of this century, and myxomatosis was introduced from the continent in the 1950s to control the numbers. It did this spectacularly, and fresh outbreaks of the horrific disease still keep the population in check, to the relief of most farmers.

Follow the wall as it climbs uphill, narrowing with a rock outcrop on the left. On the near skyline is a larch tree; take the indistinct path up the slope to this, then turn right and walk about 30m to a stile through the wall. This leads into a wood; continue along the path with a wall to your right.

This is the northern border of Lanthwaite Wood, once composed of sessile oak but now an eccentric assortment; even so there are enough oaks to attract a few of the characteristic birds like pied flycatcher and redstart. There are several Scots pines to the left, not the normal tall types associated with plantations but low-crowned trees with buttressed trunks, more like the genuine natives of the Scottish Highlands.

After about 150m the path turns sharp left, then zig-zags down via a series of steps to join a track.

This is a very attractive section of the walk, common heather and bell heather lining the craggy slopes and the tree canopy breaking every now and then to reveal Crummock Water and the hamlet of Loweswater.

Turn left along the track.

The vegetation is remarkably luxuriant, not because the soil is especially good but because sheep are excluded. Ungrazed, the floors of most Lake District woods would be like this, supporting a thick quilt of bilberry, heather and woodrush.

To the right, screened by the trees, is the river Cocker. Its name is derived from the old British 'cucra', meaning crooked stream.

Ignore any side-tracks and continue to descend, to the lake shore.

A classic view of Crummock Water suddenly opens out, framed by tall pines; looking south over the lake Mellbreak is to the right and Rannerdale Knotts to the left, with Red Pike and High Stile in the distance. The glacier that shaped the valley flowed from that direction, chiselling a wide corridor that eventually acted as a trough for its own meltwater. Crummock Water is clean and deep, and, like Ennerdale Water and Wastwater, a large part of its yield is drawn-off unadulterated and pumped south to slake the thirst of industrial Lancashire. Its shores are barren because aquatic or marginal plants find the substrate too poor in mineral nutrients, and the narrow band of shoreline pebbles shelves suddenly, sometimes precipitously, to a maximum depth of 44m (144ft). Crummock Water is a beautiful, austere lake that is not so confined or compromised as its sister to the south.

boathouse on the north-east shore of Crummock Water

Bear left along a path leading to a wide stony track with the lake to your right. Go along this until just before a boathouse, then take the path which bears left up through the wood. This bears round to the left and eventually joins a grassy track. Turn right along this, leading out of the wood.

View from northern end of Crummock Water – south-east clockwise to south-west

Suddenly Grasmoor is once again the centrepiece, impossible to ignore.

The wall to the left has a distinct gap in it, from the footing to about half way up. With such an unyielding medium, the skilled wallers who made and maintained these field boundaries displayed great skill and

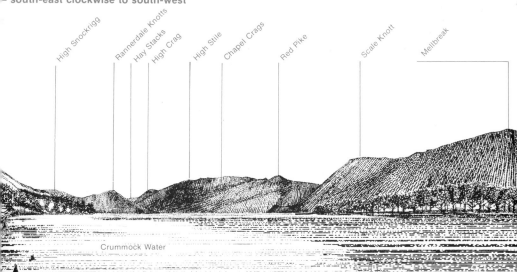

High Snockrigg
Rannerdale Knotts
Hay Stacks
High Crag
High Stile
Chapel Crags
Red Pike
Scale Knott
Mellbreak

Crummock Water

nagination in accommodating the require-
ents of farmers and landowners. Many of
e gaps were constructed to allow runnels
r streams to flow unhindered, but others
ere put there to let animals move freely
etween fields. 'Hogg-holes' allowed young
heep to reach better pasture, 'smoots'
nticed rabbits to walk into hinged traps.

**alk across the field keeping to the right of
e wall and go over a stile, then bear right
nd left towards Lanthwaite Green Farm.**

nother excellent example of a very old
rm, its origins lost in the period up to the
7th century when yeoman farmers or
tatesmen' were living through a

comfortable page of history, their
prosperity underpinned by the value of
wool. Just over the page in the 18th century
lurked disaster, bad winters, wars and
inflation, but by then many of the yeoman
families had turned aristocrat and the
farms were left to a poorer breed whose
main object was to stay alive. Thus the
body of this farm, greatly altered, remained
functional and is still a working unit today,
but the soul lies hidden in the modest core
of old stonework.

**Go to the left around the farm, then turn
right along the road and back to the car
park.**

Raven

◁ *Highland cattle, dwarfed by Whiteside End*

*If you have enjoyed these walks don't hang up your boots:
companion volumes include WALKS TO REMEMBER –
EAST AND CENTRAL LAKE DISTRICT and WALKS TO REMEMBER
– SOUTH AND WEST LAKE DISTRICT*

Published by
Polecat Press Ltd
Registered Office
63 High Bridge
Newcastle upon Tyne
NE1 1DU